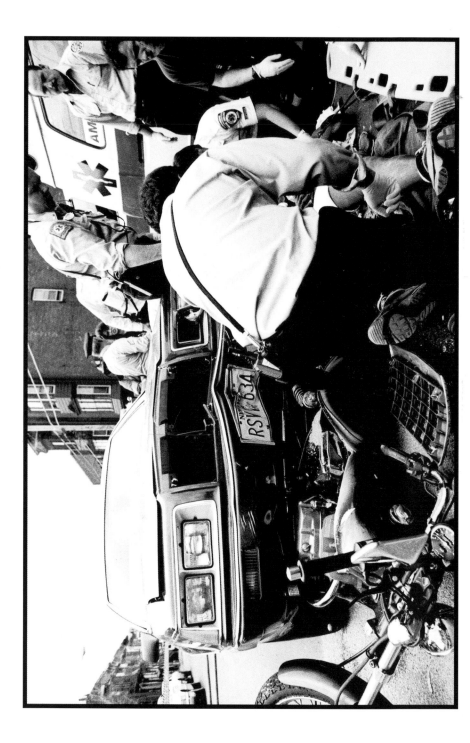

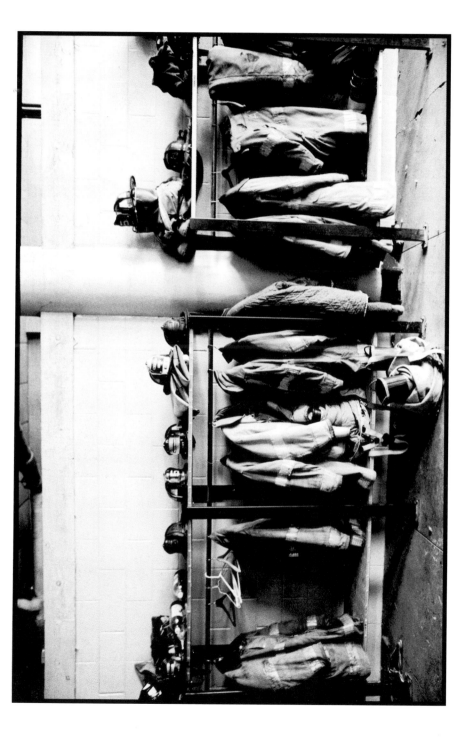

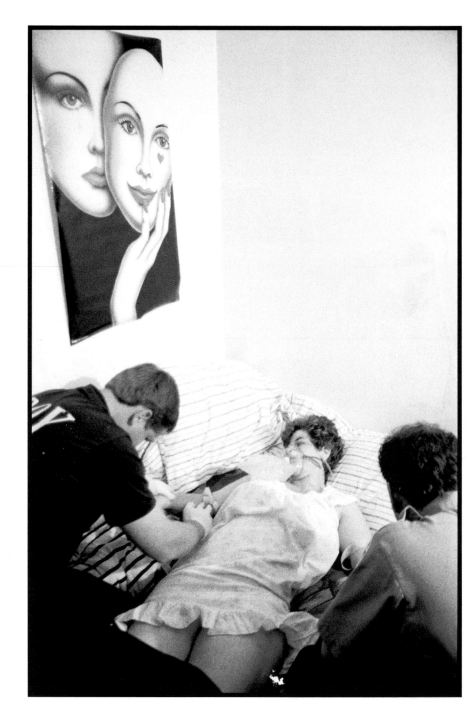

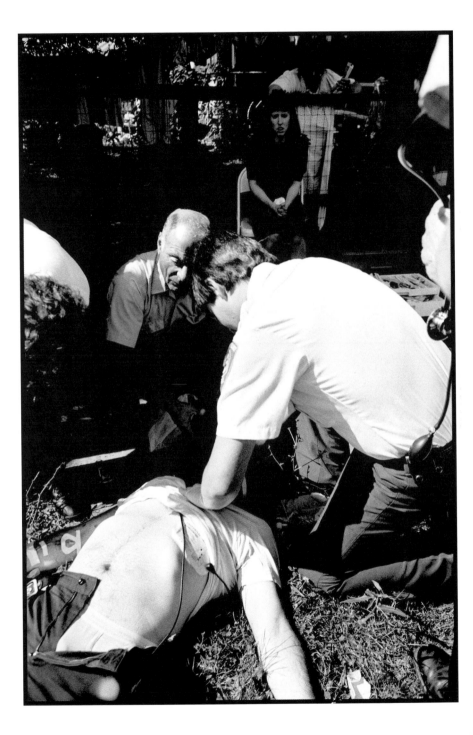

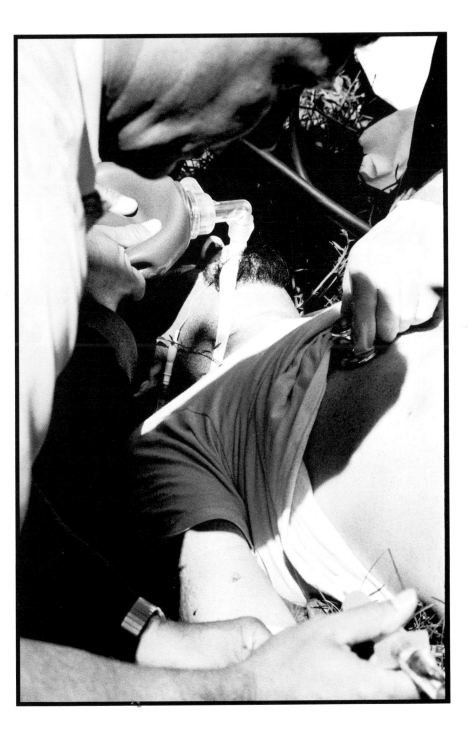

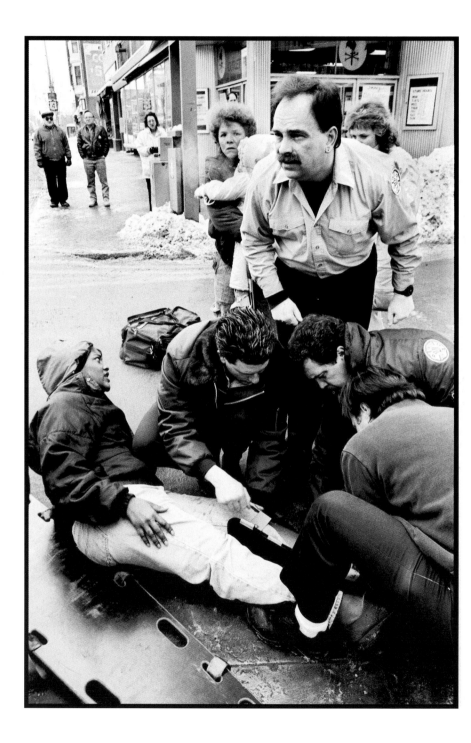

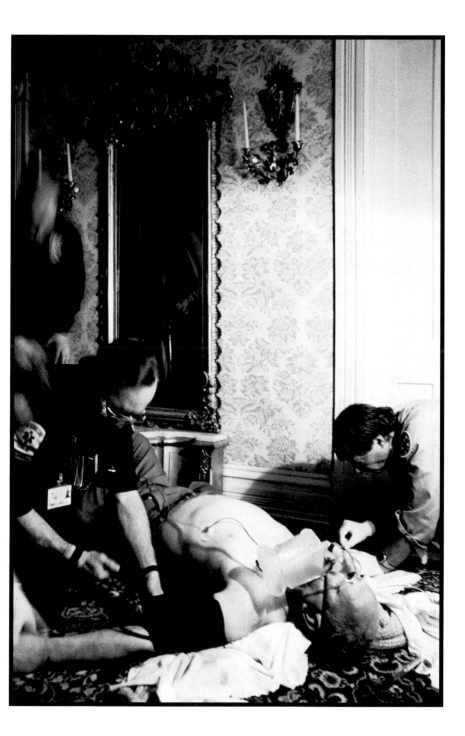

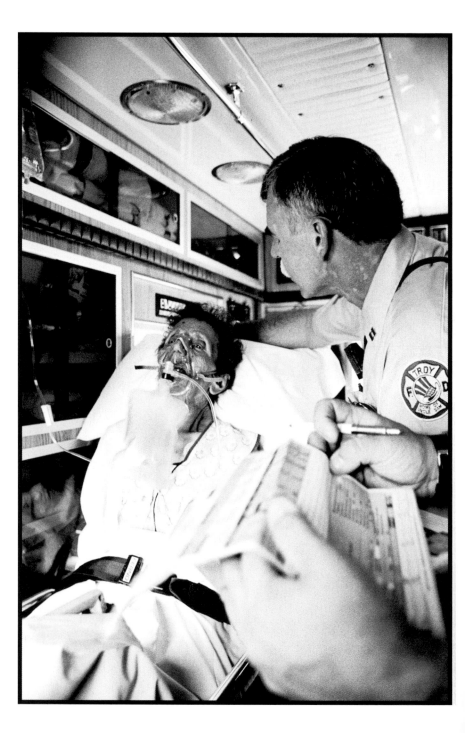

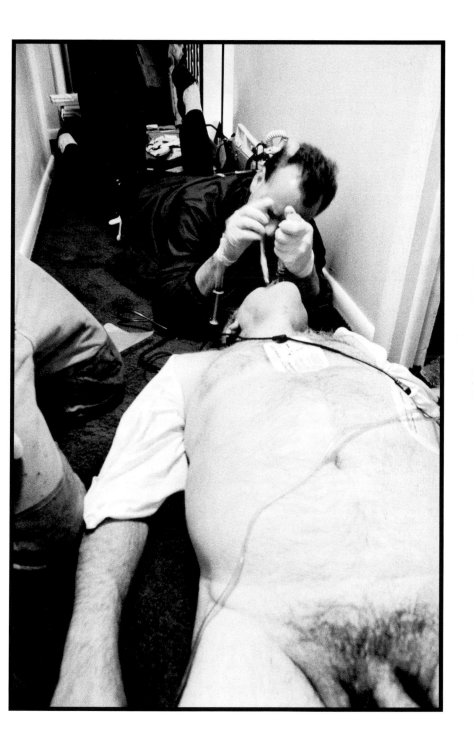

SAVING TROY

ALSO BY WILLIAM B. PATRICK

We Didn't Come Here for This: A Memoir in Poetry

Roxa: Voices of the Culver Family

These Upraised Hands

Letter to the Ghosts

SAVING TROY

A Year with Firefighters & Paramedics
in a Battered City

William B. Patrick

HUDSON WHITMAN

PUBLISHERS

Published in the United States by Hudson Whitman, LLC

Patrick, William B., 1949–
Saving Troy: A Year with Firefighters and Paramedics
in a Battered City / William B. Patrick
ISBN 0-9768813-0-6
Library of Congress Control Number: 2005930851
1. Firefighters. 2. Paramedics
3. Emergency medical services – New York State
4. Rescue services – New York State

Hudson Whitman website address:
HUDSONWHITMAN.COM

First Edition

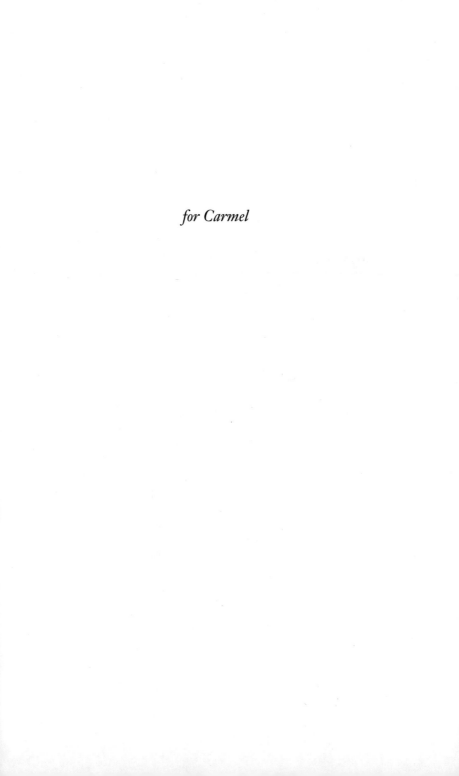

for Carmel

This is a work of non-fiction.

No dialogue has been fabricated.

No characters have been invented.

All firefighters in this book except one gave me their permission to use their actual names.

I have changed all call addresses, as well as the names of all medical patients and their relatives, to protect their privacy. The Diamonds, who also wanted their real names used, are the only exception.

If you want to talk of the whole world,
talk of your village.

— Anton Chekhov

Prologue

Mike Kelleher is sitting in the back of the liquor store, by the cooler with the refrigerated wines, when the guy shows him a serrated steak knife and says, "Get off the phone."

Until now, it had been a slow morning. A cloudy Wednesday figured to be slow. Just a couple of regulars. One who had walked down from Samaritan Hospital's alcohol rehabilitation unit, five blocks away, and was looking for some Mad Dog 20/20.

"Why were you in detox?" Mike wanted to know.

"I was having trouble with my wife and kids."

"Go someplace else, okay?"

"You can't do that."

"Fuck you I can't," Mike told him. "There are only two of us in the store, and only one of us has the keys. And I know you don't, so go someplace else and buy it."

"You can't do that," he mumbled again, but he was already shuffling toward the door.

And another regular, a professor's wife, snuck in about 10 a.m. for her pint of Romanov vodka. 10 a.m. That left her enough time to suck down her daily pint, chew some sugarless bubble gum to get any telltale odor off her breath, and still make her lunch date. Mike saw her in the Price Chopper supermarket sometimes and she'd always look away, or bury her head in the frozen pizza case until he'd passed by. The closet drinker's code — never say hello in public to anyone who knows your secret. Mike had learned quickly, the way bartenders do, about his customers' secrets.

Working at Plaza Discount Wines and Liquors, with its sign that said only LIQUOR, in the Troy Plaza on Hoosick Street, which is N.Y. State Route 7, was Mike's side job. He was a lieutenant on the 1st Platoon of the Troy Fire Department for 48 hours a week, 24 hours on then 72 off, pulling his two 24-hour tours of duty each week on Truck 1 at the 115th Street Station in North Troy. Most North Troy residents still called it Lansingburgh, or the Burgh, even though it had been part of the city of Troy since 1900.

Mike loved being a firefighter, but he wasn't thrilled about going back to the firehouse right now. His shift, the 1st Platoon, would be on tomorrow. Mike didn't much care for Truck 1 in the Burgh. It was too quiet there for him. He wanted to be downtown, at Central Station on State Street, but he was a new lieutenant, and junior lieutenants seldom got their choice of assignments. Most of the time they had to bid spots in what everyone, without the obvious irony, called the out-houses. Central Station had Medic 2, the paramedic truck which served the entire city, the Rescue Squad, which went to all the fire and trauma calls in Troy, Engine 5, and the Chiefs' cars. If you wanted to see action as a firefighter and paramedic, Central Station was the place to work, not Truck 1 in the Burgh. And he sure didn't want to be working at the liquor store today.

So he had called his friend, Phil Quandt, another firefighter, to tell him what Mike and his wife, Lori, had done on their vacation in Cape Cod when this third customer had slunk in. Customers usually just poked around, found something or didn't, and waved at Mike when they were ready to pay. No big deal. He kept talking to Phil about going back to Truck 1 the next day. Why get excited over another cheap-wine customer?

"Get off the phone now," the guy barks as he moves around the corner that houses the Scotches and Bourbons.

"I've got to go. I've got a customer here," Mike says to Phil, and he hangs up the phone, fast. *Boom. Okay, it's down,* Mike is thinking, *What does this jerk want?*

"Get up."

Mike stands up.

"You're going up to the front of the store and open the register and give me all the money. Now."

"Relax," Mike says. "You're the boss. You've got the knife."

They walk up past the Champagnes and the California wines, and Mike stops, with his back against the pint liquor bottles, leaving room for the register drawer to slide open.

"If you move, I'm going to kill you," the guy says, and works the knife tighter between two of Mike's ribs.

Mike hands him all the bills in the drawer now, but that's not good enough.

"What's in the drawer underneath?"

"Rolls of coins."

"Well, give them to me."

As Mike starts to give him the penny rolls, the guy says, "I don't want those. Give me the quarters."

"Make up your mind, will you," Mike snaps at him.

After the guy gets all the change in the bag, he asks if that's everything, and Mike nods.

"Go ahead. You've got everything. Have a nice day," Mike says.

Without smiling, he moves the knife up to Mike's throat.

"Now we're going to the back of the store."

I'm not going to the back of the store, Mike is thinking, *because I know what usually happens in the back of the store to the people that are working. I'll play the robbery game with you, but I'm not playing the homicide game.* The tip of the guy's steak knife is starting to break Mike's skin.

Mike shoves him, to get the knife away from his throat, but the guy is still behind him, and Mike feels what he thinks are two hard punches in his back. He tries to spin around to hit the guy, but he feels another sharp punch and he goes down, with the guy heavy on top of him. Now Mike spots a bloody knife on the floor, and knows they weren't punches. He grabs it, and starts swinging back.

"You want your frigging knife back. Here, take it," Mike is yelling as he swings, and he feels an adrenaline surge pump through him. The knife seems to connect a couple of times, but it's all just happening way too fast. The guy is kneeling on him, punching him now, and Mike sees Lori's face for a second. Determined to start a family, they had spent a fair portion of their two idyllic weeks on Cape Cod making love and, strangely enough, returning to Troy hadn't broken the spell. When she said goodbye to him this morning, Mike had almost decided to blow off work for the day and stay home, but he didn't tell Lori that. *I don't want to die here, not in this liquor store,* Mike thinks.

Suddenly, he hears his grandmother, dead ten years, repeating her favorite piece of advice. *Don't walk away,* he can hear her saying. *Don't ever leave home mad at somebody in your family,* and Mike is struggling to remember: *Did I forget this morning?. . . No, I said it . . . I said, Back to the old salt mines, hon . . . I love you.* Mike never left home without telling Lori he loved her. If you were a firefighter, you never knew what was going to happen to you.

Mike can't find the knife now, and he swings his head from side to side, trying to dodge the guy's punches.

If I let this son of a bitch kill me, everybody I love will be pissed off, and they're going to be hurt. He ain't killing me. That's it. One of us is walking out and it ain't gonna be him.

Mike pushes him off and grabs the counter to hoist himself

up. He pulls a bottle off the shelf next to him. It's Smirnoff 100 proof vodka. He sees the name and the blue label. That's the 100 proof. He catches the guy square in the forehead with it, but it's only a pint bottle, and the guy doesn't even blink. He's only about six feet tall, no taller than Mike, but he has broader shoulders and a prison physique.

Now the guy grabs Mike and throws him the ten feet across the store, and Mike carroms off the Cordials and Cocktails shelves. Some bottles hit him on their way down; some wobble and hit the floor next to him after he falls on his hands and knees. All the syrupy liqueur smells spring out and mix around him in the air — Sambuca, Peppermint Schnapps, something with berries, Blackberry brandy maybe.

"Stay down," the guy is yelling, and he swings a liter bottle of something that lands straight on the top of Mike's head, shatters, and runs down into both his ears. "Stay down."

Mike can see a Frangelico label, with glass and blood hanging off it, lying beside him, and now he watches the brown and yellow of a Kahlua bottle with that red, vertical stripe under the seal rise up in his peripheral vision and come around, roundhouse style, almost in slow motion, before he feels it smash above his left ear.

"Stay down, bitch. Stay down."

"I'm going to get up and you're going to be sorry you ever came in here," Mike says.

If I stay down, he's going to kill me, Mike is thinking as he struggles up off his knees and charges the guy. "Now I'm fucking pissed," he screams, and he locks a death grip on the guy's legs. "I'm going to kill you."

But now they're both down again and Mike is caught in a choke hold. He feels himself starting to black out. *This bastard ain't going to . . . If Lori's pregnant, I don't want my kid to grow up and not . . . You better think of something quick, because he's going to kill you now.*

"The cops just pulled up in front," Mike blurts out. "You're screwed. They're going to come in here and lock your ass up for this."

And suddenly, miraculously, the guy is gone, out the back door, and Mike can still see out the front windows. He can see the Key Bank branch office opposite the liquor store, and the cars pulling up to park in front of the Ames store, and a Fairbanks Express truck grinding away from the traffic light, gearing up for the Collar City Bridge, for the ribbon of Route 7 that winds west toward Latham, toward the interstates, toward the flat grey of the morning sky Mike can still see — the sky that might still, if he gets really lucky, hold a red, hazy sunset for him in about eight hours.

Off-duty firefighter stabbed
By George Pawlaczyk
The Record — September 23

TROY — A 29-year-old Troy man was charged with attempted murder Wednesday after he allegedly stabbed an off-duty city fireman during a liquor store robbery, and then hid for over five hours in the trunk of what was to have been the getaway car.

When the silver Plymouth Sundance was on Eighth Street being towed to the Troy Police garage about 4 p.m., police say William Charles Shaw, of 415 Ninth St. leaped from a rear door. The car had been under constant police guard.

They said Shaw pushed out the back seat and emerged from the trunk where he had been hiding since the 11:15 a.m. robbery of the Plaza Discount Wines and Liquors on Hoosick Street. He was captured about 20 minutes later near 121 Ninth St. after he asked a stranger to use the bathroom.

Shaw was arraigned at 7:20 p.m. in Troy Police Court where he was charged with attempted second-degree murder, robbery and first-degree robbery assault, as well as a misdemeanor count of possession of a dangerous weapon, a knife.

During the court appearance before City Court Judge Patrick J. McGrath, the defendant was uncommunicative and, at one point, slumped to one knee with his head held down and over a railing.

McGrath remanded Shaw to the Rensselaer County Jail without bail until a hearing today. He appointed a public defender for Shaw who, in a low voice, told McGrath he did not want an attorney.

The defendant wore hospital type garb, was shoeless, and had a heavy gauze strip wrapped around his head. During the arraignment, police asked Shaw to allow them to take him to a hospital to have a head wound stitched.

Minutes after the arraignment, as Shaw was being led back into the police department, he smashed his head against a wall, sustaining a new wound.

About 15 minutes later Shaw emerged strapped to a stretcher and bound for Samaritan Hospital, and then to jail.

Shaw's brother and mother said he had been released from state prison in February after serving a four-year term. The brother said Shaw, "who is a very intelligent person," was having trouble coping on the outside and has been missing appointments with a psychologist.

His mother said her son had started a new job in Menands on Tuesday.

The Troy Plaza is, for the most part, a 10-square-acre island of striated asphalt, fissured by frost-cracks and ordered here and there by pock-marked parking lines. The stores themselves, set back so far, appear to be almost an afterthought: The L-shaped, single-story row of buildings that provides the east and south borders for the parking lot is so typical and plain, with their generic signs and full-view display windows set into bland, fading facades, that you just naturally look up, at the sky, even as you walk toward them.

A Friendly's restaurant anchors the end nearest the liquor store, and the Ames department store, which squats obesely on two-thirds of the south line, is the far end. A Radio Shack, a discount sportswear store, a Chinese take-out restaurant, a card shop, a Payless Shoe Source, a beauty supply store, the Price Chopper market, a Strawberries, and a dark pub sandwiched into the corner where the two lines of tired buildings meet, all occupy the rectangular slots in between.

This is the typical strip-mall recipe we've been force-fed in small cities across the country, and it looks as anonymous here as anywhere else. Except for the Key Bank branch office marooned in the parking lot's northwest corner, it's basically an open plateau, so you would expect, on a Wednesday morning at quarter after eleven, three weeks into September, with the kids back in school and a hundred or so cars in the parking lot, that some shopper would notice a blood-soaked man staggering from the liquor store into the Sally Beauty Supply next door. But no one does.

The older woman who works at Sally begins to scream when she sees Mike. She thinks he's a robber wearing a red ski-mask. All she can see are his eyes.

As Mike slides down along the wall, he is thinking, *I must look like shit. Hey, I'm all right, lady. You get hit in the head, and you bleed a lot. It's just a head wound. Take it easy.*

"Lady, can you please call for help? Can you call the fire department?" Mike asks her.

The Sally lady is backing behind the counter, saying, "Oh, my God . . . oh, my God."

"Tell them I'm a fireman, and I think I've been stabbed."

It's hard to tell whether it's the word "fireman" or "stabbed" that snaps her out of her fear, but she stares at him for a few seconds now, and finally decides. "I'll call for an ambulance," she tells him.

For Mike, that could be a death sentence. Two commercial ambulance services, Mohawk and Troy (although EMPIRE is painted on their vehicles), are licensed to operate in the city of Troy. The overwhelming majority of their business comes from contracts to transport elderly patients between nursing homes and hospitals — "shucking lizards," in ambo-driver lingo. Despite that fact, both companies are eager to hold onto the emergency transport part of the business: Trauma calls, like stabbings, shootings, full cardiac arrests, diabetic comas, and epileptic seizures, are the more dramatic ALS (advanced life support) calls that make their employees think of reality-based TV shows and forget, temporarily, that most of them are making less than six bucks an hour to lift and carry and pull and drive, day after back-straining day.

For two years, the Troy Fire Department, with the city administration, has been trying to obtain its own license to operate emergency ambulances, not only to improve response times to calls but also to deliver better pre-hospital care to the city's residents. Unfortunately, strong lobbying by Mohawk and Empire, along with a fair amount of regional corruption, has helped defeat their proposals to the State Council. Mike and every other firefighter in the department know from painful experience how slow the ambulance companies' response times can be, and Mike knows he doesn't have that kind of time right now.

"No, lady, please. Call the fire department. 272-3400."

"What is it?" She starts to dial, hesitates, and puts the receiver back down. "What is it again?"

The only other person in the store, an elderly woman buying exfoliant and night cream, is screaming that her husband is outside, right outside, couldn't she just go out there, he is waiting to pick her up.

Mike just gazes up at her. *Hey, you go on. Don't let me stop you, but don't step on me as you hurry out, okay?* Mike thinks.

"Two-seven-two-three-four-zero-zero," Mike says now, and lets his chin flop down onto his blood-soaked chest.

The fire department dispatcher, on the third floor of Central Station, receives the call at 11:15, and sends out two tones — the first one for the BLS (basic life support) unit, Engine 2 on Bouton Road, and the second for Medic 2, the primary ALS unit, manned by two firefighter paramedics.

Over the radio, the dispatcher tells all of them that the caller is frantic, screaming that she needs the medics. That's all he's got. The police are en route. He's called for an ambulance.

Wayne Laranjo, normally the Captain of Engine 5 on Mike's Platoon, the 1st, is working overtime today, riding the backstep on Engine 2. He has a hunch it's Mike when he hears the call come in for the Troy Plaza, next to the liquor store. He knows Mike is working there and he figures he's probably been shot. He just has a real bad feeling about this one.

Now, as he arrives and sees Mike sitting cross-legged in a spreading puddle of blood, it really bothers him. Wayne has about two months left before his retirement kicks in, and seeing

Mike this way is the last thing he needs. He is already feeling burnt out. That's one of the reasons he's retiring. He's sick of watching friends and neighbors die.

Mo Catel is one of the 4th Platoon paramedics on Medic 2 today, and he doesn't even recognize Mike. He just goes to work on him. It's difficult to do the assessment because of all the blood. Where are the leaks? The patient is still talking. He's sitting upright. He has an airway, and he seems to be alert. So he's basically okay for right now, but this amount of blood means he won't be doing okay for very long.

Wayne kneels behind Mike, supporting his back with his thighs. "I'm here, Mike," he says. Mike has worked with Wayne. He trusts him. *I'm going to be all right now. Jesus, I could go for a cigarette*, he thinks.

"If you've got a cigarette, could you light one, Wayne? Let me take a couple of drags off it, okay?"

"You're not going to believe this, kid," Wayne says. "I left them back in the firehouse. But you couldn't smoke one anyway. All your goddamn blood would put it out."

Wayne finds the first gash on the back of Mike's head, and tells the hoseman next to him, "Hand me a trauma dressing. Give me that 5 x 9." He puts it on, but discovers another gash around the right side. "Give me another 5 x 9," he says now. They aren't pumping blood, like arterial bleeds, but there's a strong, constant flow from each of them. "Where's the ambulance?" Wayne wants to know.

Mo is still assessing the patient, working on the ABC's: airway, breathing, and circulation. The basics.

"What's your name, buddy?"

Jesus, Mo, who do you think it is? It's me.

"Mike," he answers.

"Okay, Mike, hang in there. We're here to help you." From that Mo knows that Mike has a clear airway, because he can talk, and his respirations seem fine for the moment.

The bleeding is the problem, and there is way too much of that. The circulatory system is a closed one, and when it gets opened up, Mo can't stay in control of his patient. He has to find all the leaks, patch them, get Mike's fluids back up, keep his airway open, and get him to a surgeon. That means a trauma center, Albany Medical Center, 10 to 15 minutes away by ambulance, depending on traffic and road conditions. 10 to 15 minutes, but that's after the ambulance gets there.

Mo keys his portable radio: "Dispatcher, get me an ETA on that ambulance, will you?"

RECEIVED, comes the dispatcher's reply.

Wayne has two trauma dressings in place now, but as he leans over Mike's shoulder to say, "You're going to be okay, kid," he sees that his forehead is laid open, too.

"Where do you work, Mike?" Mo starts to ask, and Wayne finally snaps.

"It's Kelleher, for Christ's sake, Mo. It's Mike Kelleher," Wayne barks at him, turning again to the hoseman. "Give me another trauma dressing, will you?"

Mo feels the blood drain from his own face now. He and Mike had joined the department on the same day, and he thought they were a lot alike: They were relatively aggressive firefighters; they liked the busy rigs; they had been promoted to lieutenant within six months of each other. Mike wasn't just a peer. It was like Mo was working on himself. If Mike had to die, Mo didn't want him dying in front of him. On the operating table at the Med, if he had to, okay. Mo might be able to accept that. But not right in front of him, not right here.

"110 over 70 — 21 on the respirations," Mo says, cranking up his pace another notch. "Fix me a lactated ringers, and hand me a 16, right there, second in on the top." The hoseman hands him a 16 gauge IV needle for volume replacement of fluids.

Mike is listening to everything. *Okay, at least I'm stable*, he consoles himself. *If I can stay conscious, just stay with the program . . . I can answer what . . . I'm losing blood, but if I'm . . . I must be compensating for it . . . I must be . . .*

"Where's the goddamned ambulance?" Mo is shouting into his radio. "What's the hold-up?"

MEDIC 2, NO ETA AVAILABLE YET.

"Give me two occlusive dressings," Wayne is yelling.

Mike knows what they're talking about. *Oh, the ambulances are probably doing transports,* he thinks. *The nursing home shuffle. And occlusive dressings. Wow, I must be hurting. I mean, they must think I've got a sucking wound somewhere.*

Wayne is cutting up the back of Mike's shirt and through his collar, peeling his shirt off him so he can look for more wounds. He finds some too easily. Occlusive dressings are 4 x 4 gauze pads with vaseline on them, so they stay where they're stuck, for chest wounds where air may be escaping, or where a lung may have been struck, and Wayne is already calling for a third one.

"Wayne, you're scaring the shit out of me," Mike says.

Everyone is getting worried. Wayne presses an occlusive dressing on every chest wound he finds, and by number five, he figures Mike for a collapsed lung at the very least. He hopes to God Mike's heart isn't nicked, but Mike is getting woozy now, and his blood is starting to seep through the dressings.

Mo is afraid of compensation. There's a process of shock known as compensating shock where, if a patient loses a tremendous amount of blood, his heart-rate will accelerate, and circulate whatever blood is left in the system faster and faster. His blood vessels actually contract. The pipes get smaller, to increase the pressure, so they can keep blood moving to the vital core — heart, kidneys, lungs, the brain. The problem is, the body can compensate only for a little while, and then it craps out, fast.

"Jesus, here's one near his liver," Wayne says.

Mo wipes the blood off Mike's left forearm and tries to feel his skin. In shock, the body shunts blood away from the skin, and then the skin gets cool and pale. But Mike's blood has dyed his skin, so Mo can't tell from the color.

"Mike, how you doing?" Mo wants to know. "Stay with me, pal." He ties off an elastic tourniquet. "You're going to feel a needle-stick, okay? Try not to move."

At this, Mike opens his eyes and looks down. "Jesus, I don't think I can bear to be stabbed again and have you miss, Mo. Get it the first time, will you? I don't want to be stabbed any more than I have to."

"Here's the ambulance," Wayne says.

"Troy Ambulance on the scene, dispatcher."

TROY AMBULANCE ON THE SCENE . . . ELEVEN HUNDRED THIRTY-TWO. The dispatcher states the military time, and marks on his dispatch tape the number of minutes that have passed while Mike has been waiting for that ambulance.

**Dworsky questions
ambulance response time**
By George Pawlaczyk
The Record — September 24

TROY — Steven G. Dworsky, who is determined to get a city-run ambulance service, said 13 minutes, 7 seconds is an unacceptable response time when heavy bleeding is involved.

It is the precise time a Troy firefighter, bleeding profusely from stab wounds and lacerations, waited until an ambulance showed at the Troy Plaza to whisk him to Albany Medical Center Hospital, about another 10 minutes away.

Dworsky, Troy city manager, sent a

letter Thursday to Philip Gause, president of Troy Ambulance Service, requesting that he explain why it took his company that length of time to respond.

"This is an unacceptable time lapse," said Dworsky. "We want to know why it took this long. We don't want it to happen again."

Gause could not be reached for comment.

Dworsky had a print-out made of the radio transmissions connected with the call to help Michael Kelleher, 31, a Troy firefighter and part time liquor store clerk, severely wounded Wednesday during a robbery.

Kelleher, who was stabbed, was taken to Albany Medical Center where he underwent surgery. He is in fair condition.

The print-out shows that an initial call to the fire department came in at 11:15 a.m. plus 37 seconds.

The paramedics were on their way by 11:16 a.m. plus 58 seconds.

They arrived at exactly 11:21 a.m.

The ambulance crew was called at 11:18 a.m. plus 40 seconds. They were called again at 11:26 a.m. plus 15 seconds, and again at 11:28 a.m. plus 35 seconds, and finally at exactly 11:29 a.m. Each time they were asked when they would arrive.

The ambulance pulled in at 11:32 a.m. plus 13 seconds.

A spokesman for the Regional Emergency Medical Organization (REMO), said a response time of 10 minutes is considered to be the outside limit in most medical manuals.

"But 14 minutes isn't that bad," he said.

REMO recently turned down Troy's request to establish a city-run ambulance.

The board of REMO said there is no need to augment the two ambulance services, Mohawk and Troy Ambulance Service, which operate in the city.

Mike Kelleher

On the way down to Albany one of the guys said it seemed I was like going in and out of it, but that's only because with what happened what I was afraid of was I didn't want to get sick in the back of the ambulance. If I sit in the back of a car, even if I try to ride four or five blocks, I'll get car-sick. Now, after what happened to me, stabbed eight times and hit over the head with liquor bottles, choked, I'm afraid I don't want to embarrass myself by getting car-sick in the back of an ambulance? That's what was going through my mind: Oh, I don't want to puke because I'm going to be embarrassed if I barf.

I really got scared in the trauma room at Albany Medical, when they were running the IV's, shoving a tube down my nose, down my throat, when they said, "We're bringing a cardiologist in to do an echocardiogram," and I said, "Why?" And they said, "We want to make sure when you were stabbed in the chest that he didn't nick your heart." That's when I got really scared. I thought, Oh, he hit me in the heart. *And that's when, once I was out of the liquor store and once the guy was gone, that was the time I can honestly say I was the most scared. Even with the exploratory surgery, to make sure there was no internal bleeding, that he hadn't hit any other organs inside, I said to myself,* As long as my heart and lungs are all right, I've got a chance.

When I was down there, they took my wedding band off, and that bothered me. These two fingers here were sliced open, they were laid open, and they were afraid of swelling or something like that, and that's why they wanted to take the band off then. It bothered me because that's the only one piece of jewelry I never take off, and I didn't want the band to come off.

It's like I have a St. Florian medal, too, in the shape of the Maltese Cross, and when they took the chain off my neck the medal was gone. It turned up when they were cleaning up at the liquor store, the medal turned up, so I still have the medal. St. Florian's the patron saint of firefighters, and I really figured that day, he was looking out for me. So I had those two connections: my wife gave me the St. Florian medal, too. When I thought that was gone, it really bothered me.

But as far as the care I got that day, from the fire department, from the EMTs and the paramedics, I'll never be able to thank the people that worked on me enough. My attitude now, because the doctors told me I was very lucky, that the amount of times I was stabbed, and just the number of times I was hit in the head with liquor bottles and not having any skull fractures or no damage to anything, just goes to show how thick an Irish skull is. Like I said to somebody later, "Hitting somebody who's Irish in the head, it doesn't hurt them. It just annoys them." The more he hit me, the more annoyed I got.

First thing I thought when he said to me we're going in the back of the store was, He'll kill me back there. *What if it had been the old lady in the beauty salon next door? She wouldn't have been able to fight him. What if it had been a convenience store with a 16-year-old kid working to save money for a car or college? He might not have thought that, he might have walked to the back of the store, so he'd be dead. So you know, in a lot of ways, like I said to my wife, if this guy had to go into someplace, I'd rather he came in and tried to rob me than go after some old woman or somebody like a senior citizen working in their own store, or some kid in high school. I had made up my mind when we were walking toward the back,* There's going to be one of us walking out of here and it ain't going to be you.

When I worked in the liquor store, there was a lot of poor people that came in, there was a lot of black people that came in, there was a lot of older people that came in, and my rule of thumb was: I'd try to treat people the way I'd like to be treated. When I was working in the store, if somebody came in and acted like an asshole, I wouldn't care if they were a rich, white person — my attitude was, First time I'll let you go, everybody has a bad day — *second time was,* You want to act like an asshole, okay then, I'll treat you like an asshole. Here's your stuff, have a nice day, don't let the door hit you in the ass. *I treat everybody alike, from the street people who came in every day for their bottles of wine to the RPI professors and the doctors and lawyers and Indian chiefs. Who knows what they want? I treat people the way I want to be treated. I have no animosity toward anybody because of what that guy did to me. My attitude was that he was like a meteor that fell, and I was just unlucky enough to be where he fell.*

First Platoon at Central Station — October

Terry Fox . . . . Lieutenant, Paramedic, Medic 2

Gary Hanna . . . . Firefighter, EMT, Engine 5

Mike Harrison . . . . Battalion Chief, EMT

Don Kimmey . . . . Firefighter, Paramedic, Medic 2

Wayne Laranjo . . . . Captain, EMT, Engine 5

Matt Magill . . . . Captain, EMT, Rescue Squad

Tom Miter . . . . Firefighter, Paramedic, Engine 5

Ric Moreno . . . . Firefighter, Paramedic, Engine 5

Frank Ryan . . . . Firefighter, EMT, Rescue Squad

Dave Stevens . . . . Firefighter, Paramedic, Rescue Squad

Charley Willson . . . . . . Firefighter, EMT, Rescue Squad

1

"Joe-Joe, the dog-faced boy," Don Kimmey howls as he starts up Medic 2.

Joe Reilly gives me a look that is both bemused and long-suffering and slams the passenger door. Joe is a paramedic stationed at Engine 4 usually, in Troy's urban war zone. Today he is "riding the seat," acting as lieutenant on the medic rig for Terry Fox, who is on vacation.

"ATTENTION ALL FIRE UNITS. ENGINE 3 AND MEDIC 2 ARE RESPONDING TO TROY HILLS APARTMENTS, BUILDING . . . "

As the door lifts clear and Don pulls out of Central Station, to the right, the wrong way on one-way State Street, Joe switches the black siren-knob from its 10 o'clock position at STANDBY, past WAIL at 12 and YELP at 2, and settles on the 4 o'clock, HI-LO position, which Don likens to the Bobbies' sirens in England, and its immediate wail swallows up the voice of the dispatcher announcing the call address.

Don laughs and looks past me toward Joe, who isn't rising to Don's normal bait, and past him to see if cars are coming down 5th Avenue. There aren't any, and he accelerates hard now into the turn. Ever since Don saw the Cheers episode where Carla called Cliff "Jo-Jo," after P.T. Barnum's early sideshow attraction, a Russian boy with silky yellow hair that covered his entire face, he jumps on every opportunity to toss out the hook and wait for Joe to bite. That Joe has dark hair and no beard, since firefighters can only grow moustaches, is clearly beside the point: His name is Joe, isn't it? Don even went to the trouble of cutting out small dog faces from magazine ads and pasting them onto Joe's face in the miniature gallery of firefighter portraits that hangs in each of the six fire stations in Troy.

Joe yanks the siren knob to YELP as we approach the intersection of Congress and 5th Streets, hoping the change in sound pattern will alert the drivers racing down the Congress Street hill, but Don slows there before he turns onto Congress, just in case. A lot of drivers even ignore the big Federal sirens on Engine 5 and the Rescue Squad, so why would they stop for the smaller, electronic siren that Medic 2 has?

Sirens seem mysterious and ordinary at the same time, like rivers or cemeteries. In Troy, which stretches seven miles along the Hudson River and merely two miles east, up over the hills toward Brunswick and Wynantskill, they're a common sound. Because Troy has its fair share of crime, more than its fair share of homeless and elderly citizens, and because emergency vehicles often have to race at least half the narrow length of the city to reach a call or a hospital, people in Troy are used to hearing plenty of sirens. The pedestrians we're passing, who turn or cover their ears, still look at us curiously as we flash by, but the drivers who have to pull over to let us screech by simply look annoyed.

"There's Adam," Don says, and he waves at one of the department's homeless regulars, half of him sprawled on the cold cobblestones in the Williams Street alley and the other half propped against the side of Famous Lunch, with its rows of three-inch hot dogs grilling next to the greasy front window, already steaming at 9:30 a.m.

"We'll have him before lunch," Joe says.

"Nope, right in the middle of lunch," Don counters. "Eat fast."

Joe moves to restore the HI-LO setting, but thinks better of it, and leaves it at YELP as Don turns south onto 3rd Street.

"Where we going?"

"Troy Hills," Joe answers, but his words drown in one of the siren's swells.

"Where?" Don asks again, cocking his head forward. There are two outfitted pick-ups that serve as medic trucks, and Don claims the siren on this one is the loudest. He swears riding in it for thirteen years has wrecked his hearing. "You can hear this in Watervliet," he says. That's the town where Don grew up, just over the Congress Street bridge, across the river from downtown Troy.

Joe leans in front of me. "Troy Hills Apartments, Building 5," he shouts.

"What do we got?"

"Unresponsive man," Joe answers, and sits back.

Troy Hills Apartments, at the southern tip of Troy, are near Stow Avenue, just up from the Menands Bridge. 3rd Street is the designated route south for fire vehicles from Central Station, which have almost four miles to travel if the call is at the far reaches of the city. Medic 2 and the Rescue Squad, both housed at Central Station on State Street, go anywhere in the city, while the six engines, each assigned to its own fire station, serve geographical "still" districts. That's why Engine 3 will assist Medic 2 on this call: Troy Hills Apartments are in their district.

"Who is it?" I ask Joe, as Don slows again where the tunnel under Russell Sage College funnels onto Ferry Street.

"We don't get the name," Joe says, turning to me, "just the address and the nature of the call, like this one — unknown unconscious."

"We'll go to the hospital and the nurse or doctor will ask what the name is, and that's the last thing you get. You never find that out," Don says, looking straight ahead. He doesn't address most people when he talks. He has to concentrate on driving, of course, but it's more than that. Of his nicknames — Nipper, the Little Dutchman, Duke, the Big Cat, Granite-head, Diesel Don — Nipper seems most apt: Don acts like the family dog protecting the house and family when a stranger appears. He'll wag his tail, because charm is a useful tool, but he lets you see his teeth the whole time, and you can see he'd be happy to take a chunk out of you.

"I never wonder about who they are," he continues. "You just go and take care of them. As soon as they give an address, you can tell. You know exactly what you're going on, because we may have been there, you know? The name, ah, the name might ring a bell, it might not, but the address, bang, it clicks right in."

Rows of 3-story brick houses are flashing by, many with realtors' For Sale signs on them, promising you can assume their mortgages, as we fly past Liberty Street and approach Washington. A young mother on the corner up ahead is dragging her toddler away from the curb, holding her free hand over one of her ears as the small boy jumps up and down and waves at the red, screeching truck that's whizzing past him.

"Wait till you see Terry Fox drive," Joe says now.

"Foxy starts in the center," Don jumps in, "straddling the painted line, and if someone's coming at him, he veers left, right at them, and forces them toward the curb. The cars ricochet off the parked ones at the curb and then they come back into their lane and Foxy can say, ' I didn't touch them,' you know?"

In the park that runs from Washington Street south to Adams, from the first president's street to the second, the trees have a stripped, late-November look already, even in this strong, mid-October sunlight. Only the brown leaves on the oaks are left to shiver in the morning breeze.

A woman pushing a stroller by Caprara's Auto Body Shop wheels suddenly when she hears us and hurries in the same direction we're traveling, south, as if she has had some sudden premonition that we might be heading toward a person she cares about.

Joe finally flips the siren back to HI-LO, and over the truck radio we hear the captain of Engine 3 mark its arrival at Troy Hills Apartments. Then the dispatcher comes on, repeating Engine 3's message for everyone else listening, and he ends with the time of day, 9:35.

Don laughs. "I'm telling you, I used to be really scared every once in a while, because Foxy never had control of the wheel." Don is demonstrating Foxy's style for me. "Foxy will get the gas and brake with his right foot, and then he has the high beams going with his left, and he's also got his hands busy as hell with the horn and spotlight, like this."

A driver in front of Kennedy's towing garage nods at us and heaves an armful of chains into the back of his truck. We cross Jefferson, then Ida Street. Don blows the horn a couple of times as we fly over the bridge that spans the Poestenkill Creek, throwing a wave at the closed door of Engine 6 at Canal and 3rd, but no firefighters are standing out in front to wave back.

More presidents' streets now — Madison, Monroe, where a huge, blue minaret sits atop the Ukrainian church, Jackson Street with the Carmelite Priory of St. Joseph's — and on past Van Buren, where 3rd Street merges into 4th, which is U.S. Route 4. Not far now, and I wonder if the unconscious man's family is there with him, and if they can hear our siren.

"So Ric Moreno named Foxy the one-man band," Don continues, "because he always had everything going." Then he smiles over at Joe for confirmation that it's all true.

A construction worker directing traffic where 4th Street becomes Burden bows and waves us through. We shoot up Burden, past the South End Tavern with its sign still advertising a

LADIES ENTRANCE, and onto Stow Avenue. Troy Hills Apartments appear above us now, to our left, row after row of 2-story, light-brick garden apartments with white front doors that are framed by four thin, white columns stretching the full height of each building. We can see the lights of Engine 3, still flashing, in front of Building 5.

Don turns left onto Cottage Street. Joe switches the dial back to STANDBY and the siren abruptly stops. He keys the radio.

"Medic 2 arriving."

And the dispatcher answers, "MEDIC 2 ON THE SCENE, ZERO NINE THREE SIX. MOHAWK AMBULANCE EN ROUTE."

Each identical building has its distinguishing number above its door. Don and Joe grab their bags from the side compartment and we rush in under the number 5.

Inside the living room, Harold Burke appears to still be watching *Regis and Kathie Lee*, but with his eyes closed. Except for that, he seems perfectly attentive: His long fingers, draped over the arms of the overstuffed chair, don't drum or fidget; he sits up pretty straight; his head is bent just slightly to the left, as if he wants the chance to make one final appraisal of Kathie Lee's legs; and his mouth is closed in a pale, tight line, ensuring his silent reception of every televised sound. Harold has become the eye of this particular storm, the only calm spot in a swarming room.

"Harold N. Burke," the captain of Engine 3 repeats, writing as he speaks, filling in the PCR (pre-hospital care report) which, if Harold was almost dead, the paramedics would take with them to the hospital to complete.

"M," a woman crying and holding her forehead with both of her hands says, but Regis and Kathie Lee are sitting in among the audience, stumbling through an introduction for a country and western band, and the fan next to Kathie Lee is hugging her and screaming, so the captain can't hear her and asks her to say it again. "Not *N*. It's *M*. Harold *M*. Burke." She is shouting now in her frustration and grief. "It's an *M*. in the middle."

"How old is Harold?"

"He'll be 72 next Friday."

"What's your name?" the captain asks.

"I'm his daughter. I'm his daughter, okay?" she says, sobbing hard now, staring hopelessly at the unanimated body in the familiar, flower-print chair.

Don eases back one shut eyelid, then the other, shining a penlight into each before he slides it back closed. Then he unbuttons Harold's shirt and sticks three white circles on Harold's chest and side. They're fast patches, for the monitor/defibrillator, and he hooks the white and black leads to the patches that will show any electrical activity in Harold's heart. Joe holds a finger on Harold's carotid artery and tries to look expressionless.

The curtains are drawn, creating a palpable gloom that is strobed erratically by flashes from the TV as the camera angles switch, and I can see there are five or six other people, relatives or friends or neighbors, who have arranged themselves around the room. Two older women huddle together on the couch, and a younger woman kneels by their legs. A middle-aged man leans against a far corner, covering his eyes. A boy about ten stands near the window, as far away from the body as he can get, but he watches everyone curiously. He is the only one who isn't crying, except for the firefighters, and me, and I know I'm getting close.

The country and western group is rolling now, their pedal steel accompaniment immediately grating in this stricken room, and Don throws the TV a menacing look.

"Get that off," he commands, and one of the engine crew searches for the power button a few seconds and then finds it. Don watches the dark, rectangular monitor screen, and a flat green line moves horizontally across it, from left to right, uninterrupted by a single peak or valley.

Joe tips Harold's body toward his left side to see his lower back and his right arm flops against his leg with a heartbreaking thump in the new quiet of the room. Don rolls his right sleeve back and checks his forearm for dependent lividity — the pooling of blood in the low areas of a dead body — and even from near the door anyone can see the long, purple smear there.

Don is all business here. He is the shortest man in the room, as well as on his shift at Central Station, about 5' 7", but he radiates confidence. He unsnaps the monitor leads and quickly winds them. He folds Harold's shirt closed and rolls his sleeve back down. Even in these menial tasks, he exudes a professional air. He projects the studied invulnerability of coordination, moving wordlessly in front of Harold's family as he packs up his tools. No turning to talk to a family member. No contemplative glance at the still-warm body. With the deep half-moons under his eyes, his wide forehead, a hair-line that recedes deeply on both sides of a shock of fine-brown hair that curls down and to the right, and his face far too boyish to suggest that he will be 42 in a couple of months, Don looks and acts very much like Napoleon Bonaparte's American brother.

That he is a stranger arbitrarily allowed inside a family's private grief, five feet away from a daughter sobbing for the dead father she loved, doesn't seem to register as even a passing blip on his personal radar screen. He hefts the re-assembled monitor and unused oxygen bag and strides out of the apartment, purposefully relaxed, like a veteran middleweight on his way back to his dressing room after an easy bout.

"Sorry," Joe Reilly is saying to everyone, over and over. Unlike Don, Joe is visibly shaken. A very large woman has moved a lawn chair next to the apartment door, and she squats there like one of the tenement building guards in *Soylent Green*, but without a machine gun, and Joe says, "I'm sorry," as he pushes past her as well.

Up ahead, on the sidewalk next to Medic 2, Don is laughing with Engine 3's captain.

"These shows like *Rescue 911* do us a real disservice," Joe confides to me as we walk toward the truck. "Because, you know, almost all the stories on TV are happy. There's this big crisis and the EMTs rush in and they fix everything, and then the person gets better. Very few people really get better. 90 percent of our calls, if they're heart attacks or someone who's unknown unconscious like this one, we can't save them. They're dead. And we might watch it happen five times a day."

Don slides the bags and monitor back onto the side compartment shelves now and slams the double doors. His face shows, if anything, the faint traces of a smile.

"I see every single death in this city on the days I work," Joe continues. "I can't save them. There are some streets I can't drive on anymore because I keep seeing what happened to the people in accidents there. Most of the streets in this city hold some terrible memory for me, and I live with them all the time. How do you think these reality shows make me feel?"

Harold M. Burke, 71

TROY — Harold M. Burke, 71, of Troy Hills Apartments died Monday at his residence.

Mr. Burke was born in Troy. He was educated at St. Mary's School and Troy High School.

He was employed for many years by the former American Locomotive Co. in Schenectady.

Survivors include his daughter, and several nieces, nephews and cousins.

Services will be held at 8:45 a.m. Wednesday in the John N. Clinton Funeral Home, Washington Park and 3rd Street.

Burial will be in St. Joseph's Cemetery.

Calling hours will be 4-7 p.m. today in the funeral home.

* * *

Headquarters. Central. Engine 5. Central Station. The Clubhouse. These are the agreed-upon names for the principal fire station in Troy. Disgruntled firefighters occasionally use other choice names for it, too. It's a three-story red brick building at 51 State Street. Its right side extends to where State meets Sixth Avenue and houses the Troy Police Station. The left side, set back behind a substantial apron, holds the Troy Fire Department. On the first floor, it's all doors: four tall, brown-steel garage doors, framed by ornately-carved stone panels, for the vehicles that move off the apparatus floor, and a human-scale glass door that leads to the Troy City Court, which uses the front half of the building's second floor.

Fire Chief Schultz and Assistant Chief Thompson have their offices in the back half of the second floor, as does the Troy Firefighter's Union, Local 2304. Fire and police dispatchers answer emergency calls on the third floor, in the front. Halfway up the Fire Department's side, the face of a stone lion holding a carved, drawn curtain reveals, in high relief, the date the building was completed, 1923, though the fire department didn't occupy it until three years after that.

Inside, in the common room, behind Medic 2 and the Rescue Squad and all the other vehicles parked on the apparatus floor, it's time for lunch — sausage and peppers — and Tom Miter is claiming that Frank Ryan makes love to his food.

Johnny Quest or Johnny Good Guy, those are Tom's nicknames. "Just look at him," Ric Moreno told me when I asked for an explanation: In his mid-30's, about six feet tall and a little husky, with a blonde moustache and dark blonde hair, Tom looks like one version of the quintessential fireman. He smiles now and nods in Frank's direction.

I watch as Frank diligently arranges his sausage, puckered ends curving up, like a pudgy letter "C" stretching out onto its back, relaxing down into the open torpedo roll. He laces it carefully in place with translucent onion strings and edge-blackened slices of green pepper, and then lays two straight lines of ketchup along its sides.

"Now watch this," Tom says.

Frank lifts the sandwich, squeezing gently to retain all its glistening, steaming parts, and steers one end toward his mouth. He shuts his eyes and slides it in, closing on it slowly, not just chomping off a chunk but more separating it gently from the rest, savoring it for a few seconds before his jaws go to work, and suddenly his posture reveals an unmistakable swooning quality.

"He loves it," Tom says.

"Yeah, but will he respect it in the morning?" Dave Stevens wants to know.

The 20 by 30 foot common room is uncommonly dingy. It is part TV room, with two worn, light-brown vinyl couches, and part dining room, with three formica tables shoved together and surrounded by 14 unmatched, blue and black molded chairs. The stained, off-white sheetrock walls hang above horizontal sheets of waist-high exterior plywood and lend the whole room a grimy look. A row of streaked windows set high in the far wall allows in only a vague, gauzy light. Several of the overhead fluorescent fixtures aren't working — bulbs are burned out, and faulty capacitors buzz constantly — so the glowing Pepsi machine turns out to be the brightest element in the room.

In spite of all that, though, Central has an oddly welcoming, distinctly lived-in, boys' clubhouse feel to it. An extended family inhabits this place. These are brothers, whether they're related by blood or not. The cliché about the fire service functioning as a brotherhood doesn't seem to apply as a cliché here. They even call each other "brother," and appear to mean it. There haven't been any women firefighters in the Troy Fire Department yet, and while everyone realizes that situation won't last much longer, this is still very much a guys' joint. You can burp with gusto here. You can fart and not apologize. You can walk around the bunk room naked. You can holler. You can argue. And you better learn how to "bust balls" if you want to survive in this place.

Right now, the argument about whether the general public in Troy really knows much about what firefighters actually do has displaced the earlier one about layoffs being certain if the Republicans win the election and toss the current City Manager and Democrat, Steve Dworsky, out on his backside.

Gary Hanna, at the far end of the table, nearest the television, yells out, "I think the basic majority in this city don't know anything about our job, except that we put out fires."

Ric Moreno, who has been reading the *Record*, Troy's primary newspaper, folds it up and takes off his glasses. Ric loves to play devil's advocate. "Come on. We've done EMS for 13, 14 years now, we'll run over 8000 calls this year, and every single one of those calls wasn't the same person, you know? That's a lot of different houses we've gone to. A lot of neighborhoods. A lot of next doors. I think a lot of people have been affected or touched by the EMS side of our service."

EMS (Emergency Medical Service) calls account for almost 75% of the calls that firefighters answer in Troy, and there is a continuing debate about the role of EMS continuing in the fire service here at all, especially among the fire veterans and the chiefs, most of whom were here long before they had to go out on any medical calls. A lot of firefighters just want to fight fires and handle rescues again.

"Nothing, they know nothing," two or three voices agree at the same time.

"Not nearly enough," Tom says. Tom puts his sandwich down for this. "They don't know why a hose line puts out a fire. They don't know why you're breaking windows. They don't know why you're cutting holes in their roof."

Dave interrupts to make a point. "They don't know that we're all here on Christmas Day, or what it takes to be here then, or on Christmas Eve, the emotion that's involved in not being with your family."

"They only know that when they call you, you show up," Tom continues. "And after that, they don't have any idea what you're doing. None. What do they *believe* about us? Checkers. Cards. Beer. Women. Lazy. Noisy. Football. Lots of overtime, but only in Troy, probably. What they know is that we go inside burning buildings and they know it's dangerous. I'm sure they don't know exactly what goes on in there, because all they have to go on is what they see on TV, and every fire you see on TV is a TV fire — a fire that's well-ventilated, where you can all stand up and just walk through the place and put the fire out. People know *Backdraft*. And for paramedics, they know *Emergency* from re-runs, or *Rescue 911* now."

Strangely enough, Dick Thompson, the deputy chief, who has been feuding with the 1st Platoon about almost everything for the last year or so, has decided to eat lunch with the men today, maybe to monitor what they say in front of me, a visiting writer, because all writers are as dangerous as reporters in Dick's eyes. Like many people entrusted with public safety, Dick has decided to be afraid of letting outsiders know too much. Suddenly, in a slightly mocking tone, he tosses out his opinion. "I don't think most people have the foggiest idea of what it's like to climb up a burning stairway, or what it's like to rappel into the gorge, or what it's like to be first in on a shooting, or what it's like to jump into the river," he says. "When they think about a guy jumping into water and saving somebody that's drowning, they're thinking, *Lake George, the sun's out, a nice, clean guy who's not drunk, he's not fighting me.* That's what most people think."

Charley Willson is sitting to my right, finishing his sandwich and trying not to get involved in the discussion. Like most of the guys on the 1st Platoon at Central Station, he's a veteran, with eighteen years on the job. He's on the thin side, maybe 5' 11", with a dark moustache and a haircut that makes him look a little like Alfalfa from the 1930's Little Rascals comedy shorts. Charley works on the Rescue Squad and everyone calls him Teflon Charley, because Dick never seems to blame anything on him.

He asks me what the call was at Troy Hills Apartments, and I tell him. But then I want to know how firefighters process all the deaths they witness, and why Don seemed to be acting so detached on that call.

"Other fire departments, when they have a death or something, you know, whether it's a fireman or somebody else, they bring in counselors," Charley says. "We've never done that. And I think a lot of our counseling gets done right here, while we're eating. I mean, with black humor and all, that's a big part. As bad as it is, it's a big part, and you've got to just break into the trauma, especially when we see kids get hurt.

"You'll see, if we have a kid in a bad accident, where he's mangled or something, you bring that back and you're stuck on that all night, you know? And you never know, because sometimes the guys who stay quiet about calls, you say, 'Oh, that doesn't bother them,' but they're the ones who are holding it inside. They might be the ones who are worse off, because the other guys are getting it out, talking about it. So you can never know what people are thinking."

Tom has been listening to Charley, too. "The family's a distraction on calls," he says. "Unless you're in a dangerous situation, you've got to have tunnel vision. You let the company officer talk to the family. You just do what you've got to do. And Don's the best paramedic on this job. He's got the most experience, and he really cares about the program. Not that I think I'm lousy. I'm not. But working with a guy like that, you'll never make him look bad, even if you're a bad paramedic. The worst you'll do is complement him, because he's always going to know what to do."

Charley jumps in again. "You see dead bodies almost every day you work, and it's not always traumatic. It's ordinary," he says. "Out of the ordinary is, say, somebody's mangled or something, the type of situation where how they died isn't ordinary, but we're so used to people dying. It's not that we're cold to it, but we can accept it better. It's just part of the job.

"You know, like we had this one guy. Tom, you remember the guy down at Levonian's meat plant there, he got caught in the sausage maker? His arm got dragged in. After that call, we came back here and we were having sausage and peppers, like today, and we were saying, 'I'm glad we got these before that new batch hits the racks, you know?'

"He was trapped inside this sausage-making machine. His arm was so broken, it got his shoulder, too, you know? He got pulled in so bad he even had a puncture wound on his forehead." Charley is trying to contort himself to approximate the way the guy was all twisted inside the machine.

"He's in there and he's just like this and he had all these clothes on, because down there it's freezing inside that plant. They got like two or three sweatshirts on and a jumpsuit on, like a white jumpsuit on, and we had to cut all these clothes off him to get at him because we couldn't tell what was what. And then his blood's dripping out and everything while we're doing it so you don't know what's broken or anything.

"Well, then, we get him all out, and he says, 'All right, before you lay me down, can I have a cigarette?' And we're going, 'Are you shitting me?' You know, that's all the guy wanted. 'Well, I know they won't give me one in the hospital,' he said, and the guy was in so much pain he couldn't move, and all he wanted was a cigarette. I said, 'I guess this isn't your lucky day, you know? I don't smoke.'

"So that was his mentality, and I felt bad, because he was probably in shock and he was probably thinking the only thing that was going to make him feel better was a cigarette, because he didn't even want oxygen. He was just in so much pain.

"Then we came back and, like I said, we had to sit down and we were eating the sausage and here we still had that smell like the meat, you know, the meatpacking shit. It's just got that aroma to it. And we were all laughing about it, because it's a way to deal with the trauma, right? And it's not something where you're laughing about that guy, because you know what he's going through. I know he had a bad summer. I mean, there's no doubt about it."

Everyone else at the table is still eating, or saying the city administration is talking about closing down Engine 4 on North Street. They're not even paying attention to Charley's story about blood and broken bones and life-threatening sausage machines.

"Apparently, he didn't lose his arm," Charley goes on. "He had broken ribs, he had a broken shoulder, he had a compound fracture of the arm and everything. It was the big, weaving sausage-maker. Did you ever see one of those? His clothes got caught and he got pulled in, and the machine was still going. Somebody ran over and shut the machine off, but his arm was still in there. You've just got to get that out of your system, you know, what you went through. It's just so gross to see and everything. And then, everybody always wants to know, 'Oh, jeez, how can you eat? How can you get through stuff like that?'"

"We're lucky here in Troy," Tom says. "We have a real good working relationship with the city, because of EMS. When it was just fires, you didn't talk to the people. You went in, put the fire out, and you didn't have time to talk. This is high visibility now. It's not like Schenectady, where—"

Suddenly Chief Thompson interrupts. "Wait a minute, now," he says. It looks like Tom has touched on one of his sore subjects. "It's not the EMS. The city needs a fire department. We're just doing EMS because we're already here. You can see right over in Schenectady where it's working against them. The City of Schenectady is saying, 'Lookit, we don't have the money no more. What are we gonna get rid of? Let's get rid of EMS. We don't need it. The ambulances can take care of it.' And the same thing can happen here, I'm telling you."

At this point, I ask how EMS got started at the Troy Fire Department, but I can see right away I've asked the wrong question. Dave and Tom get up and clear their places, and Ric heads for the kitchen to start the red sauce for supper. Frank becomes even more involved with his food. "Ron Baker," a couple of guys say, but nobody seems to want to talk about him in front of Chief Thompson, and an awkward silence begins.

I know Ron Baker was hired in the late 1970's to start the EMS program for Troy, I was told he left a few years ago to become EMS Coordinator for the Town of Colonie, and I learned almost right away that there had been some bad blood between Dick Thompson and Ron when he was working in Troy, but nobody's going to tell me much more right now.

Don Kimmey, in his usual seat at the head of the table, finally breaks the silence. "Know what we do?" he calls out. "The poor people in Troy, yeah, they know. They see us all the time. The rich people, nope. They just know that when they call, they get somebody right away. It doesn't matter to them, they could have a plumbing problem. They could have anything. They call the number, they're going to get somebody right away to come take care of them. The rich people, they got insurance to pay for everything. They don't care. That's why the

EMS system is the best thing that happened here, because it takes care of all incomes. Poor, middle income, high. Everybody. Because we're all going to get sick. We're all going to die."

* * *

"He wasn't making no sense," the woman in the white blouse and badly-wrinkled brown skirt is saying.

"What's his name?" Don Kimmey shouts.

He looks too old to be a student, Don is thinking. *What the hell's he doing here? This is supposed to be for students.*

We are at Campus View Apartments, on Route 4 leading east out of Troy, next to Hudson Valley Community College, for the second call of the afternoon. The one right after lunch was a dryer fire that Engine 4's crew put out before we even got there.

"He didn't have no coherence, just rolling all over like that. He was drinking all weekend," she says.

The man, wearing only a stained, torn undershirt, suddenly flops off the bed and smashes face-first onto the hardwood floor.

"His name's Wayne, Donny," Tom Miter says, and then turns back to the woman. "Are you his wife or his girlfriend?" he asks her.

"He was complaining of a headache, trying to put his shirt on as though they were his pants. I went to give him a drink and he just threw it into his own face. He was drinking, you know. 100 proof, Mr. Boston vodka. I found the bottle."

"Are you his wife?"

She hands Tom a prescription bottle and says, "Here's what I told you about, what he keeps in his drawer. I don't know what they're for. Jesus, I have kids in here. I don't want them to see this stuff."

"Wayne, come on, pal. Relax," Don is saying. "You know who the President is, Wayne?"

Tom throws the prescription to Don. "Here's what he took,

Don. She thinks the most he got was six. Most likely just five. But she says there could be other things she doesn't know about, too."

"Does Wayne act like this most of the time?" Don wants to know.

"Not unless he's really drunk," she answers.

Wayne is sitting up next to the bed now, flailing his arms, hitting the wall and the side of the bed and then the wall again.

"Who's the President? Look straight at me, pal. You know who the President is?"

Campus View Apartments, it's students mostly. It could be the booze. It could be an overdose here with all these students. I've treated overdoses here. We've been here before.

"Why did you call us?" Tom asks the woman.

"My daughter, when she got home from school, she called me at work. 'Mom, come home,' she said. 'Wayne's not right.' And when I got here, he was like this, and rolling all over the bed. He's an alcoholic, but I never seen him like this. It scared the shit out of me."

"Put your arm down," Don tells Wayne. "Here, let me hold your hand. We just want to take your blood pressure. Easy, easy. Relax, nobody's gonna hurt you. Come on, Wayne. Help us out here, buddy."

"He kept telling me he had a headache, a real bad one," she says, and Don looks up fast.

"How long has this been going on?"

"Well, Saturday, he started complaining of having a cough, a cold, you know, and he—"

"No, the head pain," Don interrupts. "Saturday it started? Did he get hit in the head? Did he fall?"

"No," she says. "He just said he had headaches, and he started drinking the vodka, like usual."

We had that kid seven, eight years ago, Don is remembering. *He was acting the same way, naked and rolling around on the bed crazy like this and then, zoom, he just shit right in the bed. We took him out of there and we were all laughing afterwards about it, and then he died that night. He had that aneurysm in his brain and it let go and none of us caught it.*

Don is animated now, kneeling in front of Wayne, between the wall and the bed. "Wayne, look at me now, right here. This is a pen-light. I want to look in your eyes. Open them big. That's it. Come on, Wayne, tell me who the President is, will you?"

"Nixon," Wayne finally says.

"Close, buddy," Don answers. "Pupils dilated and reactive, Tom. Let's get going here."

Wayne is groaning loudly now, trying to slide down onto the floor, and Don catches him.

"We want to take you to the hospital, all right, Wayne. You're acting a little bizarre. You got a pair of underwear? Let's get some drawers on you."

"Does he take any illegal drugs — cocaine, heroin?" Tom asks.

"No, he don't do nothing like that," she says.

Don finds some shorts under the bed and tries to put them on Wayne. "Put your foot in. Come on, pal. I'm trying to help you."

"I tried doing that all day, putting clothes on him," she says now, turning to walk out of the bedroom. "He wouldn't let me. He needs some help. I've got kids, you know. I can't let them see this shit."

* * *

In Medic 2, on the way back to Central Station from Samaritan Hospital, after a half hour of fighting Wayne off the ambulance stretcher and onto a hospital gurney, where he pulled his IV out and sprayed his blood all over the nurse trying to attach the leather restraints on his arms, and after the young ER doctor confirmed Don's field diagnosis of an aneurysm and hurried Wayne up for a CAT scan, Tom and Don are doing the call critique.

"We had to re-do the straps so he wouldn't yank the IV out again. You don't want to restrain a guy who's just sick. He's not a drunk that's being belligerent," Tom says. "He will die, if you leave him go like that, if that's the problem, an aneurysm, which is what the doctor thinks. I've never had a patient like that before. I mean, I've had tons of wacky patients, but usually you know why. And it's tough when you just don't know why, and you have no idea exactly what's causing it. And the only thing we had to go on was Donny had a patient like that before, and that's what it turned out to be."

For Don, this seems to be no big deal, but this aneurysm call reveals a lot about his methods: If there's a patient who is alive when they answer the call, he'll fight harder than anybody to save him. This guy, Wayne, still had a fighting chance when we found him.

"It could have been hypoxia, where you're not getting enough oxygen to the brain," Don explains, "like the people in CHF, congestive heart failure, they'll act bizarre because the brain isn't being oxygenated enough. He could have been only hungover, but you can't take a chance. Let's just put it this way, all right — he's not acting normal. And that's what I look at. When we go to somebody's home, that's the first thing you ask. Do they act like this normally, or is this out of the normal? If they say it's abnormal behavior, then you work on him. That's it."

Dick Thompson

We're here because the city needs a fire department. We're doing EMS because we're already here, and they're already paying us, and therefore they're utilizing us. If they don't need the fire department, they're not going to have EMS people. We're here to fight fires. We're like an army. You have to have an army. You need it for defense. They're not going to keep an army around to — once in a great while when there's a flood — to help out with sandbags. I didn't feel that we should drop our primary responsibility, just ignore it, which they did for about five or six years, and things really got bad here.

Well, when we got started up with the Emergency Medical Services stuff, Ron Baker's role was nothing, because he didn't work here. He wasn't here. He was non-existent at the time. My recollection of it was I had been out to the state fire academy, where I was looking for a Hurst tool at the time, a jaws of life tool for the Rescue Squad, and I had picked up some materials on EMS. When I came back, I took the stuff that I had received and I brought it to George O'Connor, the Commissioner of Public Safety, and he said he was going to look into it. Then there was a gap, I don't know how long a time period, and all of a sudden things started to happen. I think George O'Connor took that information and ran with it.

The only involvement with EMS I had at the beginning was they asked for my opinions in going over the resumes of the people looking for the job. We needed a training instructor. That's actually what Ron Baker was hired for, was a training instructor. He was a school teacher. He was involved in the volunteer EMS system over in Colonie, and he was a volunteer firefighter. He didn't have much background in fire-fighting. And also he had some — not a lot — but some background in the EMS system in the Town of Colonie. I shouldn't say some. He had a lot of background, in comparison to our level. Right now, though, we've probably got 50 guys downstairs who are more qualified than he was or is now. I mean, their level of experience. Guys like Kimmey, or Foxy, they probably have ten times the experience right now that Ron had when we hired him. At the time, we had nobody. We needed an outsider. We needed a teacher. And that's why Ron was picked. Ron did a lot, but the problem I had, after a period of time, was that Ron could see nothing else but EMS. As far as he was concerned, he wanted to close down the firehouses and everything would be EMS.

The average EMS call in this city takes between 2 and 5 men, normally three men, okay? A fire call may take 38 men, 70 men, and it may take 6 hours instead of seven minutes. So you can break it down into work-minutes. You can break it down to what happens if we do go and we don't go. I'll give you an example.

We were standing over in the City Manager's office one day, not too long ago, and a call come in for Monument Square Apartments. There was something else going on. I don't know if they were picking up from a two-alarm fire or what. And there was a delay in somebody getting there. It was a basic life support call. And about ten minutes went by, and the fire department shows up. They got an engine there. And then about another half hour went by and an ambulance showed up. Then I watched and I said, "Did you notice? Nobody cared." Why? Because that's just the normal life-cycle. People sometimes get hurt. People sometimes need assistance. Well, most people don't define that as a true emergency. But if there was a fire in that building and *nobody showed up for thirty minutes, there'd be an uprising, because fire can't wait.*

Nine-tenths of your EMS calls are not true emergencies where if you're not there within two minutes it's going to make a difference. And unfortunately a lot of your calls, even though we are there and we can make the people comfortable and we can get them to the hospital, the life-cycle is such that, you know, we can't change the fact that they're 78 years old and they're having trouble with their heart. You might buy them a little bit of time and you might make them feel more comfortable and all that's good, but I don't think it's the same thing as if you had a fire in that building and the fire department didn't show up.

That fire, if it's not stopped and dealt with immediately, can interrupt multiple lives, can interrupt multiple dollars and all that. That's what scares people, and that's why they demand an immediate response from the fire department. But on EMS calls, it's kind of like, you know. On the critical ones, obviously it's important, but on the majority of EMS calls there's a certain amount of tolerance there, or understanding if you're tied up a little bit.

See, Ronnie Baker would go into the office and somehow, him and the people who were pro-EMS, he got to them. Things aren't that simple — EMS and fire. If you only have two categories, and one's fire, and one's EMS, where are you going to put pump-outs? Where are you going to put rescue calls? People trapped in the Poestenkill Gorge? Cars rolled over? People drowning? They're rescue calls. My point is, we went on all those calls before EMS existed, so when you start to talk the differences, put everything here that we traditionally did, and then put EMS calls here. But what they're doing is they're feeding this side, the EMS side, because they got a 2% raise one year based on productivity. That's just not right.

2

Dave Stevens is pacing in Olivia Fuller's dining room. "I can't work on her in that bathroom. There's no room in there," he says. "They've got to get her out."

A case of saline bottles sits on the floor beside a soiled, green Barcalounger.

"Her legs are all discolored. They're all messed up from lack of circulation," Dave explains, motioning toward the bottles. "She's got saline home for soaking them. She's been wrapping her feet."

"How long's she been in there?" Wayne Laranjo asks. Wayne is acting captain on the Rescue Squad today.

"Two days," George Badgley, senior hoseman on Engine 4, answers. We're on 5th Avenue in the Burgh, close enough to Hoosick Street to still be in Engine 4's district. "She's laying right back against the toilet, and wedged kind of along the wall. Her husband says she's been there two days."

"Where's he been pissing?" Wayne demands. "What, did he just find her?"

He takes a few steps toward the door for a breath of fresh air. "Well, she ain't just pissing in there, that's for sure."

He's right about that. The smell of shit is overpowering in the room, acrid enough so it seems to color everything, even the dim light filtering through the dirty beige curtains in the living room. It welcomed us as soon as we hit the porch steps, but Wayne seems to be the only one willing to address it. Besides being burned out from twenty-two years on the job, he's been working a vast amount of overtime, sometimes four or five 24-hour tours a week. He was working an overtime tour the day Mike Kelleher was stabbed.

Wayne gets first shot at overtime because he's a short-timer: He put in his retirement papers almost a year ago, and he's down to ten work days left on his regular shift, as captain of Engine 5, until he's all through with the fire service. He is on the "wheel of fortune," as many of the younger firefighters enviously call it, because the "intent men," the firefighters who have filed their papers that verify their intent to retire, get called first for all overtime. The union's rank and file approved it in a union vote over a year ago, and the men who aren't retiring can see now what's happening, and they don't like it. There's a lot of over-time these days, and hardly any intent men turn it down, no matter how tired they are, and hardly any men who aren't retir-ing get to work extra days anymore. A lot of money is sliding into a few, select pockets.

What Wayne is trying to do is boost his earnings up as high as he can for this last year, because his pension will be half the amount of his final year's salary, for the rest of his life — and he and his wife are planning to move to Mexico and live on that pension — but four 24-hour tours a week are tough for anybody. So he's tired and edgy most of the time now, although he's still right about the smell in here.

Wayne walks over to monitor the action. It's a typical bathroom, with a cheap, wall-hung sink and a grimy tub shower, both in faded, Pepto Bismol pink, and now it's crammed full of fire department navy blue. With five men crammed in there, Wayne can't even see enough of the floor to calculate the room's size. He has to look up at the ceiling to figure it — maybe five feet wide by seven feet deep. Olivia is in there, too. He can briefly see parts of her as the three firefighters and two Mohawk Ambulance workers shift around each other, but he can't hear her breathing. Her eyes, sunk deep in her puffy, ashen face, are closed.

"Where's the oxygen? Get some oxygen on her, for Chrissake," Wayne says.

"We can't fit the tank in here," George answers. "We've got to come in the window with it."

In the living room, Dave is pacing. He knows Mohawk was called first, because we walked past the ambulance on our way in. This is pretty typical. The ambo EMTs couldn't handle the problem, so they called the fire dispatcher for help. Dave also knows there wouldn't be this kind of dangerous delay if the fire department had its own ambulances, but the private companies have a vested interest in keeping all the transports for themselves. One of the ambo workers sticks his head past Wayne now and asks Dave if he has a tarp covering the hoses on his engine.

"We don't have hose. We're the Squad," Dave snaps back. There's no love lost between him and the ambulance companies.

Wayne just ignores the ambo guy and turns to Dave. "What about one of our flame-resistant blankets?"

Dave is frowning harder than usual now as he scans the room, trying to discern what's usable in the monochromatic gloom. "There's a bedspread over here," he says, and starts toward it.

"I want something that's not gonna rip," Wayne says. "Let's lift her up with the air bags and slide the flame-resistant blanket under her."

The air bags are actually stiff squares of inflatable, reinforced Kevlar, about an inch thick, but they feel like hard rubber mats, fully textured on both faces with rubber points so they won't slip too easily. The Squad carries four different sizes, from the smallest, a fourteen-inch square, to the largest, which is two feet by two feet. They inflate them with compressed air from their Scott tanks — the self-contained breathing apparatuses they carry on their backs into fires — and one tank will fully inflate even the two-foot square size. The bags are thin enough to slip into confined spaces, like under damaged cars, which is where they use them most often, to lift up twisted wrecks and free trapped victims. The smallest bag can lift a twelve-ton truck eight inches off the ground. The belly of the largest bag inflates to almost a foot high, quietly, unlike the metal "jaws of life," and can lift thirty-two tons. If they stack one bag on top of another, they can lift Olivia a couple of feet up and then ease her off the toilet.

"I don't know," George calls from inside the bathroom. "The only thing, with the air bag, once you put it against the toilet, it'll break the bowl, you know what I'm saying? She's laying right back against this toilet."

Wayne isn't deterred. "We'll use the wall then. We'll inflate a bag against the wall and get her off the toilet and down onto the blanket. Then we can drag her out here and get her up on the stretcher. You can't fit her on the reeves. She's too big. She won't fit through the door. You can't make that turn."

"She won't fit past the sink," George says.

Wayne is already on his way out. "Take out the sink then. I'm gonna put the oxygen on her from outside."

"This is what you deal with, you know," Dave says. He is nervously smoothing his thick moustache, which curves down around the corners of his mouth, and I wonder if he is instinctively trying to block the palpable stench in the air.

He shoots an appraising glance over at the husband now, who is standing in a dark corner of the dining room, next to a massive oak table which is covered by empty, unwashed cans of Spaghetti-O's and four loaves of economy-size Wonder Bread, piled on top of each other. A ring of mold has a substantial foothold in the loaf on top.

"She's been in there two days, right, and she's weak now," Dave goes on. "A workout for her is probably walking to the kitchen and back. She's not in distress. She's just too big. There are five guys in with her already, and it's a small bathroom. Even if I was going to do ALS, I wouldn't do it in there, anyway. Let them do their job, which right now is extrication. There's enough people in there."

* * *

RESCUE SQUAD: ASSIST ENGINE 4 AT ONE EIGHT SEVEN 5TH AVENUE. 350-POUND CHILD STUCK ON A TOILET.

A 350-pound child stuck on a toilet: That's all we were given, because that's how Mohawk had received the call at first, and that's what their dispatcher had relayed to the fire dispatcher this morning. Medic 2 was on a call when Billy Liss, the fire dispatcher who works on the 3rd floor at Central Station, received this one, so he called to see whether the Squad was available. The Squad was the back-up ALS unit. Dave was the single paramedic assigned to the Squad, so whenever Medic 2 was busy, Dave worried about getting a difficult call. One paramedic wasn't enough for messy calls.

The Squad was busy, too. We had answered a call at RPI's student union for a man down. RPI stands for Rensselaer Polytechnic Institute, one of the better engineering schools in the country, and a school as much enamored as any Ivy League college is of its elitist separation of town from gown. Many of its students call the residents of Troy, "Troylets." Oddly enough, RPI claims tax-exempt status, as do other schools and churches in Troy, thus avoiding property taxes, yet the university receives the same city-funded fire protection and EMS care for its students and faculty as if it paid its fair share. Most of Troy's firefighters come from blue-collar backgrounds. Many are the sons of firefighters or police officers, and they resent RPI's elitist attitudes and its students' sense of entitlement. So any call at RPI has the potential to put Troy's firefighters on edge.

This morning, an epileptic kitchen worker slicing tomatoes had gone into seizure and collapsed, spilling an eight-gallon bowl of glistening, red circles all around him as he fell. He was still lying in them when we arrived. Since the hospitals no longer allow paramedics in New York State to carry valium in their drug boxes, there was little Dave could do for the worker except monitor his vital signs and wait for transport. Which is what he did. Wayne had just put the Squad back into service when Billy Liss transmitted the 350-pound child call.

* * *

No one has used the word "fat" once. Not that many of the men crowded into the bathroom, trying to extricate Olivia, are too thin. Dave himself carries some extra weight in a slight paunch, and suffers plenty of ball busting about it. In spite of that, he is quite agile. I have already witnessed his famous jumping trick, where Dave stands next to a kitchen counter, launches himself straight up, and lands on the counter with both feet from his standing position. No hands, no knees, no climbing. He simply jumps more than three feet, straight up in the air.

Nor has anyone mentioned the smell of shit that permeates the place, or made a joke about the mess everywhere. Except for Wayne's brief, indirect comment, no one has uttered a judgmental word about anything. They are simply working on the tasks at hand, and I am watching the husband to see if he feels embarrassed by the condition of his apartment, or upset about having a bunch of guys in the bathroom with his over-large, indisposed, mostly-naked wife.

Suddenly he begins to talk. "She's got a recliner chair she usually sits in. She uses her walker, goes back and forth to the bathroom."

George appears in the hallway outside the bathroom now, carrying the disconnected sink. He looks around for a suitable spot, sets it down against the dining room wall, and goes back in. The husband watches him do it, but he doesn't stop talking. "It's two days she's been sitting there. Yesterday morning, she got in there and couldn't get up. She's got too much fluid in her legs."

"What's your wife's name, sir?" Dave asks.

"My wife's dead," he answers, without missing a beat. "This is my daughter. Her name's Olivia. Olivia Fuller." He shuffles out of his gloomy corner and stands right next to me.

I can see him clearly now. He looks about seventy, with a two or three-day growth of gray stubble on his doughy face. His black, heavy-equipment cap declares him the #1 GRANDPA. His grimy T-shirt, stretched taut by his substantial beer gut, has a soaring bald eagle in its center, with the word AMERICA printed on the dark sky above it, and LAND OF THE FREE marching across the snow-draped mountaintops below.

I look at Dave. He doesn't register surprise or embarrassment at his wrong assumption, and he doesn't betray his assessment that this man's daughter looks older and sicker than her grizzled father does.

Mr. Fuller leans toward us. "We used to live upstairs, and the doctor told me, because of my wife, to get her on the first floor, so we moved down here. You fellas had an awful job moving her up and down the stairs all the time."

His sour breath is finally too much for Dave, and he takes a couple of steps away. Mr. Fuller just keeps talking. "She was overweight, too, you know, but not as bad as my daughter. One time you were taking her down the stairs and you dropped her. This is my oldest daughter here. She's forty-five."

"Easy. EASY," George is yelling inside the bathroom now. "Watch her head. Get a hand under it."

I can hear the steady hiss of the air-bags inflating, broken up by one of the men coughing, or gagging and then coughing to cover it up.

"My youngest daughter, she died in '89," Mr. Fuller continues. He touches my arm to make sure my attention stays on him. "She was thirty-three. She had breast cancer. They took her breast off. Told her she had a tumor in her breast and they took it off. Then she got the cancer in her back. It all activated. She suffered something awful."

One of the ambo guys darts past us, unhooks the orange straps on the stretcher, and goes back in the bathroom. Things are heating up in there. Warnings and complaints all scramble together and reverberate out to us.

"Look out."

"I'm losing her."

"Grab her arm, will you?"

"There's nothing to get hold of. The skin's slipping."

"All right, I got her."

"Keep her head up. Hold it steady."

"Jesus Christ."

Mr. Fuller is staring intently at me. "My wife died a year ago September," he says. "I worked 46 years, you know? I get a pension. I did labor. Construction. Worked on everything. I even took out two big smokestacks up at Samaritan Hospital. They were red brick. I took two of them down, dead of the winter, with jackhammers. We had to cut down like three or four courses of brick all around the top. If you fell, you were dead meat. Your hands would just freeze up and you'd pour alcohol on them. If you fell, inside or outside the stack, either way you were dead."

The men are backing out into the hall now, hunched over, dragging Olivia on a torn-up square of frayed carpet and a yellow blanket, bunched together and curved around her bulk. Dave hurries over to help.

"Pull the stretcher up and get ready," he calls to me. I maneuver it toward the huddle of uniformed bodies straining to squeeze Olivia out the door opening. Wayne comes back in now and grabs a piece of rug to help pull, but she's wedged, and they don't want to twist her too hard to make the turn.

Mr. Fuller won't stop talking. "Since 7:30 yesterday morning, I tried to get her out, and she said, 'Let me try myself. Let me try myself.' So she couldn't do it, and I said I'd get her something to eat, but she said she couldn't eat. So this morning she didn't fall, but she kind of went over and her head hit the sink."

I don't want to laugh, but I am starting to, and I know this isn't the appropriate time for it. Everyone else seems able to act professionally. What's wrong with me? And what am I trying not to laugh about? A fat woman stuck on a toilet for two days? The fat part? The toilet? Is it just the general absurdity of the whole scene? I have no idea. Maybe it's nervous laughter. But the more the seven men strain to dislodge Olivia, some of them trying to haul her up from behind or reaching over to shift her from inside, others bending and grunting and banging their butts on the narrow walls in the hallway outside the bathroom, the more they suddenly look like contemporary Keystone Kops popping ass-first out of some magic circus box, hauling a giant fish behind them, and the more I want to laugh, if only to pretend none of this could be real.

"She's got all the fluid in her," Mr. Fuller says, and as I bend toward the stretcher to hide my involuntary smile, they finally pop her through the opening. Quickly, they drag her over, and I can see all of her now. Olivia isn't just fat. She is massive. Lying on this blanket, she looks as if three people have somehow crammed themselves inside her skin and are all trying to climb back out. Her limbs could be torsos. She is like the Venus of Willendorf come to life and magnified by computer imaging so all of her parts flow together, demarcated only by faint creases. But she isn't moving any of the parts herself. Her eyes are closed and her mouth is hanging open.

As the seven men arrange themselves along each side of her, I am too awestruck to think this is even surrealistically funny anymore. They bend their knees, count to three, and lift, grunting hard with the strain of it. I slide the stretcher underneath and they lower her down, but she's too wide to be balanced. At least a third of her threatens to drag along the floor.

The men wrap the blanket around her, hoist the unbalanced part back up, and hook the straps over all of it, six of them staying along the sides to make sure the whole apparatus doesn't tip. Dave, listening for chest sounds with his stethoscope, looks worried.

The ambo guys start to pull the stretcher toward the door.

"Hold it just a second," Dave says. "George, hold her head up. I'm not getting anything here." Dave moves the diaphragm to the other side. "Damn it, she's in respiratory arrest. Wayne, you got the bag-valve mask with you?"

"It's in the Squad," Wayne says.

"Can you put that sink back in?" Mr. Fuller wants to know.

"We don't have time for that, sir," Dave says, and grabs the defibrillator.

The men are struggling to force Olivia and the stretcher through the front door now.

"Come on, push it through," Dave urges. "Get her out to the ambulance."

"Can somebody come back to do that sink?" Mr. Fuller is following us out. "Hinkle owns this place. You know him? Retired fireman. He don't do shit for us."

"It'll go back in pretty easily." Dave is trying not to yell at him. "George is a plumber, okay? He didn't break anything. He just disconnected it."

"Can he put the top back on?" Mr. Fuller is staring expectantly at Dave now.

For a few seconds, Dave doesn't answer. He stops, looks impatiently toward the stretcher and then back at Mr. Fuller, as if he wants some real answers. Like why has he let his daughter get so huge that she is lying immobilized in her own bathroom? Or why did he wait so long to call for help? Was he waiting until she could no longer talk? What would she tell Dave if she could talk? Who would hear Olivia tell her story, now or ever?

But Dave remembers his priorities, and catches himself. "Look, we have to help your daughter, sir," he says, hurrying out the door.

"Okay, okay." Mr. Fuller is nodding. He understands. "I'll just leave it like that. I mean, this is an emergency, right?"

We have to pick Olivia up to get her down the porch steps, and the stretcher, even with eight of us straining to hold it steady, drags us relentlessly and dangerously fast toward the sidewalk. Halfway down, with the stretcher tipping precariously back and forth, we hear Mr. Fuller shout from the doorway.

"You want me to move my car?" I look back to see him

pointing insistently at an almost new Cadillac parked dead in front of the house, blocking the quickest path to the ambulance. "I can move it," he says. "It ain't no trouble. I can move it."

* * *

Inside the ambulance, Dave is frantically trying to intubate Olivia. When a patient isn't breathing, as Olivia isn't, her airway has to be secured. It has to be artificially kept open, so a flexible, translucent plastic tube is inserted into the trachea. If the paramedic can successfully get the tube into the trachea and not insert it into the esophagus, which leads to the stomach, he can then hold it in place with an inflatable cuff that keeps stomach contents from washing up and choking the patient.

Dave lifts her tongue and slides it out of the way with his laryngoscope, and he begins to probe with the endotracheal tube. Olivia's head is tipped back, and Dave is peering in, trying to locate the epiglottis with the light and the tip of the scope.

"Call St. Mary's," he is yelling to the ambo driver. "Tell them we're bringing in a CHF patient in respiratory arrest. What's the ETA, three minutes? And tell them how big she is."

Suddenly, Olivia shudders, and a spray of dark liquid shoots out the tube, peppering the side of Dave's face and hair.

"Jesus," he shouts, and instinctively recoils.

He begins to clean her mouth out with his blue-gloved fingers, holding the tube to one side, but another blast of vomit surges out and speckles the sliding cabinet doors next to his shoulder. The bilious smell spreads through the back of the ambulance, and Dave starts to gag. "Watch her aspirate now," he says, and checks the monitor screen. "Goddamn it, she's in V-fib."

V-fib is ventricular fibrillation, the worst kind of heart rhythm she could have, the kind where the heart is quivering like jelly. Sixty to seventy percent of heart dysrhythmias that cause sudden cardiac death are ventricular fibrillations. What Dave needs to do is defibrillate her. Most people know that paramedics and doctors apply electrical shock to patients who expire, but they think the shock starts their hearts again. It doesn't. It stops the heart. It creates a ventricular standstill, called asystole. No rhythm for, they hope, a brief second, until the body's natural pacemaker kicks back in and establishes a natural, functional rhythm. It's like hitting a reset button on a malfunctioning machine.

"Look out. Don't touch her," Dave says, and he pulls the paddles off the defibrillator. He squeezes some conductive jelly onto the paddles and rubs them together to spread it evenly. He chooses the recommended initial rate of 200 joules to start, though some doctors would argue that a woman of Olivia's size will offer much more resistance to the electrical charge than a thin person, simply because of her extra tissue. Still, even at the lower settings, defibrillators deliver several thousand volts in 4 to 12 milliseconds, no matter how fat someone is. Dave hits the charge button.

The ambo worker in back with us, still holding the bag-valve mask he would have used on Olivia, is gagging now, and he moves up into the passageway to the front to be out of Dave's way.

Dave places the paddles on her chest and bears down to lower the resistance pathway. "Everybody clear," he says grimly, and discharges the current into her. She hardly moves. Dave looks at the rhythm on the monitor. "Shit," he says, and resets the charge for 300 joules.

* * *

In the emergency room at St. Mary's Hospital, one of the three hospitals in Troy to which paramedics accompany patients, the Trauma Room is just inside the automatic doors that serve the emergency vehicle entrance. It's a small room. It's set up for one patient. Next in line is the Cardiac Care Room, set up for two. About ten feet across from these critical treatment rooms are two wide nurses' stations, which are really just long desks shielded by low walls. Usually the nurses are firmly planted at these desks, filling out forms, answering phones, or talking with X-ray shuffling doctors. But from there, if the doors are left open or if the floor-length curtains have not been drawn tight, the nurses can easily monitor patients. All they have to do is stand up, and then it's hard to escape seeing them. Right now, except for Dave Stevens sitting alone at the far end of the second station, as far from the small Trauma Room as he can get, all the seats are empty. Everyone is in the Trauma Room, working on Olivia.

"She was there two days," Wayne says. He's standing in the walking space between the nurses' stations. "Us taking ten minutes to get her out of there ain't gonna do anything. You got a radio on, Dave? I'm going out for a smoke."

Dave doesn't look up. He is checking off the white boxes at the bottom of his PCR, in the TREATMENT GIVEN part.

Moved to ambulance on stretcher/backboard: check.

Airway cleared: check.

EKG Monitored (Attach Tracing): check.

Defibrillation/Cardioversion No. Times, with a box for the number next to it, 3: check.

Oxygen administered: check.

EndoTracheal Tube (E/T): check.

At *Oral/Nasal Airway*, Dave stops, considering, his pen poised above the small square. He looks up at me and says, in a hushed tone, "You do the best you can." He stares over at the closed Trauma Room door for a while, and goes on, still speaking quietly. "It's very hard with a person that big. I think what happened was she aspirated her vomit."

Suddenly, the Trauma Room door swings open and the two attending doctors, one of them a thirty-something woman with stringy, black hair and the other a large, older man, walk out together. Both of them are laughing.

Maybe they shared a little joke at the end to relieve their frustration, and I saw just the instant of release for both of them. Maybe they felt genuine sorrow for Olivia in there, and worked harder than usual to save her, so they especially needed that humor at the end of it. Maybe their laughter has nothing to do with what they've just seen and done. There's probably a very good reason for it. Dave sees them, too. But if he feels they're acting unprofessionally, he doesn't say so. He picks up the red phone, which connects to the fire dispatcher, and returns the Rescue Squad to service.

"She had long-term, chronic health problems," he says. "She was 45, but she looked 60, at least. You saw her circulation. Her heart was doing triple duty."

Now that the nurses are coming out, the noise level at the stations is returning to normal, but Dave keeps talking softly. "And it does you no good to work in that house, because you can't work in there where she was. There's no room. She wasn't just big. There was no place to even grab her. Nothing to hold onto. There's too much fat to find a vein. The nurses here couldn't get an IV in her, either. I didn't even try, because I know my limitations. I'm alone on the Squad. I'm the only para-medic assigned to it. I can't waste the time to try for an IV on her. You and I have landmarks I can find. It's very hard on a big person. I'm going to try for airway, and that's what I did. Did I do everything I could? Yeah. Did I follow the protocol? Yeah. But I still feel bad. It's hard when they're alive when you get there and then you can't save them. You just have to do the best you can."

The automatic doors swing open and Olivia's father walks in. He sees us and waves. He starts to walk over, but a nurse asks him who he is. Then the head nurse, a woman almost as large as Olivia, quickly herds him into an office down the side corridor.

Dave watches her lead Mr. Fuller away, and then he turns to me. He pauses, and I can see he is weighing how far he can trust me with delicate information. "We're set up for black and white out there, but we end up in the grey zone all the time," he says, deciding he'll remain diplomatic for now.

Dave leaves a copy of his PCR on the desk for the head nurse, and we walk toward the exit. I suggest we say something to Olivia's father before we leave, and Dave agrees.

Mr. Fuller, with his #1 GRANDPA hat still on, greets us when we appear in the office doorway. The head nurse scowls at us. I step toward him and I hold out my hand.

"I'm sorry about your daughter, Mr. Fuller," I say.

"Sorry," Dave says.

The head nurse, sitting behind the desk, is wildly waving her hands, mouthing a violent "NO" over and over, indicating she hasn't told him yet that Olivia is dead, lying naked and unattended on the table in the Trauma Room, an intubation tube still taped to her mouth. Mr. Fuller is smiling and nodding. He's ready to talk again, but the head nurse is starting to rise now, her face quickly reddening, afraid we'll say something wrong, or reveal anything at all about what might or might not have been attempted to save his daughter.

We say goodbye to Mr. Fuller, and he thanks us for helping Olivia. At the automatic doors, Dave stoops to grab the oxygen bag and the defibrillator. "Shit rolls downhill," he says, and nods back toward the office where the head nurse is working her way up to the bad news. "We be the downhill side. We're the lowest of the low. Whatever happens, they'll pin it on us."

* * *

It's 11 p.m. now in the common room at Central, and the local news has just come on. Dave is slumped in a corner of the brown, vinyl couch that sits next to the high radiator. Half a year's worth of *Reader's Digests*, topped off by a current copy of *Fire Engineering*, balance threateningly on the cold radiator next to his head.

Ric Moreno and Don Kimmey are on the other vinyl couch, the larger one at right angles to the one Dave is on. Wayne sits at one of the tables. Various sections of *The Record* and the *Times Union* and *The New York Post* are scattered across the tables and on the floor between them. A line of fire safety videos, along with one copy of *Thunder and Destruction: the NFL's Hardest Hits*, is propped against the left side of the television. Ed Dague, the Channel 13 news anchor, is running down the local election results, and the news isn't good for the Democrats.

"Wait 'til you see what happens now," Gary Hanna shouts from the doorway. He has stayed up later than usual to learn the outcome. "The City Manager will be history soon, that's the first thing. Then they'll be coming after us."

"I bet you they close Engine 4, and they lay off some guys," Ric says.

Don jumps on that one. "Good. I'll give them a list. I can name you five or six right now who aren't workers," he says, and switches over to the Monday night football game, where the Washington Redskins are narrowly beating the New York Giants.

"I don't care," Wayne says. "I'll be in Mexico."

"I can't believe he caught that," Don yells. "What the fuck was that, the guy hitting him that fast? The punk hit the bastard before he even caught it."

"With the spread, this game is in the bag. Relax," says Ric.

"Fuck the spread," Don answers. "Why do the Giants always do this? Go into fucking prevent defense and blow it." Don tosses the remote on the coffee table. "Hey, Dave, I heard you had a big one up in the Burgh. How big was she?" Don asks.

Dave still looks morose. He answers without looking over.

"The nurses at St. Mary's figured 500, maybe 550."

"Were you on that call in the Burgh with the 900-pound guy?" Ric asks Don.

"Oh, yeah. Remember, when he went to step, we were afraid his skin was going to explode?"

"I was on that call," Wayne says. "We didn't want to touch him. We really thought his skin would burst."

Don laughs, and nods at me, as if I won't believe it. "He couldn't pick his foot up this high to put it on a stool. The skin couldn't stretch anymore." Don is holding his hand about four inches off the floor.

"All he could wear was a blanket with a hole cut out of the middle of it," Wayne says. "He was so big we used three air bags to lift him up."

"He was on the floor. There was no way he could get up," Ric says. "We rolled him one way and slid one bag underneath him, and then boosted him up enough to get the next one under, one after the other like that, until we could get behind him and push him to his feet. Then he could grab hold of his walker."

"Jesus, he was big," Don says.

At the table nearest the kitchen, Charley Willson is talking to Monica, a roving reporter from Channel 13, and Bob, her cameraman. Monica is attractive, and from the frequent glances, it's clear that detail has not escaped the guys watching TV on the couches. Because *Backdraft* is being aired this coming weekend, Monica and Bob are riding along tonight, hoping to get something local and exciting to use as a promotional lead during the 6 p.m. Saturday newscast. They've been waiting for a decent call to shoot all night long, since about seven o'clock, and not one thing has happened yet.

I ask them what they usually cover, and Monica says, "Depends on the kind of day we're having. Your routine spot news. Anything weird. Never do we ever spend this much time doing a story like this. I mean, the normal story, we're in and out in no time. We don't take all day."

"We'll go to a fire if it's confirmed, you know, a fully involved fire. Shootings," Bob throws in. "We go to EMS calls where we believe a crime was committed. We go to car accidents."

I ask what their legal constraints are: "Let's say, you show up at a fire, or a serious EMS call or something unique, and somebody's coming out, members of the family are coming out, can you use their names? Can you use their faces?"

Bob is saying, "If we get it from a public street, sure. I mean, if we're standing on a sidewalk, just like you're standing on the sidewalk . . ." when Monica interrupts him.

"If you're anywhere where the general public can go, you're free and clear," she says. "If somebody's out in public, they're open game. People treat us as if we're funded by their tax money or something, or like they own us, because we're open for public consumption and it doesn't cost them anything to get us, but we're privately owned, you know? Viacom owns our station. I'm not accountable to the public. We have a right to do this. This is our right."

Bob is shaking his head in agreement. "I think a lot of times the problems I run into, it's not so much the fire department, it's the police department. It's that a lot of police officers want to be your editor. It's not their job to tell you what to take pictures of. I take pictures of everything, I mean, if somebody talks to us, they're giving us permission. Unless we barged into their house and they said, 'Get out!' and we were violating their privacy by trespassing. Like if there's a family that's been burned out and they're sitting on the street corner, watching their house burn, and we go up and say, 'God, what happened?' and they start talking to us, that's their permission. That's acknowledgement, and they're absolutely fair game."

Charley wants to know why they don't report medical

tragedies, like people having heart attacks. "Why isn't that news?" he asks.

Bob sits back. "Why isn't that news? Okay, one time on Route 787, I saw a police car and a Colonie EMS car on the side of the road, with this guy lying there. And I didn't know what they were doing, so I pulled over. I kept my distance; I didn't go up and get in their faces while they were doing CPR; I shot it from across the highway. Later, I found out the guy was just out changing his tire and had a heart attack. It wasn't news. We didn't do anything with it. We never put it on the air. I just taped over it. Now if I'm driving down the highway, and because of somebody doing CPR I get stuck in a traffic jam, that's different. If people have no idea why they're stuck in a traffic jam, they go home and watch the news to find out. That's news."

"People have heart attacks all the time," Monica says. "They're not unusual."

I remember Olivia, and Harold M. Burke now, and try to imagine what their heart attacks felt like, and if they were scared dying without any family or friends with them, and if any of that felt usual to them.

"He just had a heart attack along the side of the road," Bob says. "You know, a guy sitting in a house with a gun in his mouth, saying, 'I'm gonna kill myself,' we don't do that either."

"Who cares?" Monica asks. "I don't care about that."

"No, it isn't that we don't care," Bob says. "It's that if we shoot that, other people will watch it, and that will glorify suicide. We have this discussion two or three times a year. There will be some guy who climbs up to the top of the twin bridges over the Mohawk River and he'll sit there. He'll stop traffic for ten miles, and it will be backed up for a month, just because this guy wants to jump and kill himself. Now, why will we cover that, when we don't cover the guy in his house who's going to shoot himself? The answer has a lot to do with the traffic."

"It does," Monica says triumphantly, and smiles. "Here's the deal, too. We have eleven minutes to fill. Eleven minutes on television newscast is news, in a whole half hour. Eleven minutes of news content. The rest is weather, sports, commercials. All of those, and a kicker, a feel-good ending. In eleven minutes, I can't report Aunt Mabel's heart attack, because there were so many of them they wouldn't fit in.

"So you've got to make it spectacular, which is a word I hate to use, but it has to be out of the ordinary. It has to be different. The more unusual it is, the more newsworthy it is. We like *News of the Weird*. You can't explain it. It's not sensationalism. That's a bad word. Interesting, unusual. You want to cover things, too, that are of value to a large number of people. You're trying to make a difference in a minute, a minute and a half, you know, two minutes."

If Dave Stevens at the other end of the room can hear Monica dismissing heart attack victims as not newsworthy, he doesn't act like it. He's staring down at his hands. Don, Ric and Gary suddenly start yelling at the TV.

"He missed it."

"Jesus, I can't believe I saw that."

"He choked."

"He tripped over his own feet."

"You hold it, I'll kick it, and I'll show you how he missed it."

"I didn't see that, did I?"

"He pussyed it."

"Here. Take the ball. Watching a football game without a football in your hands is like watching a porno movie without your dick in your hands."

"They missed a 14-yard field goal. That's it. They blew

this game," Don finally yells. "That's it. I'm not a Giants fan anymore."

"Yeah," Bob says, "a while ago we started going downhill in the ratings, and we decided, 'Let's start covering the fires and the emergencies again, because people love to watch that stuff.' Whether they say they will, whether they admit it or not, people are interested in fires and emergencies. I've been to fires at 2 in the morning, and there is always a crowd of people outside, watching this house burn. Some of them walked for blocks with their robes on and their coffee. They're drawn to it, for one reason or another, and that's news."

"Or look at the fireman, Mike Kelleher, when he got stabbed," Charley says, "how much more you got out of that because he was the fireman and you had firemen working on a fireman, and there was a delay with the ambulance."

"We would have covered that story whether it was a fireman in there or if it was the governor who was stabbed and beaten up," Bob says. "What better symbol could you get for the city's argument that it needs its own ambulance service? There's a lot of weird stuff out there. Believe me, we get some pretty wacky calls. Especially in nice weather, where people say they're having a yard sale over the weekend, and would we like to come and cover it. And, you know, yard sales are like people having heart attacks on the side of the road. We won't do a yard sale unless it's a really slow day, where you could go around looking at yard sales and ask, 'Who would want this? This is garbage. Why are you buying someone else's garbage?' You could do that maybe, and people would find it funny if you did it right, if you did it tastefully."

I wander over now to watch the end of the football game, and sit down next to Dave, who still isn't watching the game.

"I wish you were riding with us when we went back this afternoon," he says. "We had to pick up our silver blanket at St. Mary's, the one we left with Olivia, and she was still in the

Trauma Room. She was too big for them to move, so they just left her lying on that table. Can you believe it? And this undertaker was running around, and he asked us if we could help carry her out to his hearse. Only the four of us from the Squad."

Dave stops for a second, looking down, and then he stands up. "We carried her from toilet to hearse in one day," he says, starting toward the bunkroom, "and isn't that extra special?"

Charley Willson

We were sitting down at Central Station and all of a sudden we got a call for Samaritan Hospital, and they said, "Go to the emergency room. The officials will meet you there." So we started up, and I was the only paramedic at the time. Going up, we never knew what the call was, and I kept saying to Duke, who was the captain, "Duke, what's going on?" Rich Caola, we called him Duke, he was the captain. I was going, "What's the call for?" and he kept saying, "I don't know. We're supposed to meet some people at the emergency room."

So we figured since we had tools, it could have been somebody was trapped, you know, like we've had them in machinery. Sometimes we've had to take the machinery apart and then the ambulance crew will take them to the hospital, and we were saying, "Maybe they need some tools to get somebody out of an entanglement or something like that." But we didn't know why we would be called to an emergency room.

Well, we go up there and the officials meet us at the door and they said they had somebody trapped in a ceiling. And I said, "Oh, all right. Is it a worker?" And they act sort of funny and just say, "No." And I said, "Did a construction worker get trapped in there or what?" And they go, "No, it's just someone caught in a ceiling." Then I said, "Well, how long is he caught?" And the guy said, "Two weeks."

"*Two weeks. That can't be. Why would he be in there for two weeks?*" Still, we were so confused, you know? So he said, "*Well, you come up with us and we'll show you.*" When he was bringing me up, I asked him, "*Well, why is this guy in there for two weeks?*" And he answered, "*He's a mental patient, and we just found him.*" And I said, "*He's been up there for two weeks and you didn't know he was gone?*"

Well, it turns out that they had reported this thing in the paper and they were telling how the guy had been missing, how they knew he had been missing, how they were looking all over and they couldn't find him anyplace. They had special search dogs come up, and the dogs tracked him from the hospital all the way down Federal Street and everything, all down to the riverbank and they found the guy's cigarettes on the riverbank and figured he just jumped in the river. So for them that justified where the guy went when he escaped from the hospital.

Now, in the meantime, this odor had started up on the third floor at the hospital — that's the mental patient floor — and a maintenance guy narrowed it down to this one bathroom area. He pushed up a ceiling tile in there and the smell got stronger. So he climbed up on top and he looked down in and he could see that this guy, who had a hospital robe on, had hung himself down a pipe-chase, using the tie from the bathrobe.

This was beginning to look real nasty for us. Again, he was two weeks down in there. The hospital official said, "*If you get up there, you can pull him back up over the wall and then lower him back down to us.*" And I said, "*Well, before I do that, I'm going to need some help.*" So I went down and got the captain and I said, "*You better get some more people up here, because this is out of hand.*" By then, the cops were there and everybody was going, "*Yes, Sergeant, no, Sergeant,*" and stuff like that, and everybody was getting a little nervous, you know. The health officials from the County were coming in and they were acting really nervous, because they could see that the lawyers were going to be the next ones pounding on the door. I mean, a *guy in a mental ward and he was able to disappear, hang himself and be gone for two weeks? Okay.*

So we went back up to cut the wall apart, to cut the wall of the shower out, and take him out that way. And they were complaining. "Hey, can't you just lift him out the way he went in?" But it was a small pipe-chase, and the guy had bloated up in there. We got our air chisels out and once we started cutting the wall apart, the odor really cranked up. It was getting hard to breathe, so we went back downstairs to the emergency room and put our air packs on.

Once we had cut a bigger hole, we could see that the guy had been leaning against a steam pipe the whole time. Now this is for two weeks he was leaning against this steam pipe, and because of the heat and everything his face was almost about gone. Between decomposing and all the rest, you know, it was burned into like jelly, and his body was completely rotund with the gas trying to get out of there. He had this flannel shirt on under the robe and the buttons were ready to burst off, and even his dungarees were popping at the seams. As well as jeans are built, and they were splitting just from the gas expanding.

At this point, one of the hospital guys says, "Can you turn him around so we can identify him?" And I looked back at him like, "Well, who the fuck else are you missing up here, you know? How many guys have you got inside walls? Are you saying you don't have a clue who this guy is?" But I just said, "No, we're not going to turn him around until we cut him down." Now we were trying to keep our composure, because it was a real ugly situation. And the guy says, "All right."

So it was me and Duke and Larry, who was standing off away from the hole we had chiseled in the wall. Now, the maintenance guy who found him said, "Look, if you guys need any help, I was already up there once, I can go up there and cut the cord for you." So he climbed up into the ceiling. He was thrilled to get up there and help us out. But once he cut the cord, all of a sudden this guy drops down and everything just exploded, you know, all his seams and everything. Well, when this guy burst, Larry, who doesn't even like nose bleeds, was trying to scale right up that bathroom wall backwards. The mental patient is oozing

all over the floor and we were all staring down at him like it was a hor-
ror movie or something. As soon as that guy dropped down, every hospi-
tal official who was there set a new hundred yard dash record down that
hallway. All we could hear were the swinging doors slamming closed.
Then, all of a sudden, one of them opened the door a crack and said,
"Can you get his wallet out for us?" And Duke and I yelled, "Fuck
you!" right through our masks. "You think we're going to wrestle with
this guy so you can prove it's the guy you lost?"

Finally, we had to get him in a body bag, which we did, and we
were carrying him down the hallway toward the elevator and the hos-
pital officials were holding the door closed and saying, "You can't come
out, because you're going to upset the other patients." And we were
thinking, "They're already nuts, what's this going to do, put them over
the edge?" They said, "You've got to bring him down the back staircase
to the morgue in the basement."

So after all that, we had to carry the guy sloshing around in the
body bag all the way down the stairs. But it was great to watch all
those guys sweating it, you know, all those top officials. They were
going to start telling us what to do until they saw that some real work
was involved, and then, zoom, they were gone. Holy shit, that was
quite a night. Talk about a memorable call, I mean, that was one of
the worst.

3

How to explain to the riverless child what a river is? Imagine
green and silver in motion, you tell him. Now add a dog's tongue
slowly lapping. But what is the real use of a river? he interrupts.
For those who live on its banks, a river is time itself, approaching,
surging past, vanishing, never to be called back. You can tell your
secrets to a river. It just carries them away.

— Richard Selzer
Down From Troy

Standing on the King Fuels loading dock, Chief Ed Schultz
looks nervously over to his left, at the shabby, sixty-one year old
bridge that connects South Troy with Menands, and then back
out to his right, at the Troy Fire Department boat that appears
and disappears by turns behind two scrap-metal barges attached
to each other by a thick rope and spinning ominously in the too-
visible Hudson River current.

"Get him off there. Get him off," Chief Schultz hollers into
his portable radio. "Portable 10, you're just going to get that
guy off, right?"

Today, Portable 10 is Charley Willson. The captain on the Rescue Squad carries Portable 10, and Charley is the acting captain for this tour of duty. The guy that the Chief wants off the barge is standing on the stern of Metro 25, the empty, 100-ton, 100-foot, blue and rust-orange barge, and he's trying to toss a tow rope to Charley Willson. He misses, drags the rope back in, jumps down onto the steel bottom, and runs toward the empty barge's bow to throw it again. He looks young, maybe nineteen or twenty, and he looks worried.

He works for R. K. Freedman, the scrap metal dealer located just up the river in Green Island that rents Metro 25 and its fully-loaded twin, the Metro 15 barge, from a company in Long Island. He was on duty this morning when the barges got loose. The fire dispatcher received the emergency call around 9:30 a.m., and this young employee claims that some kids untied the barges. He swore that they were loose when he got to work today. He says he tried but he couldn't get the two of them back into the mooring dock below Clemente's concrete plant.

R. K. Freedman rents their loading space for the barges from Clemente's, just south of where the Poestenkill Creek empties into the Hudson. It's one of the few spots where they have enough room to station a giant magnet that transfers bales of scrap metal from their trucks to these barges, and it's the only spot where the water is deep enough on the Troy side of the Hudson to load a heavy vessel.

Now it's 9:50 a.m., and these two roped-together barges are waltzing relentlessly around each other in the swift current, like a couple of canal drivers strapped to each other for a knife fight, jerking and circling toward their first two vulnerable targets — the King Fuels loading dock and the Troy-Menands Bridge.

Two other Rescue Squad members, Dave Stevens and Ric Moreno, are shouting from the shore.

"You're not even slowing it down," Dave yells.

"Get the rope and drag it. Drag it over here," Ric is yelling.

Don Kimmey, who is riding as captain on Engine 5 today, is down there with them. "We got a sixty-horse motor and they got eight fucking million tons," Don says.

"I still say what they should do is grab that rope and pull the boat, pull it toward shore," Ric says, "and just keep coming toward shore with the boat and you might just swing it enough to get it over close to us."

"You know what the thing is," Don answers, "is King Fuels has got that pipe full of oil on the dock down there."

If Charley Willson can hear Chief Schultz on his portable, or Dave and Ric yelling at him from the wooded riverbank, he sure doesn't act like it. Halfway across the swollen Hudson River, in the department's white, 17-foot Boston Whaler with its 60-horsepower Evinrude motor, Charley is leaning out over the small boat's low bow, keeping one of their life preservers centered as a bumper as Frank Ryan tries to nudge the tiny boat up against Metro 15 and coax it in toward the shore.

Charley's been on barge calls before, three or four of them. Usually kids will untie one end of a barge, and the Rescue Squad will bring a boat down and ease the loose end back into shore. No big deal. But they've all been empty. They've never had a fully-loaded barge, out in the current and moving fast. That poses a couple of immediate problems, at least.

The first problem is weight. Even with Charley and Frank on board, the Whaler weighs less than one ton, maybe eighteen hundred pounds. Metro 15 is chuck full, with a crudely rounded mountain of #2 ferrous bales on board. Sal Scattareggia, who runs the scrap yard for Reuben Freedman's son, Jake, says that Metro 15, loaded, weighs about a thousand tons — "900 ton of #2 bales, compressed, of refrigerators, stoves, car hoods, stuff like that" — so it's a hundred tons for the barge itself and then 900 more tons for the smashed-together, baled steel, or about two million pounds altogether, roped to another two hundred thousand pounds of the empty Metro 25, drifting quickly downriver.

The second problem is the current, continuously spinning the two barges *down* the river. Usually, that wouldn't be such a concern, because tidal water surging up the river from the Atlantic Ocean sets up an opposing force just about equal to the current.

Many people don't realize that the Hudson is really two different rivers. Its source is Lake Tear-of-the-Clouds, a small glacial lake set 4,000 feet above sea level into the shoulder of the Adirondacks' Mt. Marcy. Early in this century, in *Hudson River Landings*, Paul Wilstach described the upper half as "a wild, impetuous stream. It foams over rocky barriers, it plunges over waterfalls, and it accepts into its erratic channel a few lesser streams before it reaches the cities of Troy and Albany and becomes its other self."

That other self, from beneath the federal dam and lock at Troy to its mouth at New York City, is essentially a tidal estuary. Half of the Hudson River's 300-mile length lies above Troy, and is always fresh water, as we would expect, but the other half is constantly flooded with salt water from the Atlantic. The salt line is around Poughkeepsie, but brackish water allows shad and herring to spawn this far up and encourages striped, ocean bass to chase them here in a feeding frenzy. Sailors and photographers occasionally glimpse sea lions sunning themselves on rocks near Albany and Kingston, and in March of 1647, Adriaen Van Der Donck, an early Dutch settler, reported that a whale

"grounded near the great Chahoos falls. This fish was tolerably fat, for although the citizens of Rennselaerwyck broiled out a great quantity of train oil, still the whole river (the current being still rapid) was oily for three weeks, and covered with grease. As the fish lay rotting, the air was infected with its stench to such a degree that the smell was offensive and perceptible for two miles to leeward."

The whale beached itself on a now-submerged island across from present-day Lansingburgh, and since the settlers at the time claimed it was a white whale, some local historians speculate that Herman Melville, who grew up by the Hudson River in Lansingburgh, may have heard of the leviathan from his mother.

Another variable is the tide. Even though the current is always heading downriver, when the tide is coming in, you actually have pressure against your boat if you are going downstream. There can be as much as an eight-foot difference in tidal elevation in the river at Troy, whereas, downriver, they may have only a foot or a foot and a half, because the river really narrows considerably north of Albany. The tide will be at its lowest at 2:42 p.m. today, about five hours from now, so the tidal pressure against these barges is diminishing. And to make matters worse, Mike Harrison measured one and a half inches of water in his rain gauge after yesterday's storm, and the Hudson is swirling dark and high with the strong run-off today.

On a normal, sunny, November day like this, with the tide ebbing as it is, the current at Troy and Albany is about eight-tenths of a knot, according to Frank Keane, who is General Manager for the Port of Albany. "In the Spring," Frank says, "when you have run-off, you have a tremendous volume and velocity of water flowing through here, with tree trunks going by at probably 15, 16 knots." And with yesterday's inch and a half of rain, today is like Spring run-off. Add to that the 15 mph wind from the North and the 37 degree air temperature and nobody wants to fall in this river now, or get in the path of these spinning barges.

"NOT SO CLOSE. NOT SO CLOSE."

All of a sudden, Charley can hear Chief Schultz's voice from his radio, and he realizes the Whaler's motor has stopped. He can hear the life preserver scraping ominously against the barge, and the current slapping by, and the instructions shouted from the shore.

"What are you doing?" Charley yells back at Frank.

"I don't know what happened," Frank answers, and he turns to tilt the motor up, but it won't budge. "Shit, a rope's wrapped around the prop," Frank says.

"Raise up the motor. Get it out of the water," Charley shouts.

"It's too tight. It won't move."

One of the 3-inch lines trailing under the empty barge has come loose and gotten tangled in their propeller. Charley can see Metro 25 swinging around toward them now, and he knows they've got at most a couple of minutes until the two barges swing together and crush them in between.

He pulls the life preserver in and hurries back next to Frank. What he has is a pocket knife, that's it, and not much time. Holding onto a back cleat, with Frank pulling up hard on the engine, Charley reaches underwater and saws away at the thick rope. With his head down, Charley can't see how close the empty barge is, and he's glad.

They're lucky today. The rope is old, and cuts easily. Frank is able to lever the engine up now and Charley plucks the last strands out of the prop. Frank gets the engine going again and shifts into reverse, and they back out into the channel half a minute before Metro 25 clangs hard against the loaded barge.

Gary Hanna, Engine 5's driver, is on the loading dock with Chief Schultz. He keeps repeating, "I'm worried about that bridge coming down," but the Chief doesn't respond. Gary is worried about the fuel oil lines, too, but he doesn't talk about them. Everybody's worried about them. The King Fuels loading dock is where boats tie up to unload fuel oil for King's storage tanks. The fuel lines reach right down to the dock, and if the barges can't be turned away, if they swing in and rupture those lines, who knows how many gallons of #2 fuel oil will pour into the Hudson, and that's if a spark doesn't ignite the fuel and blow up the entire operation.

Chief Schultz squints up toward the bridge deck and keys his radio. "Portable 1 to Dispatcher," he says, "I can see police units on the Troy side of the bridge right now. Want to ask them to move their vehicles and back off?"

"I'm afraid of that tower coming down right on top of those barges," Gary says. "I'd get that guy off of there and get our boat clear, if I were you."

Nobody has mentioned the barge in Louisiana that hit the concrete pilings of a train bridge two months ago, the same morning that Mike Kelleher got stabbed, and caused a train wreck that killed 43 people and dangled others above a swamp populated by alligators, snakes, and bears. But no one who looks up at the scaling paint and the rust working through the faded green on the Troy-Menands bridge could miss the similar potential for a collapse here, and no one wants what would certainly be a major disruption for several communities if it happens.

Garry Mitchell
The Associated Press

Saraland, Alabama, September 22 — An Amtrak train hurtled off a bridge into an inky bayou early Wednesday, plunging its sleeping passengers into a nightmare of fire, water and death. The FBI said it was examining a barge that may have struck and weakened the bridge before the wreck.

Forty-three people aboard the cross-country Sunset Limited were killed, some of them trapped in a submerged, silver passenger car and others in a burned engine, and 10 were missing, railroad spokesman Howard Robertson said. It was the deadliest wreck in Amtrak's 23-year history.

A group of six barges near the crash site included one that had a big dent

in it, and concrete pilings on the
bridge also were dented, FBI Agent
Charles W. Archer said at an evening
briefing in Mobile. "We are looking at
a suspect barge," he said.

The Troy-Menands bridge has a bridge identification number: it's 1062850. When Dave Clements, one of the bridge management engineers for the New York State Department of
Transportation, received the emergency call for barges loose
and heading for the Troy-Menands bridge at 9:35 a.m., he said,
"Oh, my God," loud enough to get everyone's immediate attention in the office.

He looked up #1062850, and here's what he found: It was
built in 1932; it is 1,512 feet long, with a 64-foot out-to-out
width, and it occupies 95,861 square feet; on average, 30,000
cars a day drive over it; there are four traffic lanes and two six-
foot sidewalks on it.

Dave Clements' anxiety level did not drop much as he read
further. The bridge is an all-steel, 11-span bridge with lift towers that had not been raised for at least twenty years, and there
was no indication of the last date that anyone tested them. The
bridge has numerous punch-throughs, or pot-holes, in the deck
and on the sidewalks, which have been closed to pedestrian traffic for over two years. The concrete piers that support the span-
junctions are rigid-frame piers, protected by coffer dams of steel
sheeting backfilled with stone to absorb the consistent shocks
from ice, natural and manmade debris, scour, corrosion and,
infrequently, loose boats or barges.

But a two million pound barge in a swift current is something else again, especially one with built-up momentum. *The
usual 3 to 4 mph current impact, we might be okay*, Dave was thinking, but he couldn't be sure about the flow-rate today. *Physics
mass times velocity, M x V, equals momentum . . . if those barges really
get cranking, we've got the railroad bridge next, then the Dunn*

Memorial, bang, bang, one after the other . . . oh, my God. If we lose
a pier on Troy-Menands, we lose two spans. If we lose two spans, we
lose the whole bridge.

Finally, now, Charley gets the empty barge's stern line in
hand, and Frank steers close enough to shore that Ric can catch
it. With Don and Dave helping, they wrap it quickly around the
thickest maple they can find. As the rope tightens, the Freedman's guy takes off, running like crazy toward the bow again, in
case the rope breaks and boomerangs his way. The firefighters
scramble up the bank at the same time, in case it snaps back
toward them. Nobody puts a lot of trust in this rope right now.
But Charley has a yellow gaff in his hand, hooked onto the side
of Metro 15, and he seems to be working the loaded barge in
closer as the empty barge behind it strains against the line and
the two of them slow their erratic spinning.

The maple is bending, farther and farther, and the earth on
the uphill side is spurting out as the roots are dragged with
audible cracks up toward the surface, but the tree is holding.
The stern line from Metro 25 seems sound enough, and the
barges are backing up just slightly against the current. They're
swinging in toward the spot where the frigid water sloshes over
the dark skeleton of a 19th Century wooden barge that once
carried tons of the first mass-produced horseshoes from Henry
Burden's Iron Company on the Hudson down to the Union
troops fighting in the Civil War more than a hundred and
thirty years ago.

Burden invented the machine that could make one consis-
tently-formed horseshoe every second — sixty a minute, thirty-
six hundred an hour. In 1860, a good blacksmith, if he didn't
rest, could make about twelve horseshoes in an hour, enough
for three horses. In a ten-hour day, Burden's horseshoe machine
could spit out enough iron shoes for nine thousand Union
horses. Confederate officers had orders to raid any supply trains

that were carrying Burden's horseshoes, because there was no mill in the South that made them. By the end of the Civil War, in 1865, Burden's industrial buildings, all powered by a 60-foot high by 22-foot wide water wheel fed by three manmade, company-owned lakes, stretched for a mile along these banks. Now a piece of that property is owned by King Fuels.

From his vantage point on the river, Charley can see, directly above the barges, the circular, five-story, black King Fuels tower, which is the most prominent river landmark for miles. The rudiments of a face, minus the nose, are painted on it: Wide, full pink lips, one eye, its left, with a blue center surrounded by too much white, and the other eye, just a white crescent with a line of lashes hanging off it, is winking.

Suddenly, now, the three-inch line holding the two barges explodes, with a sharp report that even the people whose cars have been stopped up on the Route 787 ramp to the bridge can hear. Metro 25 and Metro 15, free again, spin slowly in the current and drift inexorably toward the King Fuels dock and the oval coffer dams that buffer the Troy-Menands bridge piers.

Local news teams are arriving, getting as close as police will allow them. Firefighters running determinedly through the woods and along the riverbanks, police on the access roads and bridge ramps, hearty cyclists and roller bladers across the way on the bike path, stopped motorists on all the roads — everyone is staring intently at these runaway barges on the river. The Hudson hasn't gotten this much focused attention from so many different people in years.

As in many of the post-Industrial Revolution cities in the Northeast, most residents of Troy seem to have basically lost much connection to their river, except to watch the environmental sloop *Clearwater* dock at the Troy marina, or to bike down along the Watervliet-Albany side, or if they take an early evening blues cruise on the Captain J.P. moored behind City

Hall. However, most people in Troy still keep their distance from the river itself, although it wasn't always that way.

* * *

The Hudson River was the primary reason Troy was settled by Europeans, and why it prospered as a rich, boisterous mix of commerce, culture, manufacturing, education, and political shenanigans during a remarkable hundred and ten-year heyday that lasted almost until World War II.

From 1609, when the *Half Moon* sailed as far up the Hudson as she could, until first the railroads and then the highways allowed more and more people and industries to move farther and farther west, this seven-mile stretch of land along the Hudson seemed to provide a steadily-growing but usually divisive American people with what they seemed to want: beaver and otter pelts, taverns, strategic military encampments, flour, beef, paper, warehouses, canal boats, an engineering college, iron, wool, a female seminary, church bells, theaters, cast-iron stoves, a station on the Underground Railroad, mass-produced horseshoes, professional baseball, beer, music halls, stagecoaches, steel, railroad spikes, surveying instruments, prostitutes, detachable collars and cuffs, labor unions, decent hospitals, and a thousand other things.

Troy's modern settlement began with the Dutch. In the seventeenth century, they were looking for a passage to Asia and "the western sea" by way of the Atlantic. They were also desperately envious of the French fur traders in the New World, who had been exclusively gathering valuable beaver and otter pelts along the Hudson, which they called the *Riviere Grande*, for most of the 16th Century. To remedy this, the Dutch East India Company finally hired an Englishman, Captain Henry Hudson, and gave him two principal tasks: Lead an expedition that would discover a northwest passage to India, and steal the lucrative fur trade from the French in America.

On September 19th, 1609, reaching only as far as the navigable headwaters just above what would become Troy, at North Latitude 42 degrees, 43 minutes, 50 seconds by East Longitude 30 degrees, 21 minutes, 45 seconds, the crew of the *Half Moon* did succeed in bartering knives, beads, and hatchets with Uncas, who would be immortalized more than two hundred years later by James Fenimore Cooper, and other local Mohicans for the precious animal skins. Robert Juet, Hudson's clerk on the trip, recorded this entry in his diary when they were anchored near the site that became Troy:

The one and twentieth was faire weather, and the wind all Southerly . . . our Master and his Mate determined to try some of the chiefe men of the Countrey, whether they had any treachery in them. So they tooke them downe into the Cabin, and gave them so much wine and aqua vitae, that they were all merrie: and one of them had his wife with him, which sate so modestly, as any of our Countrey women would doe in a strange place. In the end one of them was drunke, which had been aboord of our ship all the time that we had beene there; and that was strange to them; for they could not tell how to take it. The canoes and folke went all on shoare; but some of them came again, and brought stropes of Beades; some had sixe, seven, eight, nine, ten; and gave him. So he slept all night quietly.

It would take another twenty-five years before the Native Americans would come to understand that their friendliness and trust had actually insured their own downfall. Hudson's successful voyage led to the rapid Dutch colonization of *Nieu Nederlandt*, which by 1630 included towns all the way up the newly-named Hudson's River from Manhattan to Rensselaerwyck, where the rapids of the one "great river" and the massive waterfall at the mouth of another, the Mohawk River, had persuaded Hudson to turn his ship around. These impenetrable rapids and the seventy-foot high by a quarter-mile wide Cohoes Falls established early Troy as the natural spot where all river travelers had to stop, transfer their cargoes to wagons, and portage around to navigable waters.

That geographical reality, along with the number of spacious islands that dotted the confluence of the two rivers, suited the British perfectly during their numerous military campaigns against the French from 1686 up until the American Revolution. And it didn't hurt the colonial rebels in 1776, when they had to defend the Hudson against this same tyrannical power who had purposely not sunk any money into its embattled colony for the development of any commercial transportation routes.

By 1800, however, according to *The Artificial River*, Carol Sheriff's book on the Erie Canal, "shipping a ton of goods thirty miles into the interior of the United States cost as much as shipping the same goods all the way to England. Clearly, the situation needed improvement if the nation was to prosper." That was because the only gap in the Adirondack Mountains afforded to settlers in the northern colonies was where the Mohawk River flowed easterly from central New York and met the Hudson, and all water routes stopped at Lake Ontario. How many in 1800 could imagine actually *making* a river that could do what God had neglected to do — unite the Atlantic Ocean with the Great Lakes?

For these settlers, though, the topography of upstate New York was clear evidence of the Hand of Providence: "God, they reasoned, would not have created breaks in mountain chains or riverbeds unless Man was destined to finish the work." And the unimaginable improvement and end of that Providential work arrived in 1825 with the opening of the Erie Canal, which provided a continuous water route from the Hudson at Troy all the way to Lake Erie, 363 miles long.

Troy's financial star, poised at the eastern end of the new "Great Highway," shot immediately into the heavens. A city which had only 150 inhabitants when it was named in 1789, Troy's population surged to almost 8,000 by the time the Erie Canal opened, hit just under 40,000 by the end of the Civil War, and topped 60,000 in 1890, ten years before it absorbed the village of Lansingburgh and added 15,000 more residents to the city's tax rolls. In one year, 1923, Troy's collar and cuff industry employed more than 10,000 men and women and reported gross receipts totaling over 43 million dollars. And the city's iron and steel industry, to cite only one other, was even larger.

* * *

The stronger current in the river's channel is helping Charley and Frank out now. When the rope snapped, Metro 25 swung back out into the fast water and dragged the heavier Metro 15 along, far enough out so they missed the King Fuels loading dock. Against Chief Schultz's warnings, Frank has steered the Whaler between the barges and the shoreline now, and they're trying to ease the barges through the second opening between the piers.

They still haven't gotten the Freedman's guy off the empty barge, but the Chief no longer seems as concerned about that. He knows the barges are too high for Charley to reach their ropes, so they still need that guy up there to help.

"Portable 10, why don't you let it go. All it looks like now is you'll force it into the abutment near the shoreline. Let it go and see if it'll drift past," he says.

Frank backs off, and Metro 15 heads straight for the pier. As it gets close, though, it veers unexpectedly to the right and just scrapes noisily along the steel sheeting of the dam. Metro 25 slingshots through the opening and heads toward the shore, dragging the loaded barge clear, leaving no visible damage to the pier. One bridge still standing and two to go, as the barges head off toward Albany.

A half mile farther downriver, Charley catches the stern line from the empty barge once again and passes it off to Ric Moreno and the others on the bank, and they attach it to a thicker tree. But this time, as soon as it tightens, the rope that connects the two barges snaps almost immediately, and the loaded barge floats off alone downriver. As the Rescue Squad secures the empty barge with its bow line, the Freedman's guy is finally able to climb off, and he acts almost proud as he walks up from the riverbank. "There's a lot of weight on there. 800 tons at least," he says. "That ain't nothing, though. Barges hold a lot." It's a pretty gutsy comment from someone who may lose his job today, but it's also strangely typical bravado from a blue-collar Troy kid.

* * *

Historically, workers in Troy have often demonstrated their defiance to whatever they considered authority. Even during Troy's glorious heyday, which extended from the opening of the Erie Canal until most of the textile factories, iron mills and breweries had shut down or moved away during the Great Depression of the 1930's, there was constant unrest just beneath the social surface. A few blocks past the ornate facades of the factory owners' mansions lay row after row of iron mongers' tenements. Kate Mullany, organizer of the only bona fide female union in the country, the Troy laundresses union, battled management constantly to win wages that stitchers and pressers could simply feed their children on.

In 1853, Troy hosted the world premiere of *Uncle Tom's Cabin*, but ten years later was also, paradoxically, the site of a horrible Draft Riot, where 2000 workers wrecked the machinery and type of the *Troy Daily Times* and beat black people and abolitionists in the streets.

In 1860, an escaped slave from Virginia, Charles Nalle, working in Troy as a coachman for a wealthy industrialist named

Uri Gilbert, was arrested under the authority of the Fugitive Slave Act, and held in a house at First and State Street. Troy's Police Chief, Timothy Quinn, trying to return the slave to his rightful owner, moved the manacled Nalle toward a police wagon waiting on First Street. But a mob of over 1,000 abolitionists and freemen, led by Harriet Tubman herself, attacked Quinn and the police guards. Tubman threw her arms around Nalle and shouted, "Drag us out. Drag him to the river. Drown him, but don't let them have him." The crowd succeeded in stealing Nalle back from the police and they ferried him across the Hudson to Watervliet. When the police succeeded in recapturing him, 600 dollars was raised by the citizens of Troy to buy Nalle's freedom, and he lived the rest of his life a free man and citizen of the city.

Violent and wrongheaded or not, though, Troy in the 19th Century was a remarkable place to be. On the way to his inauguration in 1861, Lincoln stopped and addressed a crowd of 30,000 at Troy's Union Station. In 1870, President Grant, along with Meade, Sherman and Sheridan, three well-known Union generals, attended the burial of Troy's Major-General George H. Thomas at Oakwood Cemetery. The most famous singers in the world, including Jenny Lind, the Swedish Nightingale, sang at the Troy Music Hall. And after the great fire of 1862 destroyed the entire downtown, incinerating more than 550 buildings in a hellish, six-hour conflagration, it took less than a year for the people of Troy to rebuild their city. In July of that year alone, 181 new buildings were erected in the burned zone.

* * *

Ric and Don Kimmey have climbed into the Whaler now to help out. Without another barge to swing it sideways and shift its course, Metro 15 picks up speed. Everyone left on shore has to run quicker along the exposed sections of river beach or turn and go up through the woods to keep pace with it now. Up above us, on the well-tended access road to the Rensselaer County Wastewater Treatment Plant, sits a line of police cars and fire engines, their lights flashing. But in here it looks like a toxic dump site. The slanted ground between the trees is covered with almost a hundred years of coal-tar deposits that weren't halted until the mid-1940's, and there are piles of other junk that have been added more recently — portable heaters, flower pots, Pepsi bottles half full of filthy water, old tires, Budweiser cans, several black bulbs from toilet tanks scattered here and there, an old General Electric washing machine, and lots of indistinguishable metal parts. On a flat section, we find a dead, bleached dog, with a mass of colorless intestines clustered beside his stomach. He looks skinned, and otherworldly. Just past him, a battered but intact Remington typewriter sits upright in front of a tree, as if someone, watching the river go by, just finished composing a letter and left for a few minutes to mail it.

A hundred yards farther down the shore, on a sandbar, Mike Harrison is handing one end of a steel cable to Charley Willson. He and Gary Hanna cinch the other end around a massive oak that leans out where the sandbar rises to become the riverbank.

"Gary, you want to hook this other one up," Mike is saying. "Loop it around, go up here under this branch, loop it around here."

Firefighters from the Watervliet Arsenal have brought over some long, substantial steel cables. The barge is eddying temporarily in a small bay near a sandbar, and Ric and Don are perched on its gunwales, looping their end of the cable around a cleat. Frank is trying to inch the barge toward shore to give all of them time to get set. "Move back toward the middle. Keep the ass end from going out. Get to the upriver side and keep that from going out in the channel," Mike yells to Frank.

No tugs are in sight yet, and the Coast Guard has no station this far up the river. Ralph Carpino, the captain of the last working tug docked in Albany, the *Frances Turecamo*, lives down in Kingston, and there's no word on whether he's headed north. The other Boston Whaler owned by the Troy Fire Department isn't running and, because it's the middle of November, everybody else has their boats in storage for the winter.

"They say there are three tugs on the way," Mike says. "One's coming down through the lock and the other two are coming up the river, but I don't see any yet."

The barge is moving out again, tightening the cable. "Watch yourselves now, watch yourselves. That cable's got a backlash if it snaps," Gary is shouting. "Get away from the tree. Mike, all those roots and everything are right there, so watch it."

On Chief Schultz's portable radio, I can hear the Dispatcher: PORTABLE 1, COAST GUARD REQUESTS THAT WE ESTIMATE THE DISTANCE FROM THE BARGE TO THE RAILROAD BRIDGE.

The cable holds, but with a sickening groan, the tree is hauled completely out of the ground, roots and all, and dragged out along the sandbar and pulled into the water.

Mike Harrison talks resignedly into his radio now. "Portable 10, back off, you can't stop it." Then, running out on the sandbar, he yells at Kimmey, "Get off the barge, Donny. You and Ric, get off it."

Suddenly, though, the tree flips up onto its top and catches in the sand. The barge shudders abruptly and starts to back up, then holds in place, shifting almost imperceptibly in the current.

"Dispatcher, part of a tree that we had cabled the barge to is anchoring it in the river. It's at a standstill right now. We just don't know how long it's going to hold." As Chief Schultz talks into his radio, the *Leigh Ann Reinauer*, a tug with its name and, under that, New York, painted on its side, pulls into sight, blowing its horn three times.

* * *

Back at the Troy marina, a reporter, Phil Bayly, and a cameraman from Channel 13 are waiting. "When you had them tied together, then they snapped apart, boy, I could hear that from across the river," Phil says.

"That's why we were climbing up the hill," Gary says.

"What kind of thoughts went through your mind in the middle of this battle?" Phil asks Charley, who is smiling now.

"Well, this is the third one I've done, and we were able to do it before, so I knew if you could just keep it from turning, if you just keep trying to edge it in gradually, you'll get it. The concern was because of the speed at the beginning. The current's running a lot faster today than it has been before. Other times we could work with it a little bit. But once it got past the bridge, then we knew we could work it in eventually."

"Did you really worry about the damage to that bridge?"

"See, we were afraid in the beginning that, like at the Troy-Menands bridge it wasn't too bad, we had control of it, but if it got out in the middle of the current and started heading for that railroad bridge, that's the one we were really concerned about," Charley says.

"Thanks, guys, I appreciate it. Hell of a sight to see, I'm telling you," Phil says.

As they climb into the back of the Rescue Squad, Don is laughing. "That was fun," he says. "That's why you work out. You know how long we chased along that riverbank?"

"No, but I'll tell you, I haven't climbed a barbed-wire fence in a long time," Ric answers. "Enough to work up an appetite for lunch, that's how long."

"If that got out in the middle of the channel, it would have gone straight south, with all those other bridges in the way," Don says.

Charley jumps in now. "Too bad we couldn't keep it in Troy. It just got away from us. If it got downriver, it would have kept going and going, you know, and we were running out of options. We would have finally ended up in Poughkeepsie, and I don't think we know their language. We don't even have visas to get across the border down there, do we?"

Mike Harrison

I didn't want to be a fireman when I was a kid, not until I was maybe twenty, and I'm the only one in my immediate family, including my kids, that became one. See, I wanted to be a farmer. I wanted to be a nurseryman, all right? I wanted to go to Cornell, but my parents couldn't afford to send me to Cornell. They not only couldn't afford to send me there — they didn't want me to go there. They didn't want me to be a horticulturist, because my guidance counselors in high school, (now we're back in the 50's and my guidance counselors happened to be coaches who didn't have a degree and so they had nothing else to do but be guidance counselors), they said my aptitudes showed that I should be a doctor or a chemist. The aptitude tests I used to take would ask questions like, "Would you rather be in an office all day, or on a garbage truck?" and I'd put down, on a garbage truck, because even that looked better than an office. So at any rate I went to Siena, because my parents wanted me to study pre-med. I also had an opportunity to go away and play baseball. The St. Louis Cardinals offered me a tryout, and they were offering guys twenty thousand dollars to play baseball, and in those days that was big money, but my parents said no to that, too. They didn't exactly say I couldn't do it, they just advised me not to do it, and to go to Siena.

I regret that now. At 55, it's always in the back of my mind. I wish I had gone for the tryout. When I was a junior at Siena, in pre-med, I said to my parents, "Mom and Dad, I love you very much, but I really want to take horticulture, and I'm going to go to Farmingdale." They had the best program in the state at that time, except for Cornell. So I went down there and that's where I met my wife, Mary. Three years later, when I finally asked her to marry me, I told her that I played a lot of softball, that I was a volunteer fireman, and that I lived in upstate New York and that's where I intended to live, that I loved her very much and if she could accept all those things, I'd like her to marry me. This was before I joined down here and got paid for fighting fires. And Mary and I have got seven kids, so I guess it worked out.

One of the drawbacks of being a fireman is you lose a lot of time with your family. Not lose it maybe, but I think your family suffers from the schedule, although I prefer the schedule this way, 24 on and 72 off. You miss a lot of holidays. Saturdays. It always seems that every damn Saturday or Sunday, there's something going on, and you're working. Even though you only work one Saturday and one Sunday a month, you always miss something. But the stress of the job is incredible. There are individuals on the job that don't give a damn, but I would say that probably 95% of the men on the job care. And therefore if you're a caring person, you're there because you want to alleviate pain and suffering, and the more of it you see, the more it takes something out of you. It does draw life energy out of you, and sometimes you can replenish it in your three days off, but you never forget. I can close my eyes right now and see many, many ugly scenes that I don't particularly want to see. And every once in a while, they'll come up and slap me in the face, when I'm thinking about something totally unrelated.

And definitely there are health hazards. I got throat cancer, it'll be eleven years this coming March. I had radiation. I had 33 radiation treatments. I got a very sore throat. I couldn't eat. I lost about 35 pounds. I got tired, but I didn't get vomity. I'm still hoarse from the radiation treatments. I always had a gravelly voice, but when I had radiation I couldn't talk at all for over a month. But I don't really blame the job particularly for my cancer, even though I was involved with a naphthalene call once where a worker died and all us firemen who were there developed serious problems or died afterwards. I was a heavy smoker, too. I do know that throat cancer is 65% more prevalent in firefighters than it is in the general population. Also, because of my side interests, in the landscaping business, I also used every chemical that's now off the market with absolutely no protection, DDT and all that stuff. It's always nice to be able to blame your job because you get disability, blah blah blah, and when I did get the cancer, naturally people encouraged me to do that. But there were a lot of other reasons. Being in the fire department didn't help any, but neither did smoking three packs a day, and neither did all the chemicals and crap I worked with over the years. I'm obviously very fortunate to still be here, and I experienced what I always consider was Divine Intervention.

I used a lot of mental imaging during that time. For me, that's just a matter of relaxation and then being able to image my immune system. My imagery back then was Pac-Man images, remember those? I imagined them going through my immune system, eating the cancer cells and getting them out of my body. Well, the mental imaging was just something I did every day. I don't know why, but it never dawned on me that cancer kills you, or that it was going to kill me, in any event. And I just had a real positive attitude right from the get-go that I would get better. In fact, I used to bug my doctor, even during my radiation treatments, "When can I go back to work? When can I go back to work?"

But also, one thing when I was doing the radiation, I used to get these muscle spasms in my throat where I couldn't breathe. I couldn't exchange air. It only happened twice. One time I was driving my car and all of a sudden I couldn't breathe. I remembered from my EMT training that I had to extend my neck and wait for a breath to come, but I was just frightened to death. I don't know if it ever happened to you, but it felt like when you were a kid and you fell and got the wind

*knocked out of you. You're laying there and you can't breathe. I was
just driving down the road and that happened, coming back from radiation treatment one day. Another time a spasm happened when I was
out in my nursery at home, and that was an important time. That's
the time I felt I was given the sign. I don't want to sound like some
kind of nut, but I do feel I'm a spiritual person. I try to be, and I have
a lot of faith in a belief system and in a higher power, and I call Him
God. Or Her. But I have that faith. At any rate, I want to give you
some background for this story.*

*At that age, 44, three of my kids were still young. Well, two of
them were in cub scouts, and there was this deal on a weekend to go to
Plattsburgh Air Force Base with them, and I had signed up to take
them. I only did radiation five days a week, so I was off on weekends.
As luck would have it, Judy, a friend of mine, called and said there
was going to be a healing mass on Saturday of that same weekend. I
don't remember the priest's name, but he was somebody I wanted to
hear, and she was calling to see if I wanted to go with her. I don't
think I thought about dying too much back then but I can remember
saying, "Well, jeez, this is maybe the last time I'll be able to take these
kids to Plattsburgh, and God's calling me to go somewhere else." So I
was really in the throes of a difficult decision. At any rate, I finally
decided that I was going to take the boys up to Plattsburgh. I called
my friend back and I told her, and she said, "Well, that's fine. I'm
going anyway."*

*Now when I came back from Plattsburgh that Sunday afternoon,
I was out in my nursery, pruning some shrubs, and one of those
spasms hit me. I lost my breath, probably only twenty or thirty seconds, but it seemed like an eternity. And that was the only time in my
whole treatment that I broke down. I went in the house, started crying, and said to Mary, "That's it. I'm not going back. The damn
treatment's worse than the disease." So I cried, and Mary was trying
to calm me down. During this conversation at the kitchen table, the
phone rings. I answered, and it was Judy. She said, "Mike, something funny happened yesterday. What the priest told us to do when*

we went up to receive communion, not to say anything out loud, but just in our hearts and our minds, to give to the Lord the healing that we want. So I did that, and absolutely nothing happened. I didn't feel any different or anything. I guess I was kind of disappointed. Then we were about to leave and the priest said, 'Wait a minute. Before anybody goes, I have this nagging vision in my head. It means absolutely nothing to me, but it might mean something to somebody out there, to one of you people. And it's a vision of a firefighter, and the water coming from his hose is clear.' "

When Judy told me that story, I felt so strange. Believe it or not, I immediately felt healed. I felt like everything was okay. I got off the phone and of course then I was crying with a different emotion, and I told my wife, "Okay, I'll go back. I'm going to my treatment tomorrow and I'll finish up." I think I had another two or three weeks to go.

Speaking of my faith, I was on a call once, and it was a funny call, especially in light of the fact that about this time in my life I was involved in what we call a corsillo, which is a short course to christianize Catholics. It's a Spanish movement within the Catholic Church. So anyway our particular mission, Mary's and mine, was to help Christianize our environment, right? This was back in '73 or '74. We got this call, and there was heavy snow, and we were working splits — 12 hours on, 12 off, and then back for 12 hours overtime, for which we didn't get paid in those days but you had to come back anyway. So this box came in about 2 o'clock in the morning. We get to the fire and the place was going pretty good in the front. I was on the Squad with Murray Dempsey and Danny Rokjer. We had to go through this back lot, and Murray was a short, stocky guy, so he gets only about halfway across the field. We can hear this woman yelling, "God help me, God save me." Clear as anything. You could hear her really well on a cold, snowy night like that. So we look and we can see that she's in a doorway, but she's got it pushed only partway open, because they never shoveled. She couldn't get it open. She's yelling like crazy, but she's really relatively safe. The front of the building was going, but she was in the back. Anyway, Murray can't move and he yells, "I might as well be a fucking fire hydrant," because he's stuck there. So Rokjer and I have to climb over a fence, and then slog through all that snow with the gear on and we were absolutely out of breath when we got up to the woman, to tell her she's okay. Now she never stopped her, "God help me, God save me." We were yelling back, "Look, ma'am, we'll get the snow away from the door, and we'll get you out of there in a minute." We got the snow away, and the woman had to be about 300 pounds, and then this guy appeared there, too. So I said to him, "We'll get your wife out and then we'll get you. Just relax." And he's screaming and shouting at us, "She's not my wife. She's just a tenant." Which means like, "Frig her. Get me out of here."

So we get her turned around so she's facing up the stairs, and I put my hands under her shoulders and I said to her, "Okay, just step back." When I said that, I stepped back, then she stepped back, and I fell. She landed on my chest, and all I could do underneath her was make like a snow angel. I couldn't budge. And she's still shouting, "God help me, God save me," this whole time. She never broke cadence. I said to Rokjer, "Danny, get her off me." And he's laughing so hard he can't do anything, right? Finally I screamed, "Get this fat bitch off of me," and he's laughing and she's still saying, "God help me, God save me." And the guy is still up in the doorway yelling to get him out of there, when he could have just walked right out the door. Danny finally got her off, and then she started yelling that she was cold. Here I am, trying to be a Christian, right, and I say, "Well, you're not getting my coat. You're going in that ambulance." That's a call I'll never forget.

I hope I act differently as a fireman because I'm a Christian, but I fall short on that aspect. But I accept, see, I accept the fact that I'm not perfect. I think my religious beliefs and my profession, especially here, kind of dovetail. I believe that we're all put here for a purpose, and it's for us to figure out what it is. I'm still working on that. But my faith is never challenged by what I see on the job. I think we're all human, and suffering is part of the human condition. I think free will, which is the greatest gift God could give anybody, is really important. God doesn't direct all the terrible things that happen. Because we're humans, we're not perfect, and terrible things happen. I don't know why they happen. I guess the way I feel about it all is that God's ways are not necessarily mine. I take a lot of faith from Einstein, who was an agnostic or said he was. Einstein had a much better brain than I do. At the end of his life, with all of his brilliance, he said, "There's something beyond that I don't understand." So that's kind of how I paraphrase my life, really.

I feel remorse, I feel sorrow, I feel anger sometimes at the tragedies, but I don't ever judge it or question it. I would have liked to try baseball, though, just to see what would have happened. I used to spend 50% of my life fighting with people and then the other 50% going around apologizing. And that made for a pretty full life, you know? I'm very satisfied with my life now, to tell you the truth. I'm very happy. I think I've got a great life. Keeping in mind that it's not perfect and nothing ever is. Yeah, I wish that I had more money. I wish when I retire from here, in eight months or so, that I could retire without money problems, but that's not going to be. I'm going to be strapped for money until the day I die. But I wouldn't do anything differently. I've been very fortunate. I've done almost all the things I wanted to.

4

Like that thing last night, those guys are so good that they're too aggressive. I mean, they're not afraid of nothing. And then you get to a point where you can get in trouble because, you know, you're just willing to challenge anything. And I think they've always been good. They've always been successful. They've always been able to do the impossible, but I think they got themselves in trouble last night. I think they just tried to do the impossible again, and you can't keep winning trying to do the impossible. It was a hell of a thing.

— Dick Thompson

It's the 16th of December, at ten of five in the morning, and it's still dark out. At 2312 Eleventh Street, Joe DeNatali has been awake most of the night. First, the four RPI students who rent the apartment above his were playing music too loud, as usual, stomping around up there until way past midnight. And then a freezing wind started up, smacking against his back windows, and wouldn't stop. Finally, all those sirens for something pretty close began around 1:30, and that was the clincher. He got up, and once he was up, he almost always stayed up. He watched some kickboxer movie on cable, and about 4:30 he got really hungry, so he decided to cook up some french fries.

But now the smell of those fries popping in all that peanut oil on his gas stove is actually making him a little drowsy. Maybe he'll just plop down on the living room couch and rest for a few minutes, just long enough to let those french fries brown up nice and crisp.

ATTENTION ALL UNITS: ALARM OF FIRE IS BEING TRANSMITTED FOR BOX 429. THE ADDRESS IS 2312 ELEVENTH STREET. THAT'S AT THE DEAD END NORTH OF HUTTON STREET. CALLER STATES THE BUILDING IS ON FIRE. UNITS RESPONDING: ENGINE 5, ENGINE 4 IN PLACE OF ENGINE 2, TRUCK 2, RESCUE SQUAD, MEDIC 2, AND CAR 4. I REPEAT: ALARM OF FIRE, BOX 429, IS BEING TRANS-MITTED. 5 ZERO 2. DISPATCHER 9.

As the first alarm sounds on the monitor in the hallway out-side his bedroom, Charley Willson doesn't wake up completely. His wife, Joyce, pulls the covers up higher and rolls over, hop-ing a second alarm won't follow. Her clock says a little after five in the morning, and the 1st Platoon isn't on duty until eight a.m., so Charley's safe for about three more hours. The 4th Pla-toon can handle the fire. Unless a second alarm goes out, and then they'll probably issue a recall, too, and the next platoon on duty will have to go in early. That would mean Charley, because the 1st follows the 4th. Along with all the other wives and girl-friends of guys on the 1st, Joyce was happier when any other platoon caught the working fires. Not that she didn't care about the men on the other platoons. She did. She'd just rather listen to Charley grouse about missing out on the action than always picture him inside the flames.

The dispatcher hasn't bothered to mention Car 2, which is Assistant Chief Dick Thompson. He doesn't need to. He knows Dick has been supervising the clean-up at the Arrow Cash

Market fire, which came in about three and a half hours ago. The Arrow Cash Market is on 15th Street, only a few blocks up the hill from the location of the 11th Street fire, and he knows how Dick operates. He's sure Dick was at the new fire scene before he finished his dispatch.

As Chief of Operations, Dick is completely responsible for the fire ground. It's his job to make sure every firefighter under his command gets to the fire scene and back to his station without getting hurt. It's also his job to see that every fire in Troy is put out as efficiently as possible. If anything, Dick takes his job too seriously. He almost lives at Central Station. Some of his detractors on the 1st Platoon often accuse him of trolling for calls — driving around and watching for any possible emergencies — even when he's off-duty, just so he can maintain control. No matter how much his enemies complain about him, though, they all agree on two things: He's a great firefighter, and he knows how to manage a fire ground.

At 5:02 this morning, as Dick arrives at 2312 11th St., his gut instinct tells him this fire is serious trouble. "Car 2 arriving. We've got heavy smoke," he radios the dispatcher. There's a fierce wind blowing over the hill, pushing the smoke down so it blankets the street. It's so thick he can't even see enough to drive his car all the way to the dead end. As he approaches, he can barely see the burning house, although he can certainly hear the fire snarling somewhere behind the dense smoke.

He can also hear hysterical shouting. "Hurry up. He's still in there." Three college students dressed only in sweats pile out of the smoke and surround Dick, pointing. "Our roommate's still in there, in the back bedroom, up there. He's still inside."

"Car 2 to Fire Alarm," Dick immediately says into his portable. "We have a report of people trapped. Put out a second alarm."

A second alarm in Troy means that two more engines and another truck company will respond to the fire, and the dispatcher calls now for Engine 6, Engine 3, and Truck 1. With the exception of Engine 2, which is still mopping up at the earlier fire, only Engine 1 in the Burgh has not been sent to fight this one.

The 4th Platoon's Rescue Squad was making its way back to Central Station with a load of re-filled air tanks when the box alarm went out. Around 2 a.m., after they had knocked the Arrow Cash Market fire down, Dick had kicked them loose to take all the empty Scott tanks over to Engine 3 on Campbell Avenue and fill them up, just in case another fire came in. Two other bullshit calls came in after that, so they've been awake the whole night, too.

Mike Murnane and Carl Campbell, two of the 4th Platoon's Rescue Squad veterans, have worked as partners for almost ten years. They search fire floors as a team, orchestrate rescues with each other, and ride together in the back of the Squad. They've both been working out on their treadmills at home a lot lately, and they feel like they've pretty much reached fighting trim. Walking out of the first fire more than three hours ago, they had started laughing. "Hey, I could handle another one of these tonight," Mike said, and Carl answered, "Yeah, we could take one more of these easy." Now as the Squad inches up 11th Street in the billowing smoke, though, neither of them is laughing.

Engine 4's crew is attacking with a line at the front door of the house, working to hold the flames in the back so the Rescue Squad has some chance to use the stairs, but the orange wave of fire is surging closer and closer. The wind is gusting at 25 or 30 miles an hour, pumping superheated air toward the front, eddying the steam from the hose's spray, and slapping the whole, volatile mixture back in their faces as they advance up the porch steps.

Dick runs along the south side of the building now, down through a vacant lot to the street, and catches a glimpse of the Squad as the wind parts the smoke for an instant. He starts toward it, and almost runs into Mike and Carl hurrying up from the curb.

"Jesus, you can't see your hand in front of your face," Mike shouts.

"Lookit," Dick says, leading them up the side, "these kids swear on a stack of bibles there's a guy left in there, up in that bedroom." He points to the last window on the second floor. Even with the swirling smoke, they can see that ten feet past it the entire back porch, top to bottom, is a mass of flames. "I think it's too far gone for an interior search, but maybe we could try a ladder to that window, you know? You might get a chance to search the one room and then get out," Dick says.

As Mike looks at Carl for a judgment, Walt Schouler, the captain of the Rescue Squad, runs up. With him is Rich Cellucci, a probationary firefighter who is training with the Squad and whose first actual fire was the Arrow Cash Market fire a few hours ago. Mike and Carl both know that throwing a ladder to that window will eat up two or three minutes at least. With this volume of fire and the wind stoking it, whoever is in there doesn't have much time left, if he's still alive at all.

"We'll try the stairs," Carl says without hesitation.

Dick doesn't want to hear that. There's no more aggressive firefighter in the department than Dick, but this fire is more than dangerous. It's a flashover waiting to happen. And the 4th is Dick's old platoon. Walt Schouler is Dick's best friend in the department, and Dick was Battalion Chief on the 4th before he became Assistant Chief. He doesn't want to see his friends go into that building, but he knows it's their call. He just has a bad feeling about this one.

"Be careful in there," Dick says, and the four men hurry toward the front steps.

Dick turns to transmit the exposures — or what surrounds the fire structure on each of its four sides — to the dispatcher. He keys his radio, hunches over to shelter it from the wind, and speaks fast. "Exposures are the following: 1 is the street; 2 is a two-story frame with 10-foot separation; 3 is a rear yard; 4 is a vacant lot. Fire building is a two and a half story frame. Heavy fire in the rear of the structure, covering both the first and second floors. Two lines deployed in the front. Trying to extricate the last person reported in there."

Mike Murnane hits the interior stairs first. He sees that Engine 2's crew is in there with a line, too, and he figures Dick must have pulled them off the clean-up before the Squad arrived. An uncharged hose line is lying in his path. He hears Captain Garrett yelling they should take the line up with them, but Mike steps over it and keeps moving. *Humping a line will just slow us down*, he thinks. He can see the stairs easily now. They're pretty clear, and he looks back to check on Carl, Walt, and Rich, to make sure they're still close. Carl's there, but his head is down as he ascends, and the others are right behind him. *The smoke in the street is a lot worse than this*, Mike is thinking. *We'll be okay.*

By the top of the stairs, though, Mike can see the smoke on the second floor is much worse. It's most of the way down the wall. Carl bumps into him from behind, and mutters something inside his mask. Together they drop to their knees and begin the search. From where the stairwell empties out, the room they want is up a little and to the right. As they sweep their gloved hands in front of them, following the baseboard to the first opening, Mike is oddly soothed by not only the usual crackling and snapping of the fire eating the house, but by the dim roar of Engine 4's crew attempting to keep the stairwell open for them below. At least these are familiar noises in a burning house, not the ominous near-silence that no water and an imminent flashover might bring.

Mike can feel the heat pinching his ears, but it's not scalding yet. Of the four Squad members there, only Rich Cellucci, the probie, wears a Nomex hood to protect his neck and ears. When Walt, Carl, and Mike joined the department, they weren't issued

Nomex hoods, and they just never got around to buying them on their own. Usually, Mike is glad he doesn't have one, because his ears serve as a heat barometer — if they're really burning, it's too hot to be wherever he is. So far, his ears are holding up.

Inside the bedroom, the Squad members comb every surface, but none of them finds more than the usual college-kid stuff — piles of clothes, heavy books, CD cases, flimsy furniture. The students outside seemed certain, but there's no roommate in here, at least not where they said he'd be. Suddenly, a loud rumble shakes the building and a burst of orange light flashes out past the hallway. Just as suddenly, the comforting hose sound from downstairs disappears, and Mike's ears start to burn.

Outside, as Dick watches, every window in the downstairs, one by one from back to front, explodes into flames. It looks and sounds like a steam locomotive barreling through a black train-bridge, grimly outlining the structure as it tears by. As it reaches the front of the house, the three hosemen from Engine 4, trying to back away from the fireball, are knocked head over heels down the porch steps and land on top of each other in the narrow front yard, their turnout gear steaming in the 15-degree cold.

"Squad, are you able to give me a report?" Dick shouts into his radio. Nothing comes back, and Dick tries again. "Portable 10, if you're in the building, be careful. The whole back of this joint is going. Get to a window and get out now."

Dick holds his radio tight to his ear to hear Carl's answer: "Car 2, we're upstairs, on the second floor. We can't find anybody here, and we're turned around. We're not sure how to get out."

"Car 2 to Rescue Squad: Evacuate the building. Get out of the building." Dick waits about ten seconds, but he doesn't hear an answer, so he calls the dispatcher. "Car 2 to Fire Alarm. Get everybody out of the building."

Three years earlier, the Troy Fire Department initiated an emergency evacuation procedure, whereby the dispatcher would issue a general evacuation order and one of the drivers on the scene would blow three long blasts on his air horn, but until now they have never had to use it. The dispatcher transmits the three extended tones and then says, ALL FIRE UNITS: OUT OF THE BUILDING. REPEAT. ALL FIRE UNITS OUT OF THE BUILDING.

Inside, Mike feels like they're just crawling in circles. He hears the dispatcher's three tones issue from Carl's radio, and then his evacuation order. As the blasts from the air horn start, an intense wave of heat knocks him flat. Mike's face-mask is pressed tight to the carpet now, and he can feel his ears shriveling and singeing. *Jesus, this might be it*, he is thinking. The thought surprises him, though, and he realizes he's never thought of that on the job before this moment.

Carl is moving again, and Mike is trying to stay close. He keeps swinging his hand against Carl's leg to remind them both they're not alone. "We don't know how to get out of here," Mike can hear Carl yelling again, and then he hears Dick's voice, "Go to a window. Go to any wall and find a window." Now Walter is screaming, "We're trapped. Get us the hell out of here. Can anybody hear us?"

So this is what it's like, Mike thinks, and he feels too heavy to move any more. He imagines the heated air as some giant, dark iron pressing him into this carpet, and he can feel the heat even through his turnout coat. "We don't know where we are. Help us. We don't know how to get out," Carl keeps calling into his radio, and no one is answering now. Mike can't hear Walter anymore, and he doesn't know where Rich Cellucci, the new kid, is either. *They're probably gone*, flashes through Mike's mind, and for an instant he lets in the real possibility they might not make it out of here. But then, *Hey, you can't even be thinking that way*, he scolds himself. *Move! You've got to get out of here.*

Outside, Dick is hollering, "Find a wall," but he knows the four firefighters inside are running out of time fast. He hasn't seen a Troy firefighter get trapped and die in a burning house for 27 years, since his first year on the job, but he's afraid this morning he may have to see it again.

The dispatcher has picked up another distress call from the Rescue Squad, and he radios Dick — FIRE ALARM TO CAR 2: PORTABLE 10 IS ON THE SECOND FLOOR. THEY'RE NOT SURE HOW TO GET OUT.

"Fire Alarm, sound a 3rd alarm," is all Dick answers. No matter what happens now, he's going to need more men. "And recall the 1st Platoon," he adds.

Rich is having trouble with his breathing. He's afraid his Scott tank is almost empty. The warning alarm that signals low air hasn't gone off yet, but what if it's broken? What if he runs out of air in here? Carl and Mike are gone. He can hear Dick yelling, "Go to the front of the building," on Walt's radio, but it's too hot in that direction. They tried it. He keeps telling himself this is just like the smoke house at the fire training tower up in Wynantskill, but he knows it really isn't. It's way too hot for that, and the heat keeps building. He can feel it squeezing down on him. Pretty soon he won't be able to breathe at all. *Calm down. Breathe slow. You're not alone*, he says to himself. *Calm down. Just do what you got to do.*

All of a sudden, Walt grabs him. "Hey, I've got a window," he yells through his mask. Walt is dragging him now, screaming, "This way. It's a window. Come on," and Rich isn't thinking about breathing anymore. He can see lights flashing outside, and firefighters looking up toward him, and then Walt dives head first out the window. "One, two . . ." Rich counts, and dives after him.

Dick is running along the south side of the house again, peering up. "Jump out any window," he yells, not even bothering to use his radio now. He is screaming up at the black, empty rectangles above him, hoping to see a gloved hand or a helmet appear in any of them. "Jump out the window. Jump out."

Mike can't find Carl anymore. He throws a hand forward, sweeping side to side, and feels nothing there but carpet, so he drags himself half his length, and sweeps again. *Don't give up now, goddamn it.* He drags again, sweeps. This time there's something hard — wood or metal, a leg maybe — and above it something softer. *Must be upholstery.* Quickly, he runs his hand along the front. *Three cushions — a couch, for Christ's sake.* He crawls quickly past it and finds a wall, and then a shattered window. He sticks a hand out and feels the cold air. As he hauls himself up by the windowsill and shoves his head out to look down, he sees flames from the window below are blowing out at a 45-degree angle, straining up toward him.

"Oh, man, out of the frying pan and into the fire," he says out loud. It seems at that instant like the funniest line in the world to him, and he starts to laugh and cry at once. He begins to pound his hand on the siding, hoping someone will hear, and within a few seconds a 14-foot ladder slams in place below him. Suddenly, Carl grabs Mike from behind and throws him through the broken window.

On the north side, nobody saw that Rich Cellucci was caught upside down, hanging by one foot from wires near the top of the ladder. Dave Judge had already caught Walt Schouler when he came out. In all the smoke and darkness, no one saw Rich, and it took him a couple of minutes to work himself free and climb down the ladder on his own. By then, word that he was still trapped had spread to the other side.

"Cellucci's still in there," Dick is yelling, and a couple of guys start up the ladders to find him. When Rich hears his name being shouted, he runs around to the other side and calls, "Hey, I'm out. I'm okay."

Mike Murnane is sitting in the snow, blood oozing from a cut on his nose. When Carl followed him out the window, he landed on top of him, and his Scott tank smashed into Mike's nose. Carl is sitting next to Mike now. Both of them are black as burned shingles.

As Rich walks up, Carl looks at him and laughs. "I thought you were the one I threw out the window," he says. Then he turns to Mike and shakes his head. Carl's smile quickly switches to a look of mock concern and he tells him, "If I knew it was you, I would've gone out first."

Pulse of the People
from <u>The Record</u>
Praise for Troy Firefighters
They define 'above brave'

It was shortly after 5 a.m. on Dec. 16 that I was abruptly awakened by the scanner in my home.

It was the frightened and out-of-breath voice of a Troy firefighter calling for help for his crew that was trapped on the fire floor of a structure fire on 11th Street. I said to myself, you're dreaming, go back to sleep. But I heard his voice again and it was more frightening and more scared.

Being the son of a deceased Troy firefighter, I've been through this scenario before. Many times I escorted my mother to a Troy hospital because my father had been injured at a fire scene. One such injury ended his career and led to his death in 1985 at the age of 54.

I write this letter to the people that think a professional firefighter works a 24-hour tour just sitting around the firehouse doing nothing except waiting for the "bell to hit." When that bell does hit, the firefighter doesn't know what he is going to encounter from the time he throws his shoes off to dress in his turn-out gear until he returns. People shouldn't criticize the firefighters, because they don't fully understand this dangerous career.

There is no word in Webster's dictionary that defines "above brave," but it means the same as firefighter.

D.M.CHRISTENSON

Thank you from RPI
This letter was sent to Assistant Fire Chief Dick Thompson.

I am writing to commend the bravery of your firefighters for their heroic rescue efforts at the fire on 11th Street early Thursday morning. They showed a selfless devotion to their duty, risking their lives to enter a building where they knew conditions were already extremely hazardous.

As the president of Rensselaer Polytechnic Institute, I want to express my particular gratitude because these heroic efforts were undertaken in the belief that one of our students was trapped inside. It is reassuring to know the extent of the training, professionalism and bravery of your officers, but it is harrowing to think how much more seriously they might have been injured.

Again, on behalf of the entire Rensselaer community, please accept my sincerest thanks.

R. BYRON PIPES
President — RPI

"You missed it," Joe Reilly has been saying to everyone who walks through the door, except for the firefighters who were actually at the 11th Street fire and the TV and radio reporters who keep showing up to interview them. It's 9:30 in the morning, and Joe has been repeating, "You missed it," for almost two annoying hours now. Joe is at Central Station today to ride on Medic 2 for Don Kimmey, who is on vacation.

Dick Thompson has been holed up in the 10-foot square Battalion Chief's office, at the far left corner of the apparatus floor, fielding questions since he came in about 7:30.

"Okay, which fire?" he says abruptly to one of the AM radio reporters, who keeps looking down to make sure the water dripping off the Rescue Squad truck isn't draining toward her shiny, black Etienne Aigner boots.

"The second one," she answers.

"Awright, the second fire was on 11th Street," Dick begins, rolling his eyes a little and shifting some papers on Mike Harrison's desk. "Right now I'm looking into the strong possibility that the fire started as the result of careless cooking on the first floor. The building is probably gonna be torn down. The damage is extensive."

A bunch of guys from the 1st Platoon — Terry Fox, Tom Miter, Ric Moreno, Dave Stevens, and Charley Willson — are hanging out with Joe Reilly at the watch area, up near the front of the building, by the door to the firefighters' parking lot. They were called in early, about 5:30, to help out at the fire and to man Central Station. Because Carl and Mike and the other members of the Squad from the 4th Platoon were taken to the hospital, Ric, Charley, Dave, and Frank Ryan, all working the Squad on the 1st Platoon today, had to take their places at the fire.

But by 5:30, the worst was over, and they had several hours of overhaul and clean-up after the fire — pulling ceilings, raking through the charred furniture and appliances, hauling the ruined possessions out of the house — finishing the filthy, mundane work of making certain the fire was out. The 4th Platoon got the danger, the challenge, the excitement, and the adrenaline rush that many firefighters thrive on at a fire, and the 1st just got cold and dirty, as far as they're concerned.

Charley is on the phone with Joyce, his wife, who has been watching the alarming coverage of this fire on the morning news, and he's trying to calm her down. Ric, who has been feuding with Chief Thompson as much as anybody on this shift, is staring down toward the Battalion Chief's office. He turns away from watching Dick talking to the reporter with a disgusted look.

"The 4th is Dick's shift," he says. "He wouldn't be doing that for us. He was a captain on there for a long time, with Walt Schouler, before he moved up. That's his shift. It's always been his shift. But whenever he's got any special stuff to do, he asks us to do it."

For the last year or so, most of the big fires, what they call the "workers," have been occurring when the 4th was on duty. Just coincidence, without a doubt, but for the guys on the 1st who really like fighting fires, like Ric, it's getting hard to take, and they're stuck looking for other ways to prove themselves.

Terry Fox snorts with laughter. "Yeah, of course," he says. "Hazmat, some extrication, something to put together, he'll ask us. He knows if he says to go pop the A-post, cut through the roof, and then flop it back so we can haul the driver out of a car wreck, he won't get people on the 1st leafing through manuals to find out how to do it. He just doesn't like us getting up in his face if we don't like something," he says. "Only problem is, with the 4th, he's got to bend over and pluck them out of his ass most of the time."

At 46, Terry Fox, who answers to Foxy most of the time, is the second oldest man on the shift at Central Station, nine years younger than Battalion Chief Mike Harrison. At almost 6'3", he's the tallest of the group. With two former wives, three kids, and Protestant roots, he's broken the mostly Catholic and once-married mold of this group. His usually unruly salt-and-pepper hair, his white moustache, and his solid Irish build make him appear the quintessential, ever-trustworthy, veteran firefighter, but Foxy also counts on a bemused countenance and playful behavior to belie his stormy past and occasionally violent present. With his history as a boxer and a semi-professional football player, the numerous tales of his local bar brawls, and the two harrowing years he volunteered as a crew chief on a helicopter in Vietnam, it's no surprise that most guys bust his balls — about talking incessantly, about his erratic driving, about pacing around over-caffeinated and wild-eyed most nights he's on the job — from a safe distance.

Today is Foxy's second-to-last official day as the paramedic lieutenant on Medic 2. He and Charley Willson are being promoted, and he's feeling feisty, as usual, but he's beginning to feel nostalgic as well. Foxy will stay with the 1st Platoon at Central, assuming the captain's spot on Engine 5 since Wayne Laranjo is retiring and moving down to Mexico, but his promotion also means he won't be working as a paramedic anymore. And after almost fourteen years on the Medic rig, understanding the inevitability of change isn't much of a consolation for him.

Charley Willson would like to stay with the 1st Platoon, but as a new lieutenant he has no seniority, so he is bidding an open spot on the 3rd Platoon. Most everyone on the shift likes "Teflon Charley." But Frank Ryan and Ric Moreno are especially upset about him leaving the Rescue Squad. They've all worked together on the Squad for almost fifteen years, and they don't just like Charley — they absolutely trust him to save their asses in a tight spot, and that's the highest compliment any fire-fighter can pay another.

And, to add insult to the injury of the 1st Platoon's family being split up, somebody from the 4th Platoon is taking Foxy's place on the Medic rig. Jeff Gordon, a young lieutenant on the 4th, has the seniority to take Foxy's spot. He'll be coming over right after Christmas. Don Kimmey, who will be off on vacation until New Year's Day, has threatened to bid off the 1st Platoon if Jeff is allowed to do what he clearly wants to do — work as a firefighter paramedic on the 1st Platoon.

Don is one of the old guard. Though he's only 41, he has been on the job for almost twenty years, and Jeff is, comparatively, pretty new. He's been working as a firefighter for about eight years, and has only been a paramedic for the last two. But it's not just how long Jeff has been on the job. Don has two other problems with Jeff.

Number one, he is a lieutenant, a rank above Don, who is still a hoseman — his veteran status, considerable experience, and his position as one of the department's best paramedics notwithstanding. Jeff Gordon will be in charge of Don, and won't let him forget it. Jeff's reputation for arrogance, for condescension, and for pulling rank at the wrong moments has preceded him. And to make matters even worse, Don has never much cared for authority. It's true that Foxy was also a lieutenant on Medic 2, but he and Don were able to work together as equal partners.

And number two, firehouse rumor has it that Jeff is gay, even though he was married once and now dates women regularly, so at the very least the rumors claim he's bisexual. For Don, who may be the most macho firefighter on the 1st Platoon, in spite of or maybe because of his height, either rumor is the kiss of death if the fellow in question is going to be his partner.

"How did Kimmey get vacation over Christmas?" Ric wants to know.

"He signed up for it," Terry says, and Ric shoots him the Okay-thanks-a-lot-I-think-I-knew-that-you-jerk look.

"I used to be afraid I'd miss a fire when I went on vacation,"

Ric says, "but we don't have any fires on the 1st anymore. Half a dozen Signal 30s a year, maybe, and most of them are bullshit fires. Almost nothing worth anything. We hardly ever get one blowing out the windows when we pull up. The 4th is getting all of them. Shit, I even miss the idea that I might miss a fire."

Foxy breaks in. "This fire last night came as close to a fucking reality check as this job has had in a while. You get in there and find yourself caught like that, you feel your asshole pucker, you know? The pucker factor definitely goes up."

"Thompson should never have let them go in," Ric says suddenly, and uncharacteristically.

All the guys there know this is more about Ric's personal animosity for Dick than about Dick's decision to let the Squad search inside that burning building this morning. They also know it would have been Ric charging into that building if the 1st had been working, and they suspect sour grapes — that he's disappointed it wasn't him in there — without saying it. On top of that, Ric works with Carl at Sidelines, the sports bar in South Troy that's owned by three of the Troy firefighters, including Ric, and they're pretty close friends. "The fire was too far advanced," Ric says, trying to shore up his point.

"Oh, bullshit," Tom Miter jumps in, "it's the middle of the night and it's somebody's house. I don't care if a hundred people come up and tell you there's nobody left in there. You can't take their word for it. And they had three guys swearing the guy was still in there. They had to go in."

"Yeah, but where was the guy?" Ric demands. "He wasn't in there, was he? He was at a friend's house, and the Squad almost bought it. Dick should never have let that happen."

Tom looks toward the Battalion Chief's office and lowers his voice. "Look, Ric, you know how I feel. A guy like Dick, he can't be happy. He's on site, he sees what happens, he's got to find something wrong. I was watching a show about the fire department in Chicago the other day, and these guys are ventilating a roof and their Chief calls up on the radio, 'Have you got that roof open yet?" And one guy on the roof says, 'Working on it,' and then a few seconds later, 'Okay, Chief, we got it open,' and the Chief calls back to him, 'Attaboy.' And that's it. Nothing more. No 'How big is the hole?' or 'Where did you put it?' or 'What are you doing now?' Just 'Attaboy.' Around here, we do the job perfect and Dick'll still find some way we fucked up. But Carl and Mike wanted to go in there, and somebody had to do a search for the guy."

"Yeah, and if Carl and Mike were dead now, you'd be saying what I'm saying."

"Come on, Ric, they just got caught in there too long," Dave Stevens says. "There was no water on the second floor. Fire doubles every minute it's left to free burn. You know that. One room, after a minute, it's two. Two rooms, after another minute, you got four. After three minutes, eight rooms, and that's the whole second floor. Those guys were in there nine or ten minutes with that fire really working."

"You would have done the same thing," Tom says to Ric. "You'd have gone in there, too, and you know it, whether Dick said it was okay or not."

Like a select few on each shift, and like Chief Thompson himself, Ric has a reputation as one of the most aggressive fire-fighters on the job, and he folds his arms across his chest now, not answering, conceding Tom's point, but Tom goes on.

"And you know what it's like in there, the smoke and heat and bumping into shit and the noise with everybody screaming and it's just chaotic. I can't believe they got out of there. What did I hear Jeff Gordon call a fire? A ballet? It ain't nothing like a goddamned ballet. I don't know, Gordon's really out there. It's barely organized chaos, that's what a fire is."

At the mention of ballet, Foxy, who often wears a towel around his neck, pulls it off and starts to pirouette with it toward the middle of the apparatus floor, between the Rescue

Squad truck and the Battalion Chief's car, chanting in falsetto, "Oh, Jeff, the fleet's in. Yoo hoo, the fleet's in."

All of a sudden, Mike Kelleher walks through the door, and Joe Reilly says, "Hey, Mike, you missed it." Mike hasn't been back to work since he was stabbed during the liquor store hold-up in September, and today is his final day of sick leave.

"Yeah, and I'm glad I did. Fuck you, Joe," Mike answers.

"Hey, Kelleher, productive vacation or what?" Ric says.

Mike's wife, Lori, is two months pregnant, and everybody begins yelling at him, congratulating, razzing, speculating about the size of his balls, all at the same time. Tom grabs him around the shoulders to give him a playful bear hug, and Mike tries to squirm away.

"Watch the head. Watch the head," Mike says, laughing. As he pulls loose, he lowers his head, and you can see the lines of stitches crisscrossing his scalp through his thinning hair.

"Who knows how to use a vacation?" he asks. "Not you idiots, that's for sure. At least I know what to do when I'm out of this joint."

Unpleasant memories may hurt elderly on holidays

By Gladys Alcedo
The Record — December 24

TROY — The holiday season is usually marked with a festive mood, but for some, the celebrations are tainted with unpleasant memories.

According to staff from Troy's James A. Eddy Memorial Geriatric Center, some of the elderly experience difficulty during this time of year. They offered some helpful advice for people coping with the season.

Due to the holiday tradition of

family get-togethers, older adults recall unpleasant memories of family losses.

"In many cases, they are isolated from the people that they love, through death or people moving away," said Eddy's Director of Social Services Naomi Goldick. The Eddy staff recommend community involvement to beat those holiday blues.

Some can find comfort in extending themselves in the service of others during this Christmas season, said Eddy's Director of the Adult Home Patricia Hasan.

"If you can turn it from 'How can I make myself happy' to 'What can I do,' then it can become special," she said. "All of us have this need to be needed."

Music can help the elderly, Goldick said. "Music is very important for a lot of people."

But the greatest remedy for older adults is to find someone with whom to share their memories, Hasan said. "Sharing those happy and sad memories with someone is comforting, to have someone to understand and just listen."

Geraldine is slumped in a grimy, beige, overstuffed chair that must have once had clean upholstery with bright maroon and pink flowers blooming lavishly along forest-green vines. If you look really hard, you can still catch tiny spots of color hiding here and there among the spreading stains.

It's Christmas Eve, and this is the fourth ALS call of the day. Terry Fox kneels by Geraldine's chair, taking her pulse.

"Now, when you took the nitroglycerin, on a scale of 1 to 10, what did the pain —"

"10," Geraldine interrupts. "10, for three days. 10."

"All right. Now you just said you had some relief, right, Geraldine, from the nitro?"

"Geri," she says. "Call me Geri."

Geri is probably about 80, moderately overweight, still dressed in her flannel bathrobe at 3 in the afternoon, her grayish-white hair curling wildly in this overheated apartment, but her skin color is truly alarming. To set the heart monitor patches, Foxy has to open her robe, and a long, still-pink vertical scar shines garishly where it bifurcates the gray skin of her chest and abdomen.

Paramedics talk about performing an initial visual assessment as soon as they see a patient — it's called the "look test" — and they often instinctively base some of their treatment decisions on it. Geri isn't cyanotic: She doesn't have that bluish skin shade she would have if her blood wasn't being properly oxygenated. But she is a kind of sickly gray, and she definitely failed the look test. Failed it big time, as the paramedics say, and now she's beginning to cry.

"I want you to relax," Foxy says. He takes her left hand and holds it between his. "Now Geri, I know you've had open heart surgery. Do you have a pacemaker?"

Geri nods, and tries to shift in the chair, but the springs seem to be bad and she can only roll back and forth a little, whining, and she sinks even further into it.

"How long ago was your open heart surgery?"

"Two and a half years." she answers, squirming in her chair. "But the pain I used to have, it's coming back and it's worse."

"Okay. Two and a half years. I want you to relax. You're not helping yourself if you're breathing through your mouth. Close your mouth and breathe through your nose. Have you had a cold recently?"

"I just came out of that goddamned hospital. I can't go back there. You see, I just want to die. I don't want to go. I'm 69 years old."

Hearing her say she's 69, Foxy steals a glance at Joe Reilly, who's preparing a catheter for Geri's right arm, and Joe arches his eyebrows.

"I don't want to live anymore," Geri says suddenly, and grabs Foxy's arm.

Directly behind Geri, a picture of two young men hangs on the wall. They're standing side-by-side, in matching T-shirts and jeans, but one has close-trimmed hair under a floppy leather hat and the other has long hair and no hat. They're outside on grass somewhere, on a bright day, with a small pine tree in the background, holding a double-barreled shotgun together, horizontally. The one in the leather hat holds the barrel, and the long-haired one holds the stock.

"Oh, Geri. Don't you want to see the Holidays?" Foxy asks her.

"No, I lost my boy, twenty years ago at Christmas. My son got killed," she says, and she lets out a piercing wail.

"Geri, I want you to calm down here. You're creating more aggravation for yourself," Foxy says, standing up.

Geri grabs the arms of the chair and pulls herself forward a little, staring up at him. "I want to die, don't you understand? I don't care if I die here. I've got nothing to live for. Do you understand what I'm trying to tell you?"

"Yes, I do, Geri, but I also understand that someone called, or you called, and we're required to do a certain number of things because of that."

Joe is sliding the needle into Geri's arm now, and she pulls her arm away. "What are you doing?" she snaps at him.

"Trying to get this line started for you, hon," Joe answers, and draws her arm back toward him, though the veins are almost imperceptible in her age-spotted, wrinkled skin. "You know, there's somebody that loves you and cares about you, to call us to come and help," Joe continues. "You should want to live for them. They want you around, you know."

"Well, I don't want to be around. I hate it."

Foxy rests a hand on her shoulder, trying to console her, and then positions his stethoscope diaphragm on her chest and listens for a second before he moves to another spot. "We're initiating an IV, which is part of our required treatment, okay, Geri?"

"I know," she says. "I'm a nurse."

"Well, if you're a nurse, you know what we have to do. I can hear your heart rate slowing down. Where were you a nurse?"

"At Leonard Hospital."

"Well, you must know Gwen Fox? She's my mom."

"Oh, I know Gwen, yeah."

"Okay, good. How long were you a nurse, Geri?"

"32 years."

"32 years. Now you know there are a lot of people who care about you, all those people you helped in all those years."

Geri is crying again now, and she grabs Foxy's arm again. "Let me talk to you. I thought if I didn't go to the hospital, I'd just die. But it don't happen. I keep coming back."

Foxy drapes his stethoscope around his neck now and leans down closer to her. "I only want to tell you this because of what you've expressed to me here. There are avenues. There are *Do Not Resuscitate* laws."

"Oh, I've got that all written out," Geri says quickly, and sinks back into her chair.

Foxy walks to the monitor now and studies the heart strip for a few seconds, and then he turns back to her. "You're not in need of that at this point, though. You're in sinus rhythm, and your breathing is starting to slow down somewhat. What we're going to do is let the folks from the ambulance service come in here, and they'll put you on a stretcher, and take you up to the hospital again, just as a precaution. Is that okay?"

"Yeah, that's okay," Geri answers quietly, resigned now.

"I want you to remember to breathe slowly through your nose," Foxy says. "Let the oxygen help you. It won't do any good for your nasal passages if you don't take it in."

"You're a sweet man," Geri murmurs, but she turns and looks back at the picture behind the chair as Foxy answers.

"Well, I try to be," he says, with real sincerity, as he tears off the monitor strip and puts it on the clipboard for the doctor at the hospital. "You know, the advice they gave me back when I was in kindergarten, *Do unto others as you would have them do unto you*, I try to remember that. It doesn't matter whether you're in kindergarten or out in the world, facing whoever it is you have to face. I want you to try and calm down. I can appreciate your emotional trouble, but anyone who's done 32 years as a nurse has done a lot of good. Try to remember that."

* * *

At Samaritan Hospital, Foxy leans against the end of the nurses' desk and stares at one of Geri's chest X-rays hanging in the light cabinet on the wall.

I ask him if he'll miss working as a paramedic, and he nods without turning. Then he straightens to his full height before elaborating.

"It's change," he says, "and I accept that. Change is inevitable. I'll still be answering EMS calls, but I won't be functioning as a paramedic. That will be different, and difficult. My job as captain of Engine 5 will be to oversee the operations of an engine company, inside and outside the firehouse. On a call, I'll have overall control of the scene until, if it's an ALS call, the paramedics come and take over control of that patient from the engine crew. In my case, I'm a paramedic, and I'm supposed to function up to the level of my training, but I can't just usurp the position and interaction of the paramedics who are there. They have to develop their teamwork, because they're not going to be with me every time. They have to be able to be co-dependent."

A nurse walks out to the desk from the small room that serves as a lounge and scrolls through a Rolodex, and Foxy moves down the hallway a few steps, out of earshot of any nurses or doctors, to give me his less official answer.

"I like people. I like the fact that there are people in this world," he whispers. "Good, bad, or indifferent, I like them. And I don't like the idea of having done this so long, at what I feel personally is some level of proficiency, and it's frustrating to have to give it up. Most of the people we treat, they don't have a family doctor. They don't play golf with doctors. They don't have regular check-ups. More times than not, we find these people at the end point of whatever is causing their problems, because they don't have two dimes to rub together to take the kids in and find out what that cough is about. They need us.

"These are human beings, no different than me, and at some point in my life, I may need somebody to just reach out their hand and put it on mine, or lay a hand on my shoulder, and just supply some physical contact. Somebody there, looking in my eyes, talking to me, knowing I'm in there, observing the window of my soul. So if I'm in the same room as a person, whether it's their last breath or just a breath which is causing them agony for whatever reason, sometimes when I'm with the people who are really in the worst shape, I can see they just want someone to touch them. I've been able to put myself there for them, and I'm going to miss that."

As Foxy moves back to the light cabinet, the ER receptionist, a petite, attractive woman named Connie, appears at the far end of the hallway and tosses him a seductive but scolding smile as she strides past.

"Pretty clear except . . ." he begins to say, but stops to smile quickly back at Connie, who waggles her index finger at him and hustles back to her desk.

"Like Geri here, you know?" he says, as he points to her X-ray. "She's got this heart problem, and she's obviously alone. This is a tough season for her, like for a lot of folks. You could see the way it affected her emotions. Physical problems become that much greater. I was wondering, when I saw that picture behind her, if her son took his own life, and that would make it even harder this time of year.

"I don't know if she's serious about dying or not, but this season definitely gets to people. I've seen plenty of deaths from hanging, or from self-inflicted gunshots. And I've had at least two calls during the Christmas holidays where the people even stabbed themselves. That's a very difficult thing to do, because the body pulls away from the knife, and they ended up puncturing themselves three or four times in the belly, but they're only into the muscle wall of the belly. Unless you're intent to jump hard on that sucker, you just make superficial wounds. And they're screaming at you the whole time, you know? And if they're willing to cut themselves, how willing will they be to cut me? Probably more willing. This time of year, you never know."

Foxy moves around the desk now and peers toward the receptionist's area, but Connie isn't in there, and he waves hello to a young Indian resident who's coming down the hall.

"When I first got on this shift, I saw way too many suicides and attempted suicides, and I wasn't doing too well myself. I don't do too well with relationships, I guess. Maybe that's why I'm getting divorced now," he laughs. "But back in the 80s, it was my attitude. I had a bad attitude at one time. Scared the hell out of me when I spent five days in the hospital from taking on all the stresses and worries. I decided I was much too young to die, and I also realized there were still going to be bills after I was gone. Unless Providence smiles on me soon and I end up with a rich uncle who owns a gold mine or I play one of these lottery numbers and win and I get some breathing room for four or five years.

"I had palpitations. A lot of people with stressful jobs get them, but they were getting to the point for me where they were getting kind of violent. I used to drink a lot of beer, and I quit. Then I started drinking a lot of Pepsi and coffee and staying up late, worrying about bills and kids and a house and I drove myself into a state of frenzy. My heart just couldn't take it. It was when I was breaking up with the woman I lived with for seven years. I just turned around and said to myself that the stress was killing me. You can recognize it. Or at least now I can."

The resident has been examining Geri's X-ray, grinning foolishly, and Fox turns now to point out an oblong shadow partway down the right side, near the center.

"If you look over here," he says, "just outside the line of the ribs, you can see the enlargement of the heart. Her heart's working overtime, and —"

"Yes, yes, I see," the resident says, "but listen, Foxy, I have this good joke for you. A fireman came home one day and he said to his wife, 'We have this system at the firehouse. When Bell #1 rings, we slide down the fire pole. When Bell #2 rings, we put on our fire jackets and fire boots. When Bell #3 rings, we get on the truck and race to the fire. I want a system like that starting here now. So when I come home and say, Bell #1, I want you to undress. When I say, Bell #2, I want you to jump into bed. And when I say, Bell #3, I'm going to jump on top of you and we're going to screw like crazy.'

"So the next day the fireman came home. 'Bell #1,' and she stripped. 'Bell #2,' and she jumped into bed. 'Bell #3,' and he jumped on top of her and started humping away. All of a sudden, she yelled, 'Bell #4!' And he said, 'Bell #4, what the hell is that?' And she shouted, 'More hose, more hose. You're nowhere near the fire.'"

As the resident howls with laughter at his own joke, Adam, a homeless alcoholic who is one of the fire department's regulars, and who seems to be passed out on a gurney in Holding Room 1, sits up, rips out his IV, and starts hollering for a drink.

"Christmas holidays," Foxy says. "Hell of a season."

Terry Fox

When I came back from Vietnam, in March of 1970, I went down to Florida for a year, just to try and find myself, because I really wasn't socially acceptable. I had been in country for 30 months. People would ask me, "What did you do over there?" And I'd answer, "Flew every day. Picked up people and put them into the jungle, went back and picked them up and took them out of the jungle. Sometimes they were alive and sometimes I had to pick them up dead. Sometimes I picked up pieces of them. Sometimes I flew up water and batteries in the middle of the night, screaming on the radio, needing help. Sometimes we accomplished the mission. Sometimes we just couldn't get there. That's what I did for two and a half years."

I could have told them what actually happened, but most people didn't want to hear what actually happened. What I did over there had a significance to me that was so great I'd become angered by people who wanted to belittle it. Where the significance to them might turn into a nice political argument, to me it was life and death. Where I had just come from, it was only measured that one way — life or death. Somebody would start going off on what we were doing in Vietnam and I'd tell them, "You say that again, I'll kill you," and I really meant it. They didn't mean what they said, but I knew I meant what I said. You know, if somebody drove me to the point, I was just going to break someone's neck. I was socially unacceptable.

When I finally came back to Troy, I did have some political value, because I came under the title of "war hero." My dad had been a police officer back in the 50's, so they wanted me to be a cop. They offered me a job as a sheriff's deputy, or whatever I wanted, because of the medal I'd won in Vietnam.

I was a crew chief on a helicopter, and back in the northern area of the Ashau Valley, we were called out to a recon extract — a recon team of thirteen people caught out on the top of a mountain. They had been chased out of Laos by probably a battalion of NVA, and they had significant information. For three days, other guys had been trying to get them off the mountain. This recon team had been in close, hand-to-hand combat. The thirteen of them had been fighting a battalion, at least. They were pretty interested in keeping their asses together and alive, and these were tough guys.

So command had tried for three or four days, and had lost something like four aircraft trying to get them out. It became a priority mission, where anyone who was capable of doing it would be directed there, and people were being diverted from other missions. It was under order of this one-star general. "They cannot last out there. I want them out." That was the direct order sent to all the other general officers around, including our bird colonel. The recon team had significant information that they needed; they were fighting their asses off to stay alive; and leaving them dangling out there wasn't right. Earlier on the particular day that we went in, the sister squadron that I was with at Quang-Tri had a plane shot down and lost a crewman and a pilot. Nobody got out alive, and the plane was gone.

We just knew it was a shit sandwich, to use the vernacular. Jan Garringer was my partner. He and I flew a lot together, the two of us in different aircraft, but going in together. Usually we flew in tandem, two helicopters to a flight, and we were both crew chiefs. Usually we ended up being paired because they knew we worked well together, you know? We watched each other's ass. That's the reason why you fly two — if one goes down, the other one gets you. If you both go down, two more come and get both of you. And you never leave anybody out there, if at all possible.

Now Jan was in the lead plane that day. He went in and landed on a rocky ledge, and I counted six or seven people go into his plane, and then mortar rounds started landing. I told the pilot to tell him to get the hell out. They had him zeroed. I mean, there was just no way — the next one was going to be on his rotors. He had gotten seven out, and there were six more guys in there, and two of them were the team leaders, with most of the information that they had gathered. The important people. They had to come out.

I knew I didn't want to put us in the LZ that my partner had landed in, because I would have been blown up immediately. I saw another rock ledge sticking out of the side of the mountain that was probably twice the size of this table. I knew my pilot was good. All of our pilots were great, but this was a precipice at 1300 meters up — a sheer cliff straight down to the ground — so I knew it would be tough. I had the Hueys smoke the zone with white phosphorus, Willy Pete, which formed a cloud to cover us somewhat.

I needed it to shield us from the ground fire that was there. We could hear it and see it, and I told him I wanted to get onto this other ledge. I was going to give him control of the ramp, which was very unusual for me to do, to let somebody else control the hatch that I was going to be standing on. I wanted him to hover, holding the right, main landing gear on that rock, and just swing the plane next to the mountain with the rotor blades overlapping the top of the cliff. So we were protected from direct fire by the mountain itself, and as long as we didn't hit anything with our rotors, we were safe, except from mortars.

My right gunner was sort of useless because he was looking at this cliff face four feet away from him, so I had him available to help me and I had him belt off. We got in, and we started taking some fire. I went out on the ramp, then out onto the rock, and when I climbed out there I looked down. About five feet below me were the heads of the rest of the recon team. I had told them over the radio that was where we were going to land, and if they could, to make it there. If they couldn't, we'd find another spot, but they had made it there.

So with that adrenaline punch that comes with people in a tough situation, and I don't know where it came from — these guys were all my size, if not bigger — I reached down to them and, with their arms stretching up, I was grabbing them and throwing them over my shoulder into the airplane. There was some strong motivation there, because the bullets going by were pretty scary, and I was just tossing them up. I had to unplug from my cord, my radio connection with the pilot, because there wasn't enough cord to reach to the end of the rock. I was out there with no communications, and I didn't want the pilot to get shaky. I just kept shouting he should hold, and my crewman was relaying the information the best he could.

The last guy down there was the recon team leader, and he had this look on his face like I would imagine someone having if you were dragging him straight out of a shark's mouth. I could hear the snap and fire all around us. He had a hand on him, a meat-hook, and we just latched ourselves onto each other. I felt almost like we were an extension of each other when I grabbed him and tossed him onto the plane, and he turned and started firing at the NVA coming up the hill at us. I yelled, "Let's get the fuck out of here." Exactly my words. The pilot said, "We're clear?" I yelled back, "Yeah, I've got the ramp," and we lifted off and the ramp was coming up and I could see the pilot look back and he was shaking his head. We were still being shot at. We were definitely taking fire. We took several small-rounds hits as we lifted off. Now this team leader's face was a few inches from mine. He was right there looking at me, both of us laying exhausted on the floor, and I said, "Don't kiss me, all right?" I had a couple of Rum Crooks in my flight pocket, so I took them out and handed him one. "Here, have one of these," I said. As I lit mine, I could see Jan's helicopter was circling out, too, over some clear air, so together we got all thirteen of those guys out.

When we got back to the reconnaissance area, they had their own compound. There were 500 people there, and this was a brotherhood, *much like this one in the fire service. They're very close people, very well-trained. They'd lost too many people over there. At times they'd lost whole teams, and it was a real bad feeling picking up their dead. When these thirteen people came back and not one of them was wounded, and they came back to their LZ on our planes, their general met us and told us to shut down. "You're now my guests," he said, and we commenced to get a party going. "These people are not flying tomorrow; they're my guests," he told our colonel.*

Well, we partied our asses off, and he told our pilots and crews collectively, he said, "I have recommended you for the highest commendation that I can possibly offer you. I've put you all in for the Congressional Medal of Honor for this act." Now, because of the fact that no one was wounded or killed, we couldn't get that one, but we all received the Distinguished Flying Cross, which was significant to me. It was the second highest award that I could have won anywhere in regard to my job at the time. It wasn't put in by anyone that had anything to gain by putting us in for it, either. It was the general's full move, and he assured us that anywhere anytime that we needed anything, call upon him or his people and it would be done.

Unfortunately, my partner in the other plane, Jan, the other crew chief, was killed there on my last day in country. We switched places. Yeah, I carry that with me, too. I was leaving, and it was my last day, and there were two missions up. One of them was a night mission, and it was so, so dark over there. Scary. I hated night-times. Night missions. I told them I would fly right up to my last day, but I would not fly at night the last night.

Jan was being made NCO, and he said, "Lookit, Foxy, I've got to qualify a crew chief," and I said, "No, Jan. I told you I'm not flying the last night. I'll fly my last day, and that's it. I'm done after that." He said, "All right, I'll take the night mission." It was a night Medevac mission at Phu Bai. They had troops engaged, and there were wounded. They tried to get out, and there was a weather front, so they went IFR, instrument flight requirements. Well, they were flying north and the shoreline was to their left, or to the west. They were gaining altitude in a climbing left-hand turn, and unfortunately Jan's plane ran straight into a mountain.

All of them were killed. I flew off the records, out of the squadron, the next day, to go and pick up their bodies. There wasn't much left. They were beat up, burnt. But I picked him up. We promised each other we would. It was the last promise I had to fulfill to him. We promised each other that if either of us bought the farm, one would get the other. A lot of parts of me died with a lot of friends over there.

Same kind of people are in here. And we all in our own way say a silent prayer when we go out the door. I don't care what the call is. Especially when you pull around the corner and you see something that's blowing out the windows, obviously you know there's a life danger there, and you just hope nobody gets hurt, because fire isn't very forgiving. It takes a lick at you. I don't care how big or how small, it hurts. It's like Vietnam — very destructive, beautiful in its own physical sense, but very destructive.

But there's a character that weaves itself throughout the individuals that you see here that includes a call to service, and an edge. There's that edge in this job. It's probably the most socially accepted challenge that's still available. It's only worth living if you can do something worthwhile, you know? You can be a doctor, or a damn good lawyer who follows the law, or do some other social service things. But there's a threat here — that's part of the significance. There's an edge here.

5

Cardiac arrest and sudden death account for 60 percent of all deaths from coronary artery disease. Sudden death is a death that occurs within one hour after the onset of symptoms . . . The risk factors for sudden death are basically the same as those previously presented for atherosclerotic heart disease (ASHD). In a large number of patients, cardiac arrest is the first manifestation of heart disease. Causes of sudden death other than ASHD include: Drowning; Electrocution; Electrolyte imbalance; Trauma; Hypothermia; Acid-base imbalance; Hypoxia; Pulmonary embolism; Cerebrovascular accident; and Drug intoxication.

— Bledsoe, Porter & Shade
Paramedic Emergency Care, 2nd Ed.

"Heroin. Heroin, okay?"

The slight man, about twenty, with a neatly-trimmed goatee, stops for a second to spit the words out at the nurse, and then he resumes his pacing. This room is small, maybe only 8 feet square, so he can just take a few short, frantic steps before he has to turn and go back. It's hot, too, and he pulls his scarf free and unzips his jacket, keeping his eye on the nurse the whole time.

"Okay, okay, that's what we need to know. We have no idea," the nurse is saying, holding her hands out in front of her to keep him at a safe distance.

Jeff Gordon, the new lieutenant paramedic on the 1st Platoon, knocks a couple of times and then opens the hospital examining room door. "They sent me in here to —"

"All right, come on in," the nurse says, "I need some men in here anyway."

An older man, still wearing a paint-spattered Carhartt coat buttoned right up to his neck, has been watching quietly from an empty corner of the room. His face is ashen, except around his eyes, where the skin is pink and swollen. Suddenly he takes a step into the center, toward Jeff, and points at him.

"What happened to my son?"

Although Jeff, at six feet tall and over 190 pounds, is a head taller and probably thirty pounds heavier than this clearly older, definitely much smaller man, Jeff steps back in surprise against the closed exam room door.

"Well, I don't know who was in the apartment," Jeff answers quickly. "There were two other people in the apartment when we got there."

"Josh and Abbie," the younger man says.

"Wait a minute, Tim," the older man says.

"It was Josh and Abbie, Dad. They take heroin," Tim says, having to pace around his father now.

"There was a girl and a guy in the apartment," Jeff says. "The engine company was there. We pulled in right behind them, and he was in full cardiac arrest when we got there."

"They shot him full of heroin, Dad."

"No, he didn't do those things." Tim's mother says. Wrapped in her dark winter coat, she has been leaning against the examining table for support, but now she grabs Tim's arm to steady herself, and her words burst out in sobs. "He didn't do them."

"We did everything we could," Jeff says, frozen in place,

with his back still against the exam room door. "We worked on him for —"

"Are they here?" Tim interrupts.

He stops pacing, and he shifts his feral, brown eyes back and forth between the nurse and Jeff.

"The police are at the scene, though, so —"

"Oh, those kids are here?"

"No, they're not here. They're not here," the nurse says. "You're so upset, it's just not sinking in."

"No, it's sinking in, because I told Robert not to fuck around with that shit," Tim says.

Tim is pacing again, and his mother covers her face with her hands and moans loudly as she cries.

"Are you all right?" the nurse asks Tim.

"Yeah, I'm all right," he says, and looks down at his mother. "Don't worry about it, Mom, I'll get those bastards."

Suddenly, Tim starts for the door. "I'll be back soon," he says.

"You're all we've got now," his mother cries out and clutches at his coat, and his father grabs Tim by the shoulder.

"Stay here," his father says.

"I'm going to get those motherfuckers."

"You stay here. I need you here. Stop it," the father pleads. "Stop it."

Tim pulls away from them and the nurse steps in front of him.

"Look out. I'm going to get those fuckers," he tells her.

"Stop it. You're all I got left. I need you. Stop it," the father shouts, and throws his arms around his son from behind.

Tim slumps a little now and turns, reaching out for his mother, bringing her in, and then all three stand in the middle of the small room without moving. For half a minute, the only sounds are the muffled howls of the woman crying into her husband's coat.

"Hang onto each other," the nurse says. "Hang onto each other. This is what you need. Hug your parents. They need you right now, buddy."

"I want to see my son," the father says firmly, looking up.

Tim pulls away from his parents and wheels around to face the nurse again, his eyes glistening with rage. "Where is he? Can we see him?"

"Just a minute. Just a minute," she says. "We have to —"

The mother turns now and holds her hands out, palms up, to the nurse. "My son didn't do drugs. He told me he didn't do drugs."

"Was it drugs?" Tim wants to know.

"We can't tell yet," the nurse says.

"We're not sure," Jeff breaks in. "They'd have to do an investigation into the death, you know, to determine the —"

"We've called the coroner," the nurse is saying, overlapping Jeff's words. "The coroner is going to do an investigation."

"Yeah, we had no way of telling at the scene, you know, why he died or anything," Jeff says.

"Well, I want those kids brought down. I know they're dealing drugs. I want the fucking police there. I'm gonna rat those cocksuckers out tonight," Tim says.

"The police were there before we left the house, so they're there," Jeff says.

Tim begins to pace again, back and forth in the tight corner behind his parents, who are still holding each other in the center of the room.

"I'll take every one of these motherfuckers down. Fucking scumbags and their nigger fucking drugs."

"Stop it," his father says

"Fucking nigger fucking drugs is what it is."

"Will you stop it, Tim?"

"Don't worry about it, because I'll take care of this tonight."

"Let him get it out," the nurse says. "Let him get it out, if this is what he needs to do."

Suddenly the mother shrieks, "Robert wanted to be a doctor," and then she collapses to the floor and lands, sobbing, against her husband's legs.

"Didn't I tell you not to let him go with those fucking scumbags, those fucking niggers, didn't I? Didn't I?" Tim demands of his parents now. He stops pacing and stares at both of them. "Didn't I?"

Jeff's knuckles, gripping the brown clipboard with his half-finished Prehospital Care Report on it, are stretched white.

* * *

Today is New Year's Day. It's Jeff Gordon's first day riding as a lieutenant and paramedic firefighter with the 1st Platoon, and he has been paired, as threatened, with Don Kimmey on Medic 2. All of which now means Jeff's the officer in charge on all advanced life support calls in the city of Troy when the 1st is working, and that means Don isn't. Apparently, Don changed his mind about bidding off the shift when Jeff came on, but he hasn't given anyone his reasons for staying. Everybody on the shift is waiting for the fireworks to begin.

Earlier this morning, huge slabs of ice in the Hudson River just beyond the low-income Taylor Apartments had been shoved into haphazard geometric stacks by a Coast Guard ice-cutter, and the slabs' ragged angles were shining ominously in the sun as the second call of the day came in over Medic 2's radio — man down on 14th Street. Full arrest.

The first call had been at the Taylor Apartments, one of Troy's infamous public housing projects, for a woman with a broken jaw. "Walter," Don had said as we walked out of the building, referring to the woman's husband, who towered over her in the unframed pictures tacked onto their living room wall. "We've been here before, for the same thing. Walter's a regular."

Domestic abuse and a full arrest, both before noon on the first of January — what a great way to usher in a new year.

Two police officers, the crew of Engine 2, and two kids in their late teens, a boy and a girl, were in the 14th Street apartment when we got there. Mark Fleming, the captain on Engine 2, was dragging another teenager by his ankles into a cluttered, filthy living room as Don and Jeff hurried into the apartment. A wide, glaring line of blood and sputum snaked across the olive, wall-to-wall shag carpeting, running from the boy's face all the way back to the second room on the right off the hallway.

As Mark dropped the kid's feet, he backed into the round, formica coffee table. An empty Yoo Hoo bottle tottered and then fell off onto the rug. The table, as well as the ratty couch with no cushions next to it, were both littered with glasses half full of orange juice or dark soda, overflowing ashtrays, opened and empty CD cases, crumpled napkins, and paper plates with jelly smears and sandwich crusts on them.

"Look at that shit coming out of his nose. That's all blood, see it? I don't know if he's got a head injury or what," Don said.

Jeff knelt down next to the body and felt for a pulse. "Yeah, he's cold, too," he answered.

"There was nothing there when you, when you came in, right, Mark? I mean, he wasn't . . ." Don asked, standing back and surveying the whole scene.

"What's that?" Mark said.

"You found him in the bedroom?"

"Yeah, he was just laying on the bed. We pulled him out into the hall."

One of the cops was standing in the kitchen, about ten feet away, with the two teenagers. Jeff looked up at them and the kids looked away.

"Nobody knows anything, huh?" Jeff asked.

"Nope," Don answered, shaking his head.

"I don't know what he did last night," the boy suddenly offered.

"Were you with him last night?" Don asked.

"I was with him at the beginning of the night, but then we —"

"Okay, hold on for a second, Peter," Jeff said. Pete Fleming, Mark's brother and a hoseman on Engine 2, had been performing cardiopulmonary resuscitation (CPR) since his brother dragged the kid into the living room, but Jeff had some leads hooked up and needed the body to be still so he could read the heart monitor.

"You got asystole or what?" Don asked.

"Oh, man, very, very flat," Jeff answered, and the green line moved horizontally across the heart monitor screen with no hint of a spike, as remorselessly flat as the metal edge in a wooden ruler.

"Okay," Don said, pulling on his latex gloves and kneeling down on the other side of the body, opposite Jeff, "We don't know what's going on here, so let's do what we can. Let me take a look."

Even though Jeff was officially the paramedic in charge of this call, he was still 32 years old, with a baby face that fooled a lot of people into thinking he was even a few years younger. For a 22-year veteran like Don, youth in this case didn't add up to pragmatic knowledge. As far as he was concerned, his experience made him the one in charge. "Let's just run the thing," Don said.

The *thing* Don was talking about was the full arrest algorithm. An algorithm is any particular procedure for solving a certain type of problem. The Regional Emergency Medical Organization of the Hudson Mohawk Valleys (REMO) publishes a handbook of regional treatment protocols and procedures each year, as a supplement to the statewide protocols published by the Emergency Medical Services Program of the New York State Department of Health. These required handbooks establish the baseline of standardized treatment protocols for EMTs and Paramedics, and are intended to establish a model or minimum standard by which all patients should be treated by emergency medical care workers in the state.

REMO's Cardiac Arrest Management Algorithm for a patient with asystole, or the absence of all cardiac electrical activity, begins with CPR, then moves through intubation and establishment of IV access, and stops after administration of Epinephrine and Atropine — drugs which might get the patient's heart going again. When paramedics finish all that, they should transport the patient to the nearest hospital, though REMO does state the following in the fine print:

"Some patients may require care not specified herein. This algorithm should not be construed to prohibit such flexibility."

What Don and Jeff had this morning required flexibility.

"We're going to need some suction, I think," Don said, and Pete Fleming ran out to the Medic rig to get the suction kit.

"I'm going to set up a lactated ringers, Don," Jeff said. "Let me know when you're ready for drugs. We'll put them down the tube."

As Don worked to set up an intubation tube, Jeff started an IV in the kid's right arm with an 18-gauge needle. The cop in the kitchen began to question the boy who had volunteered the information a minute before.

"Did you see him this morning?"

"Yeah, I woke him up. It took us a while to wake him up, though, and I told him —"

"Bag," Don yelled. "Where the hell is that bag? Jesus, he's all filled up with shit. Listen, listen, hold it, listen . . ."

Pete came back in with the suction kit.

"Okay, Pete, thanks. Let me clear this crap away and then you bag him, all right?" Don said. "I just wanted to make sure it was in. He's got a ton of shit coming up."

A red and white froth had been running continuously from the kid's mouth and nose, and now it was oozing around the intubation tube Don just set up, moving the way lava does.

Jeff has two brothers in the Troy Police Department, Peter and Paul. Paul had been on the scene earlier, but he had gone outside to talk to neighbors. Now he was back.

"Full arrest, Paul," Jeff said to him. "He's been down for a while. There's roommates here, but they're not saying much, you know."

Don was trying to suction off enough fluid to stabilize the intubation tube. "I need that white tape," Don said. "You got some of that heavy white tape, Mark?"

Pete started to get it but Don caught his arm.

"Let Mark get that. I need you to be bagging."

"Don, are you ready for an eppie yet or no?" Jeff asked.

"Hang on a second. Don't start the compressions yet," Don said, still suctioning the fluid that was bubbling and frothing out of the kid's nose and mouth. "He's all full of blood and, oh, come on, what is this shit?"

Paul motions to the boy in the kitchen. "Hey, bud, you got a back door I can get through, because I don't want to disrupt these guys?"

"I don't live here," the boy said. He looked suddenly terrified.

"Meet me out front," Paul said.

All of a sudden, the dispatcher's voice blared from Mark and Jeff's portable radios: ATTENTION ALL UNITS. ENGINE 1 AND THE RESCUE SQUAD ARE RESPONDING TO NUMBER 770 3RD AVENUE, BETWEEN 121ST AND 122ND STREETS, FOR AN EMS CALL. TIME IS TWELVE ZERO FOUR.

"Jesus, turn that down, will you, Jeff, " Don said, and Jeff lowered the volume on his portable radio.

"The back door is nailed shut," the boy said. "But I don't live here."

"You don't live here?" Paul said.

"No, I don't live here."

"You know this guy?"

"Yeah."

"Who lives here?"

"He lives here."

"Who else?"

"He's got two roommates, but they're at home on school break."

"How old is he?"

"He's 19."

"You don't know anything about his history at all?" Jeff asked.

"I just know he's asthmatic."

"What, were you guys partying last night or what happened?" Paul wants to know.

"Yeah, we were partying with him last night and then we came back here this morning. We weren't with him all night, though, so I don't know," the boy said.

As Pete continued to bag, to pump air into the kid with the bag valve mask, some of it got trapped inside his torso, and the skin on his stomach began to bulge tight with the strain. Suddenly, Pete stopped bagging and vomited off to the side.

"Donny, I've got that epinephrine here," Jeff said. "I'll set you up an atropine."

"Did you find him on the floor?" Paul asked the boy.

"We were here, we went to bed, and then he was in the chair when we came out, because I heard him, like, not breathing right, so we woke him up. It took a while, and he woke up, and then he was up for a while, then he went to bed. And we went to bed in his friend's room, and a while later I heard more of him breathing wrong. We tried to get him to wake up, and he wouldn't, so we stuck him under the cold shower, but he still didn't wake up. Then we called you guys."

"Don, let me know if you're ready for that eppie," Jeff said.

"All right, let me see it now," Don said. "I just wanted to clear enough crap out of his mouth and throat."

Jeff handed the first dose over. "That's the eppie. I'll give you the atropine when you're set with that."

"What the hell are these on his arms?" Don said all of a sudden and looked up at Jeff. "I don't know what the fuck I'm dealing with here. This is all black and blue." Don was pointing to red, swollen spots on the kid's arms. See this mark here. See that? That mark there. He's got marks all over him. Jeff, get on the horn."

"Is he breathing at all?" Paul asked.

The 16-gauge catheter Don was using for the epinephrine fell apart in his hands.

"What the hell happened here? Give me another catheter. It just fell apart. No, he's not breathing."

Paul began to walk around to the other side of the dead kid, and Don pointed to the discarded needles on the floor.

"Watch your feet there, okay? I don't know what this guy's got or what, you know?" Don said.

Paul moved back toward the front door and turned to Jeff. "So when you got here he wasn't —"

"Full arrest when we got here, yeah," Jeff answered without looking up at his brother.

"201, send a supervisor up here, all right?" Paul said into his radio.

Two Mohawk ambulance drivers came in the door and Don motioned again behind him.

"Watch all these needles. Don't come near them. Give me that atropine now, Jeff."

"All right, there's a clean sharp in the box, and I've got another sharp in his other arm on this side," Jeff said.

"You guys ready to go?" Don asked the ambo workers.

"Yup, we're all set whenever you are."

"Let me just get this. I want to do this and another eppie and then we're out of here. Go ahead and wrap him up."

"Another eppie? Donny, where are your sharps?" Jeff asked.

"Right behind me."

"Two of them?"

"I see two."

"Okay, and I got another one, makes three, this one here makes four," Jeff said as he collected the discarded needles.

Don pulled the clear lactated ringers bag up higher and made sure Mark kept it taut, so they could keep replacing some of the fluids the kid had lost.

"Keep that right up there, Mark, because I want the gravity to help take the fluid down. Keep pumping it as we go," Don said, showing him how hard he wanted the IV bag squeezed.

Jeff stood up and looked around as the Mohawk drivers finished packaging the boy. "I'm just going to leave that sharp right in his arm, Don. You want another atropine before we move?"

"All right, set it up," Don said, "because we'll both be going."

"You going to St. Mary's or Samaritan?" one of the ambulance guys asked.

"Samaritan. We already called them," Don answered. "Yeah. Let's get going. We'll be there in about five minutes. Somebody grab the oxygen."

Jeff held up a stethoscope and asked Don if it was his, and Don nodded. Then Don stopped for a few seconds and wiped the sweat off his face with a towel, scraping it hard along his skin, and then wrapped the towel around his neck. As the two ambulance drivers wheeled the kid out on the stretcher, Don stared blankly down at the mess of discarded catheter parts, plastic caps, occlusive bandage wrappers, strips of bloody clothing, and other junk scattered on the rug. He kept his face expressionless as he looked over at Jeff.

"Did you talk to anybody yet?" Don said.

"No, not yet," Jeff answered. "I've got the APCOR, though, so whenever. How old did they say this kid was?"

"Nineteen."

* * *

In the trauma room at Samaritan Hospital's ER, the doctor on duty asked how long the boy had been down, how much epinephrine and atropine had been delivered at the apartment and en route in the ambulance, thought maybe two milligrams of Narcan would be a good idea, looked somewhat resigned at this stage of the situation as he watched the flat line trudge relentlessly across the monitor, and finally decided to give the kid one final effort.

"I'd like to defibrillate him anyway, once, just to try it," he said. "We'll defibrillate him once, and we'll give him one round of drugs, and that's it. So one defibrillation. Let's just go right ahead to 360, then one after the eppie, one after the atropine, and if there's no response, I'll call it."

* * *

A few minutes later, at the nurse's station, Jeff was explaining why the police were called to the apartment in the first place.

"On an unattended death, and that's considered an unattended death, at the house, then we have to call the police. Even though those people were there. In this case, because there was nobody else in an official capacity there, it's considered an unattended death, and the police have to go and investigate and check for foul play. Nine times out of ten it's routine, where an older person dies, or whatever. But in this case, this is obviously not a routine type of death, just because of his age, if for no other reason. But they may find any number of things at the house now, drugs or who knows what they could find."

The cop who was with Jeff's brother at the scene came over and held up a driver's license for the nurse behind the desk.

"He had a fake ID in his wallet," the cop said, "because he's only nineteen. He's got his brother's ID." He pointed to Jeff and said, "After you guys left, the girl gave us his real name. It's Robert. The brother is Tim. This is his ID. The kid we've got over here is Robert Coates." Then the cop handed a phone number to the nurse and walked back to the trauma room.

The nurse picked up the black phone that hung on the wall behind the desk and dialed the number.

"Yes, is this the Coates residence? Yes, I'm looking for the parents of Robert Coates, please? . . . Who might I be speaking to? . . . Yes, and your name is? . . . Well, um, we need to get in touch with them right away . . . This is Samaritan Emergency calling. Your brother is here in the emergency room . . . Well, you need to come here and then we'll explain . . . Okay, calm down. Samaritan Hospital. Come to the emergency room."

"Who was that?" Jeff asked.

"Brother," the nurse answered.

"Hang up on you?"

"Yeah. Screaming. He didn't even find out why his brother's here. He was screaming just because he is here at all. What's it going to be like when he gets here?" she wondered, and looked up and down the hallway. "I'd sure like the cops to be here when he shows up."

* * *

Back in the exam room, looking into Jeff's unfocused eyes,

it isn't hard to believe that he's remembering everything that led up to this moment. The father is sprawled in an empty corner, trying to cry quietly now, his head jerking convulsively every time a loud sob escapes. The mother is up on her feet, pleading with the nurse.

"I want to see him, all right? Can I go see him?" she asks.

"You can go see him," the nurse says, "as soon as you calm down just a little bit." She looks uncomfortably over at Jeff.

The mother turns to Jeff now, too. "Just on the possibility, on 14th Street, where was he found?"

"2236. Is that where he lives?" Jeff says. "That's his home?"

"Okay," the mother answers. "He would have like three silver earrings?"

"Yeah," Jeff says, "he did."

Now the mother turns and moves distractedly over toward her husband, beginning to mumble. "He's an RPI student. Okay, so it is the same Robert Coates. I just wanted to make sure. I hope Josh is happy."

"He'll be happy tonight," Tim says.

"Do you think you're calm enough now?" the nurse asks, and none of them answers her. "Listen, he doesn't . . . well, Mrs. Coates, he's intubated. He has a tube down his throat. That's what looks bad. Okay? Come on. Come on."

The nurse takes the mother by the arm and moves her slowly toward the door, and Jeff steps further into the room, out of their way.

"Come on. Why don't you and your son come on and see Robert," she says. "Let Mr. Coates just sit there until he feels better. Don't get him up."

By the nurse's desk, Don Kimmey is watching the nurse lead the mother and brother toward the trauma room door. As she opens it, Mrs. Coates falls against the jamb and says, "That's not him under there, is it?"

"Jesus Christ," Don says.

Now she starts into the room and says to the nurse, "Just wake him up. Just get him up, okay?"

Don turns to the ER doctor, who is filling out his own report now, and says, "Remember that guy at Christmas, the young guy, 25 or so, with the three kids, he got electrocuted, where the wife comes in and she goes, 'Come on, Jerry, get up, we're going Christmas shopping tonight. Come on. Get up.' Boy, was that something. He was operating one of those booms and he hit a high-tension wire with the boom, and what he did, he had the thing right against his chest and it came back and got him, went right through his heart. Dead dead dead dead. He never had a chance. But we worked on him for 45 minutes, at least."

Don motions toward the trauma room. "Just like this guy, we worked on him a long time, too. Even with the fresh marks on his arms, where you figure unless he had fresh blood work done the other day, there's something else going on. A 19-year-old usually doesn't die of a heart attack, you know?"

Drugs may have ended promising student's life
By Carmen Napolitano
The Record

TROY - To his family, Robert L. Coates had it all. The 19-year-old Rensselaer Polytechnic Institute sophomore was a promising student with aspirations of being an orthopedic surgeon someday. While at Troy High School, Coates was named to the National Honor Society and graduated in the top 10 of his class.

He was a star on the football field, too. More than two dozen universities across the country offered him scholarships if he'd play ball for them.

But Troy police said his parents and many of his friends didn't know that Coates had been using drugs for the past two years. And detectives suspect that he may have been using drugs when he collapsed in his home and later died New Year's Day.

Troy Police Capt. Jack Mahar said he believes the drugs were purchased Friday in New York City where Coates and two friends traveled to ring in the new year.

"We are still investigating the case, but it has been reported that the three men were using drugs," Mahar said. "We have talked to several witnesses and are pushing forward with our investigation."

An autopsy was conducted Sunday morning at Samaritan Hospital. Mahar said it could be a week, perhaps longer, before toxicology results are made available.

Mahar refused to say what type of drugs Coates may have been using.

Friends told investigators that Coates was having difficulty breathing earlier that day. Police are withholding the names of Coates' two friends.

No charges have been filed in connection with Coates' death.

Coates' father, James R. Coates of Troy, said there's no way his son was involved with drugs. James Coates said his son was too busy with a heavy class load. When he wasn't at RPI, he worked part time for a shipping company in Albany.

James Coates said the teenager he knew was responsible and was loved by his family. "The boy we knew was a happy boy. He was a caring kid," James Coates said. "He was a talented young man. He and I were awful good friends."

On Monday, James Coates and his wife did what they never imagined they'd do. In the empty bedroom where the teenager once slept, they picked out the clothes their son will wear to his grave. And then they drove to the funeral home where they purchased a coffin.

"There wasn't a day that went by that we didn't tell Robert we loved him," James Coates said. "What hurts the most is that we will never see him again."

It's just after dinner, and Don Kimmey is feeling well-fed and feisty. He wants to take a vote to see how many think Jeff is a ten-percenter — if he's really gay. The vote is a close one. 5 vote yes, 4 vote no, and Battalion Chief Harrison abstains. Jeff doesn't vote. So that confirms Don's suspicions.

But now Don says he has figured out a plan to let Jeff prove that he's straight. One of the older nurses at Samaritan Hospital, a pleasant but decidedly unattractive and usually garishly made-up 60 year old named Bonnie is at the center of this plan.

"Bonnie told me this morning she thought you were 'quite handsome,' those were her words, and she thought maybe you were flirting with her in the nurse's lounge when she brought you some of that holiday cake," Don says. "She wants me to set her up with you."

Jeff begins to blush, and then he turns completely red. "You're an asshole, Donny," he answers, but he is smiling a little.

"No, no, wait a minute," Don says. "I told her it's all just a big act. That most of us think you're gay. Then she said, 'Oh, come on, he can't be gay, not with the way he acts around us nurses.' I swear to God, that's what Bonnie said.

"So, I've got this idea," Don continues, extending his hand toward Jeff. "Most of the guys here think you're gay, there, bucko. I really don't care. But Bonnie's got a thing for you, and the best way for you to prove you're a man is by banging Bonnie."

It's hard to hear Jeff say, "Fuck you, Don," as he leaves the table, because Ric, Tom and Dave, among others, are laughing so loudly, and all trying at once to determine which of Bonnie's personal articles would verify the conquest — her dentures, her support hose, or her walker.

*   *   *

Now it's almost 2 a.m., and Terry Fox can't sleep, as usual. He's still drinking coffee from his thermos, but he turns the television volume down so he can tell me about his first day as a paramedic on the job.

"New Year's Eve of 1981, that was my first year with paramedic papers, with Chief Leroy, Craig. The first night I worked as a paramedic was New Year's Eve. It was a sort of a run of the mill day, with a few calls here and there, but then we were here on the floor, and it was counting down to midnight, and we got a call. It was supposedly a guy having a heart attack. They sent us to Griswold Heights, Building 13. When we got there, a bunch of people were milling around outside and we asked them about it. They said, 'Well, he doesn't need help anymore.'

"It was a cold day, like it is today, a very cold day. And Captain Leroy said he had to see him anyway, and he stepped inside the apartment and walked down the hallway to the kitchen to talk to the man. In the meantime, our equipment was out in the cold air, and I asked if I could step inside to get it out of the freezing cold. When I stepped inside, I saw Craig get hit, and then he went down under a whole crowd of people. And so I started in toward the kitchen, and I got nailed by this kid who was on the stairs in the hallway. So I shook that off and I went in to try and help Craig, who fortunately at the time was the captain on the Rescue Squad, and he was the only one other than the chiefs who carried a portable radio. He had it with him. There was a crowd of people on top of him, and I started pulling them away, and got into a hassle with several others in the room. Finally I got him up, but he had been able to yell out a message, 'Send help,' or whatever. The dispatchers had never heard any noise like that in their lives, they said later.

"We got beat up pretty good inside, and then Craig went out after the guy who hit him first and the next thing I know, I didn't see him or hear him, and I heard what I thought were the sounds of a fight outside. I went out to find two men pinning Craig's arms to the ground and a girl kicking him in the groin, so I stepped out and pretty much ended the mindset that I had that we were there to help. My mind said, 'This is no longer an EMS call. This is survival.' And I went out and punched one of the guys to get him off Craig, and helped Craig up. Then we stood there, back to back, pretty much like one of the old black hat, white hat cowboy movies in the saloon, nailing people.

"They were punching us, we were punching back as best we could, and there had to be twenty of them. The apartment next door, which had an adjoining porch and doorway, all of a sudden they all came out of there, too. I would say they were all 19 to 25 year olds, probably ten more that joined the fray, and just the two of us in the middle. God knows what it was all about, other than they were all cock-eyed and it was New Year's Eve and they thought somebody was being hurt. They just jumped us. We were the ones with the uniforms, so they came after us.

"Finally, an ambulance pulled up. There were only four or five police officers on duty that night and they were at a fire with most of our guys. But the ambulance crew came to help. And the radio transmission that Craig got off, which was to immediately send the engine and truck crews from Campbell Avenue over on an investigation, those guys showed up about a minute after the ambulance crew got there.

"When the ambulance crew came around the corner of the building, one of them was an off-duty fireman and the other was an ambulance driver, somebody kicked the ambulance driver in the balls and he went down hard. He stayed down, too. The off-duty fireman grabbed two handfuls of people, one by the throat, and he slammed both of them up against a wall and got them both out of it. Then one of the housing authority cars got there, and there was one cop who was going out on Pawling Avenue for an investigation and he stopped because of the radio transmission, and he started handcuffing people.

"So that was the last call of the night for us. My clothes were ripped off of me. Craig was pretty well beat up. He took an awful lot of punishment. For two or three weeks after that, because of the kicking he took, his gonads swelled up and he had bruising around his groin and his upper legs. And he passed blood in his urine for several weeks after that incident. And on top of that, we were accused of being drunk, so we had to take breathalyzer tests next door. Those tests saved us from counter-charges that we had assaulted all those people.

"As a result of all of it, there was an investigation and there were charges filed. The whole thing went on for almost a year, I think. The end result was that three men were singled out and identified as the prime movers in the group. The guy who originally was involved in the call and hit Craig first, and then two brothers, two guys pretty much known for their attitudes. The judge in the case, citing the omnibus law that was passed after the riots in 1968 to protect police officers and firefighters who were hurt while they were doing their jobs, took the narrow view that we were not performing our duties on the scene. He said that firefighters' duties were to suppress fires. That narrow interpretation disallowed the charges under the law of felony assault.

"But because of that incident, the law was subsequently changed in a petition that was passed by an overwhelming majority of votes — I don't think there were any dissenting votes in both houses of the State Legislature — which stated that in the State of New York it would be considered felony assault on firefighters and/or ambulance personnel responding to any emergency call. That certainly widened the spectrum of function. But all three of these guys were acquitted. They weren't even convicted of a misdemeanor. The charges that they went for were the felony charges, and the misdemeanor charges were bartered away before they went to trial.

"So that was a fairly difficult beginning. It was a shock to my system. I'm not unaccustomed to fighting, you know. I have somewhat of a reputation, and a temper. I can hold my own. But when I went on that call, I was wearing a uniform. I went there with an entirely different mindset. I went there with the mindset of helping somebody who was possibly having a heart attack. When it turned out to be something entirely different, I was still in the mindset that I was representing the city. I had a uniform on. There are things that you can do and that you can't do. But when it got to where Craig was pinned on the ground and they were beating the hell out of him, I said, 'That's it. No more Mr. Nice Guy.' I was actually somewhat scared, though, because something of a mob mentality took over and I couldn't tell what was going to result. And I didn't have Kelleher here to help me fight them off. I told Craig later on, 'If it gets any better than this, I don't think I'm going to last as a paramedic too long.'"

6

Incident Report — Scott Savaria

On January 28 at approximately 0110 hours I was at Station One having a cup of coffee with the on-duty crews. At this time we heard a loud rapid banging on the door of the house. I went along with the men there to investigate.

We discovered a woman dressed in a nightgown and barefoot. The overhead door was immediately raised and while we ascertained that a home on 116th Street was burning, the truck and engine companies responded. There had been an immediate reaction and response even before all the information was gathered from the woman I later learned was Susan Mason.

When Truck One and Engine One departed I was left alone with Mrs. Mason. The first thing she said to me as I was helping her to a chair was "I called you people fifteen minutes ago. Didn't they send you?" I then replied that we knew nothing about the fire until she came to the firehouse. Mrs. Mason was very upset and concerned for her children.

She was also suffering from frostbite and cold exposure. While I was treating her for the two problems, I asked her how long she had

155

been exposed to the cold while barefoot. This was done to attempt to get an idea of the extent of her injuries. Mrs. Mason stated that she had been outside the house screaming for at least ten or fifteen minutes before running to Station One. While I was treating her, she stated that she had been sleeping and was awakened by a loud boom and awoke to a smoke-filled house. After I wrapped Mrs. Mason's feet in warm towels and her in a blanket, I called dispatch and requested an ambulance and police assistance.

A short time later Mr. Mason entered the fire station, followed by two police officers. While I treated Mr. Mason for cold exposure, I heard a conversation between Mr. and Mrs. Mason. She repeatedly asked him what happened. Mr. Mason answered several times that he did not know. I also heard him ask her how she got out of the house. Mrs. Mason replied that she ran out of the house. Mr. Mason then began to relate to her how the fire started and what he had done. Mr. Mason stated that he had been cooking french fries and hamburgers. He further related that a fire started on the stove and he thought the fire was out and went back to the living room. He stated that a short time later he noticed the fire again and went to get a fire extinguisher. He further related that when he discharged the extinguisher on the fire, the entire room seemed to burst into flames. After he used the extinguisher he stated that the fire was out of control and he left the building. He said he then circled the building yelling. Some time later Mr. Mason said that he had gotten a ladder and put it up to a window and pulled Janice Trent to safety. Mrs. Mason continually asked him about the children. He said that the fire was too hot and the smoke too thick and that he couldn't get to the children. Mr. Mason stated that he was standing outside of the house when the fire department arrived and then found out that Mrs. Mason was safe. He stated that he was then taken to Station One. It must be noted that Mr. Mason smelled strongly of alcohol.

This statement is being given to the best of my knowledge and recollection.

from the Deposition of Susan Mason

Q: All right, was there any discussion about your husband getting something to eat?

A: Not that I recall, no.

Q: Was it unusual for him to cook at night after you went to bed?

A: No.

Q: Was it unusual for him to cook french fries?

A: No.

Q: And where would be the oil for the french fries, where was that kept?

A: In one of the cupboards.

Q: And how about the french fryer, would you describe that for me?

A: Pan with a, like a colander type basket in it.

Q: Now, were there french fried potatoes prepared?

A: Store bought.

Q: Where would that be kept, in the refrigerator?

A: Yes, freezer.

Q: Before you went to bed, had any preparations been made for eating?

A: I don't remember.

Q: Now, when you went upstairs, what did you do?

A: Went over and gave the kids a kiss and went to bed, gave the kids a kiss and went to bed.

Ed Cummings
Battalion Chief, 3rd Platoon

It was after midnight, and Fire Alarm was still on the third floor of the building, and the dispatcher called downstairs and said that she'd just had a report, and I believe it was from the telephone company, that there was a fire at such and such an address on State Street. It was Mary Jane Hanley, and the change up in Fire Alarm occurs at 11 o'clock, so it was certainly after the second shift went home. In any event, she said, "I punched it into the computer and there is no such and such an address on State Street." I think she told me 106 State Street. So what we did is we sent Engine 5 out to drive the length of State Street and see if there was anything going on. And they reported nothing.

I was a little bit concerned, because usually that time of night you don't get false alarms. You don't get mischievous false alarms. So I thought there was some event somewhere in town, but I had no idea, and it was just a few minutes later that I think Engine 1 came on. At about the same time, Fire Alarm came back on, and something about a fire on 116th Street. So that's where some of the confusion may have occurred. When this lady in the Burgh telephoned, supposedly she used a 911 system, and I think it was picked up somewhere else in the state, because there was no 911 in effect here. Now whether they turned it over to the phone company, or whether the phone company gets it right away when there is no 911 service — but somehow there was a telephone operator involved, and he relayed information to Fire Alarm. Now, after the fact, 116th Street and 106 State Street, you can see some sort of parallel there, okay?

In any event, right off the bat, we knew there was a serious fire up there. We started north, and I knew it was serious from the radio transmissions. I got there behind Engine 4, which was still on duty at the time. It was a small house. I'd call it a story and a half cottage, bedrooms on the second floor, wood frame. Back end of the house was almost totally involved, as I remember it. There was a tremendous ball of fire coming out the back end of the house, and that would be, as the hose lines advanced through the building, because they were forcing the fire out the back end, so that would follow the normal circumstances of how a fire progresses.

Grease fire caused deadly blaze
By George Pawlaczyk, Dawn Fallik
and Eric Drexler
The Record

TROY - A cooking oil blaze spread with brush-fire speed to trap four children and one adult on the second floor of a home at 73 116th Street. All five died early Friday in the worst fire in 30 years in this city.

William Sims and his 1 1/2 - year-old son, James, died in the fire, as did all three children from the Mason family - Sam Rizzo, 9, Heather Mason, 2, and Jennifer Mason, 3 months.

Thomas Mason, who had been cooking French fries about 1 a.m., told fire investigators that a stove fire re-ignited, leaped to the ceiling and sent flames across a wall which shot quickly up a stairwell. Mason said he shouted to the seven people above, where his two small daughters were sleeping, to run, and then was forced into the street.

His wife, Susan Mason, told fire officials that she mistakenly dialed 911 to call the Fire Department and then jumped out of the home's front window. She dropped about 15 feet.

The frantic woman then ran shoeless through the snow and slush to the nearby 115th Street Fire Station and pounded on the locked door. Firemen immediately answered and tried to calm her as she shouted, "My children, my children." A precious minute may have been lost because Mason initially could not be understood.

When firefighters of the station's rescue squad broke into the inferno it was too late. In minutes, the intense heat reduced the small home's interior to unrecognizable black char.

Sims, 30, and his 1 1/2-year-old son were found in an upstairs room. The little boy was in his father's arms.

Jennifer Mason, 3 months, and her sister, Heather Mason, 2, were found in a middle room.

In an upstairs front room near where Susan Mason had fallen out of the window, Sam Rizzo, 9, was found. The handicapped youth used a wheelchair but was not found in the device.

"This is the worst fire I've seen. I hope no one has to see another," said Assistant Chief Jack Sheehan. He said he could remember only a single worse city blaze, a 1963 fire in which seven died.

Troy firefighter Eric McMahon, 26, managed to break into the second floor from the rear of the house and tried to feel around for the children he knew must be there somewhere. The rescue squad member, equipped with a breathing apparatus, stayed on the second floor until his clothing caught fire.

He then jumped out a window, "rolled in the snow and went back up again," said Troy Fire Chief Edward J. Schultz. McMahon, who could not again penetrate the intense flames, was later treated for a burned hand.

Troy Police Sgt, John Waters, a member of the arson squad, said Friday afternoon, "At this point, it doesn't look like there's anything suspicious. But, we are continuing our investigation."

Waters said Susan Mason "was upstairs trying to call in the fire to the Fire Department. She called 911 and ended up with an operator, then the address got all fouled up. I don't know if she was in a panic or what, but the Fire Department lost some time there."

A cooking oil fire erupted. Thomas Mason grabbed a fire extinguisher, said Schultz, and put out the flames. The extinguisher was empty when Mason said he went back to the television. It was the proper type for such a fire and was packed with gas-propelled powder. When Mason returned to the kitchen the oil had reignited and, said Schultz, "A fire like that can really travel quickly. We've had several recent fires including one that trapped some of our firemen. It's a dangerous thing."

Friends said the two families shared the house amicably and were well liked in the neighborhood. They said Sims, Trent and their son had moved in with the Masons about two weeks ago.

from the Deposition of Thomas Mason

Q: When you got home, what did you do?

A: We sat around the bar, just talking about my father, because he died a year ago to the day.

Q: What bar was this?

A: In my house, my parents in Maryland gave us a bar set and a card table and all this stuff.

Q: Who was sitting around talking?

A: They and Susan and Bill and Janice.

Q: Was anything to drink?

A: Yup, we had a few beers there, we had a tap unit there, too, and we were just having little cups, little glasses.

Q: You remember how many you had?

A: Very few, because I was drinking half ones because I didn't feel much like having anything to drink, I was drinking half ones because they get too warm and it's just a waste.

Q: How long did you continue to sit there at the bar and drink beer, your best recollection?

A: Maybe an hour or so, because we were watching television from there too, we just got cable hooked up that day.

Q: Then what happened?

A: Susan had gone to bed and Janice went up to try to put James down, I think because they went to bed, and Bill and I were sitting there too for a little bit watching television. And I said I wanted to get something to eat, I was getting hungry because I hadn't had anything to eat all day, and he, I think he went up to help her put James to sleep because he was up and down.

Q: What happened then?

A: Started cooking, heating up the oil on the stove to deep fry some french fries and I was walking back and forth from there, and I went through the changer thing for the television in the living room . . . I got a big commercial deep fryer, it's a stovetop deep fryer . . . well, in the living room, I was standing there, I went back in the kitchen and the thing was all in flames. I never smelt nothing or heard anything. As soon as I seen that, I went back into the living room. I have a fire extinguisher next to the fireplace. I grabbed that and went back in the kitchen and tried to put the fire out. And I was yelling there was a fire. It didn't look like much of a fire, first thing in my mind was grab the fire extinguisher and try to put it out. I didn't see no smoke or nothing really where I thought anything was of danger.

from the Dispatcher's Tape
73 116th Street Fire

01:09:22

Oper: This is the NYNEX Operator. I just got a call in for a fire at 106 State Street.

Disp: OK. They didn't say anything else?

Oper: No. She has kids, she was trying to get them out of the house. I told her to get out of the house herself.

Disp: OK.

Oper: They were screaming in the background.

01:10:32

B.C.:   Cummings.

Disp: Hi Chief, Mary Jane. I just got a call from NYNEX operator. I played the tape back. She said somebody called in a fire at 106 State Street. There is no such address. It only goes up to 67. Ah, I said, you know, "Did she say it was a fire? Did she give you any information?" She said, "Well she said she was trying to get the kids out."

B.C.:   Yeah, 106 State Street.

Disp: There's no such number.

B.C.:   Yeah, I'm just trying to think of other cities that have a State Street. Schenectady's got one and Albany's got one, but supposedly it was Troy?

Disp: Well, she, all she said was this is the NYNEX operator, I just talked to somebody who said they have a call at 106 State Street. A fire. But I'm wondering if it wasn't us. They hung up on me before I, I didn't get anything from the operator.

B.C: Yeah, it could be, I don't know. Let's send our Engine 5 over just to make an investigation the length of State Street.

Disp: OK.

B.C.:   I'll go tell them.

Disp: I'll tone them out and get them.

B.C.:   And then just call the NYNEX people back. I don't know if you got a call back number. And tell them it may be another city, okay?

Disp: OK. Thank you, Chief.

01:14:30

Disp: Troy Fire Department.

Male: Hello.

Disp: Hi.

Male: Yes, 116th Street between 5th and 4th Avenue, there's been a person yelling outside and I see some smoke coming out of the top floor.

Disp: OK, where's this?

Male: 116th Street in North Troy, between 4th and 5th Avenue.

Disp: 116th between 4th and 5th.

Male: Yeah, yeah, hurry.

Disp: OK, thanks.

01:16:37

E1:   Dispatcher?

Disp: Engine 1.

E1:   Heavy smoke from a story and a half frame. We have a report of 4 kids on the 2nd floor.

Disp: Message received. Car 4, did you receive that?

C4:   Received.

Incident Report
L.J. McConnell

At about 0114 I was on watch at the 115th St. Fire Station. I heard a loud banging on the overhead doors, where I heard a woman yelling that her house was on fire and that her 4 children were trapped on the 2nd floor. Acting Capt. J. Carboni transmitted an alarm for 73 116th St.

Truck #1 responded at that time with myself, F.F. Gavitt and F.F. Kevin Gordon. When we arrived at about 0116 I saw heavy black smoke coming from the 2nd floor front window and heavy fire in rear of building. Engine #1 crew were laying 1 and 3/4 lines. The truck crew started to put a ladder to the 2nd floor front window. When entry was attempted, but not possible, we then put a ladder to 2nd floor window on east side of building. Then we started to lay line to said ladder, where entry was attempted but still not possible. After that we just again started to fight the fire.

from the Dispatcher's Tape

01:18:15

Dispatcher telephones Car 2 at his home.

C2:   Hello.

Disp: Chief, it's Mary Jane. Did you get any of that?

C2:   No, what?

Disp: We've got a fire. They didn't call a signal 30 yet, but Engine 1 got it verbally. At 116th and 4th a one and a half story frame reported 4 children up on the 2nd floor.

C2:   They didn't give a 30 yet or anything?

Disp: Ah, no, Carboni just yelled it out, Heavy Smoke.

C2:   All right, okay.

Disp: OK?

C2.:   Yeah.

01:18:43

Police report children trapped on 2nd floor.

01:23:59

C4:   We have a story and a half wood frame. Entire rear of the structure is engulfed in fire. We are operating lines in the front door. We are using outside vent and search on the 2nd floor.

Disp: Message received.

Ray Davis
Lieutenant, Medic 1

The fire came in, and I'm pretty sure it was called in by Carboni. Originally, a call came in for a fire on State Street. The address didn't jive. The dispatcher sent out Engine 5 for an investigation. I was on the Medic rig with Billy Miller. The original call came in as a 911 call, but at the time there was no 911, so they called 911 and they got beeped out to Syracuse. Syracuse called it into the dispatch center, and gave a wrong address. The address just did not jive. It was nowhere close. They had State Street. They didn't have 116th Street. I don't know why they had it, but they had it. Engine 5 went out and found no fire, and then the alarm came in. Carboni at the same time came in from the firehouse, "We have a fire on 116th Street, fully involved." That's the way it came in.

Snowing like a bastard. There was snow everywhere, probably about 6 to 8 inches, maybe more, on the ground. Slow moving. There was no way you could pick up any speed whatsoever to go from downtown Troy to Lansingburgh. You just couldn't do it.

The reports over the radio were that there were people trapped, and that they were having trouble gaining access into the building because the fire was so involved. I talked with Billy Miller on the way up, and we were saying to one another, "There's kids in there. We're going to have to go in. Gotta find a way to get in." And we talked about that on the way up.

We parked over by St. Augustine's Church to stay out of the way, came around the corner, and proceeded to help move some hand-lines at first, I believe. And then we were told by Chief Cummings that the kids were in that window, "Inside that window are the two kids." So the ladder was already in place. Whoever had put the ladder in place had dropped it through the window, and they put it in place to drop it through the window, using it to vent, so they smashed the window and left it in place. Placement of the ladder was probably not appropriate. It should have been off to the side so you could have gained access to the window, but because there were two windows I thought I was going to be able to gain access into the other window, so I just left the ladder in place. It was myself and Billy Miller. Midway up the ladder, we hit heavy smoke, heavy fire conditions. MIDWAY up the ladder, not even in the window. Heavy smoke and heavy fire conditions, all the smoke was pumping out this window because it had been vented. You couldn't see anything. There was no seeing. I broke out the rest of the window and attempted to get into the other window, it was a foot or so away from the ladder, but there was something in the way. I just couldn't get in. There was no way. I couldn't push whatever it was over. I could see what appeared to be a crib off to one side. Actually it looked like bars, bars from a crib. I didn't know at the time that it WAS a crib, but it ended up being just that. I could see it a little bit, but I just couldn't push what was in the way of the window over.

I tried for a couple of minutes to get in, but I couldn't get in. Every time you tried to get in through the one window, you were getting burned. There was no two ways around it. Billy had burns on his wrists when we got done, because he tried, too. They always tell you that if you can't get in, to let somebody else do it. So I jumped off the ladder and let Billy have a try and he couldn't get in either. We found out afterwards that they had a dresser in front of the window, and we just couldn't push it over. We couldn't get enough leverage off the ladder in snowy conditions to push the dresser over to get in the window.

We had a hose line for a short period of time, and that was at the same exact time that Eric McMahon had made entrance through the first window. He met heavy fire conditions. He was only in for less than fifteen seconds, and then he came flying back out, jumped out the window head-first and they grabbed the hose-line out of my hands to put him out. His coat was burning. When he hit the ground he was burning. He did a very good job. He got into a position that nobody else could obtain, and missed one of the children by about three feet when he made a sweep on the floor. He made one sweep and then jumped back out the window.

Now this place was all cut up into different rooms, but after you got into the building, you ended up finding out what they did was they put paneling on studs, no wallboard, okay? That's why it burned so fast. No wallboard, paneling on studs, through the upstairs. The stairway to the upstairs had a door on it, and came in off what was at one time an enclosed porch, but they were using it as part of the house. And that stairway couldn't have been any more than 20 inches wide. It was real small, that stairway. And the other thing that they didn't do when they rehabbed the house, they never took the gasoline siding, which is the asphalt shingle-type siding, off the interior of the house. So they had vinyl siding on the outside of the house, but they left the asphalt shingles on the inside of this room, which was an enclosed porch area. The fire came right out, scooted right up the stairs, and trapped all the kids upstairs, and the gasoline siding was just too much. That siding burns extremely fast. It looks like red, fake brick. As far as firefighters go, it's just a term used to describe it — gasoline siding — burns terribly fast.

from the Deposition of Thomas Mason

Q: And, where was it that this fire took place?

A: At my house, 73 116th Street, North Troy.

Q: Will you describe the house for me, please, as to stories?

A: It's a two-story, it had four bedrooms upstairs, a bathroom, one of the bedrooms you had to go, we kind of used it for a nursery for the babies, and downstairs was a living room, dining room, sun porch had a fire, a kitchen, was an eat-in-kitchen and a partial cellar.

Q: Who was the owner of that house?

A: I was, my wife and I.

Q: Were you employed at the time of this incident?

A: Yes, I was on workers compensation but employed by Acme.

Q: In what capacity?

A: In the warehouse.

Q: Now were there other people living in the house at the time of the fire?

A: Janice Trent and William Sims and their son James.

Q: How long had those people been residing there?

A: About a week, week and a half, they were staying there because their apartment — the baby was coming that is Susan's godson — it had real high lead levels and the landlord was giving them a hard time about cleaning it up. So they didn't get exposed to lead, he said they could stay somewhere else. So we said you can stay in our spare room till you can get it fixed and stay in our apartment.

Q: Do you remember what day of the week the fire was on?

A: I was on workers comp. I didn't pay any attention to days. Every day was like the one before.

Ed Cummings

There was a full crew on both Engine 1 and Truck 1 that night, and they had a line on the fire, and the guys on the truck had ground ladders up to the second floor windows, trying to get into the building because they were aware that there were people inside. As the subsequent crews arrived, they just continued to fight the fire in the same pattern that the gang from the Burgh had established.

As the Rescue Squad arrived — Pat Hughes, he was the captain on the Squad — he took another line in to back up the initial line that the gang from Engine 1 had on the fire, and some of the other gentlemen on the Squad and Engine 5, I had them throw another ground ladder. In particular, Eric McMahon and Mark Galuski had volunteered to go right up into the thick of things. There was a lot of boiling smoke, almost to the point where the second floor was just about to flash over, and McMahon and Galuski said they'd do it.

It was almost obvious to me that no one could survive the conditions that I witnessed when I first arrived. Nobody on the inside could survive. The fire had progressed past the point of survivability. Prior to flashover, you get a boiling smoke, that's the best way to describe it. Not a lazy smoke coming out the windows. There's a turbulence to it, almost. The smoke rolls over, violently rolling. It's just the high heat. The temperature is increasing inside the rooms, and what was burning initially is giving off not just smoke but combustible gases, and what's being given off will eventually become a fuel for the fire itself. So it's a physics thing, and it's in a confined space. Sometimes it doesn't take a long time for those combustible elements to explode. It depends on the conditions, all right? Flashover is a temperature thing. When the temperature reaches a certain point, that's when you experience flashover, when all of those chemicals that are in vaporous form explode.

So I saw boiling smoke, but firemen are all alike. We can't just stand there and do nothing. They had lines on the building. Guys were ventilating the windows in the back end of the second floor. So we made an attempt. A lot of time when you do find someone, they're very close to a point of exit or entry. They try to get out, and it's not uncommon to find an adult anyway, or somebody who's capable of escaping, getting as far as a doorway or close to a window or whatever.

So McMahon and Galuski went up a ground ladder into the front bedroom. Well, McMahon got inside. I don't know if Galuski ever got off the ladder, but McMahon got inside and he must have recognized the conditions, because he was just able to get out of the window again before the front half of the building flashed over. It's lucky he wasn't killed at that point.

from the Deposition of Susan Mason

Q: What is the next thing you remember?

A: Waking up and seeing smoke.

Q: Do you know what caused you to wake up?

A: I heard a loud noise, like a bang.

Q: What did you do then?

A: I ran downstairs to see if Sam was in the playpen and he wasn't there. So I ran up the stairs screaming for Janice to get her and Bill out and the baby.

Q: Okay, when you went downstairs, where was your husband?

A: He was in the kitchen standing by the back door with the fire extinguisher. I just seen the flames and ran upstairs and tried to get people out.

Q: What did you do when you went back upstairs?

A: I yelled for Janice and she met me at the top of the stairs and I tried opening windows to get the kids out and the windows were frozen and I called 911 and told them there was a fire.

Q: Now you say you dialed 911?

A: Yes.

Q: Is that the first time you attempted to call the fire department?

A: Yes, I didn't know there was a fire, I didn't realize there was flames.

Q: What happened when you dialed 911?

A: They answered some emergency, can I help you, is this an emergency? I told them my house was on fire, I was a block away, I had kids and I couldn't breathe. I just kept saying there was a fire in the house and I have got to get my kids out and I was only a block away from the firehouse.

Q: Did you give a street address?

A: I tried, yes.

Q: Did you succeed?

A: I don't know, obviously not, because they didn't get there.

Q: Were you aware that you were talking to Syracuse?

A: No.

Q: So you're not certain as you sit there that you gave them the address of the house?

A: I remember what I said to them — 116th Street, a block away from the firehouse.

Q: And then what happened?

A: And I hanged up the phone because I wanted to try and get my son out . . . I couldn't . . . I tried getting my breath long enough to get to him so I could at least pick him up by his arm and try and throw him out the window.

Q: Then what happened?

A: I just felt heat and I had to jump out the window. My bedroom window . . . I ran around the house telling Tom the kids were still in there . . . I realized the fire company hadn't gotten there, so I ran down the alleyway to the firehouse and banged on the doors.

Eric McMahon
Firefighter, Rescue Squad

That fire was intense, to say the least. We weren't first in. We were coming from Central Station. It was about 1 in the morning. When you jump on the rig, all you know is that it's a box alarm and you're going to someplace that is possibly on fire. So then it came across that it was true — we definitely had five people trapped in this building, and it's going. So everything's on: The mask is on, the hood's on, and all's you've got to do is just snap the regulator on and . . .

We had to park on either 3rd or 4th, but we couldn't get onto 116th Street. We didn't want to go on there anyway, because we had no water. I was on the Squad, and we were first in for search and rescue. So we just went running up the street, and I seen Ed, and he just said, "Get in that window right there." So I went up and stuck my head in, but it was hotter than . . . You know, I had a hood on, a helmet on, and it just fucking burned unbelievably right through all of it, and I climbed up a couple of extra rungs on the ladder and just dove in. It was hot, but I figured I'm wearing a lot more stuff than the people inside.

So then I landed on the floor, found the bed, searched the bed, swept this side of the floor, swept another side of the floor, hit a wall, hit a wall, hit a wall, I knew that this was the end of the bed, this is the window I just came in, I can't find anybody, you know, I'm getting lower and I'm getting lower and I can't find anything, and then the fire starts coming from the first floor window into the window that I'm in. Now I'm trying to get out, and it was just a real intense thing. And then come to find out, right where I went in, there was a kid right there, like I must have like landed on the kid on my way in.

If I had found a door . . . I couldn't find the door, you know, because there was a dresser and then there was another dresser, and then the door was in a corner between the two dressers. I mean, you really had to know where the door was. There was absolutely nothing I could have done. But if I had made it through there, there was two kids in there.

I went in the front window, on 116th Street, I just went right through that window, but they had gone up with another line and they just pushed the fire right down and it came right back up the window I was in. I knew there was the ladder there, the one I had just come up, so I took a calculated risk. I was banging on the wall with the flashlight, signaling that I was ready to get out of there, because the flames were just getting bigger and bigger and bigger and bigger, and then the whole window was just like a big curtain of flame, so I was like, "Ah, fuck it. I know there's a ladder there. I know it's up against the side of the house." So then I threw the flashlight out and dove out and grabbed onto the ladder. That's when I burnt my hands. I remember, I hit the ladder and just went straight down to the ground and there was a bunch of cops there. I was trying to get my fucking gloves off, because my hands were all burnt up. My face felt like it was on fire, so I ripped my hood off. Then I pushed my hands into the snow, and I heard somebody say, "Holy fuck, that's my brother." My brother Jack is a Troy cop, and he was on the call, and he bugged out when he saw me.

from the Deposition of Thomas Mason

Q: Tell me how the fire progressed based on what you saw.

A: After I hit it with the fire extinguisher, that wall where the stove is, where the cabinets, they are all wood cabinets, they went up and it was going across the ceiling and at that point, as I was standing by the back door, I went out the back door. It was hot enough where it burnt my face and I was standing by the back door.

Q: When you went outside, how were you dressed?

A: Socks, I think I had sweat pants on and a T-shirt.

Q: What did you do when you went outside?

A: I grabbed the ladder that was in the yard, we were putting a roof on the house, I knew when I left the house that was my best bet of trying to get upstairs was going through a window or something when I went out. I don't know what made me go to the back window, if I heard Janice yelling or what it was, but I put the ladder up on the sun porch, to the little porch over the back door. I broke the window to the bathroom and I pulled Janice out.

Q: Did you attempt at any time to go through the bathroom window?

A: No, I fell off the porch, I was trying to get neighbors to get the fire company there, I was yelling for neighbors to call the fire company, I figured when Susan went up, everybody was getting out. I didn't know. We always had the plans, fire extinguisher is here, the smoke detector is up there, and go out the window on the sun porch and jump off of that.

Q: What happened after you fell off the roof?

A: I hurt my arm, got caught, used to have a dog run, metal dog run caught underneath my arm . . . I tried getting back up on the roof and there was so much smoke coming out of the windows and you could see the smoke coming out the back window, a lot of it and the whole, looked like the whole kitchen was in flames.

Q: Then what happened?

A: I ran back to the house to try to get back in and I couldn't get back in . . . I tried, tried the front door and that was locked... I had it locked up for the night. I couldn't kick it in, I was going to try to get on the roof again and I don't remember why I didn't or couldn't. Short time after that I think was when the fire company started showing up. pointed out which rooms I thought people were in, I still didn't know where Susan was.

Ed Cummings

The last thing I want to be is overly graphic. When we found the bodies, all of them were smoke-stained. How can I say this in a way that isn't offensive? They were blackened, smoke-stained. Some, but not all of them, were recognizable as human beings. Closer to the front of the building, it seems to me there were two small children, 2 or 3 years old I guess, definitely smoke-stained but human forms.

Then up in the front bedroom, the room where McMahon went in, there was a handicapped boy. I don't remember seeing him, but I would imagine he was in a similar shape, because the fire hadn't totally consumed that whole area. So definitely the smoke was a factor in their deaths. But in the back of the house there was an adult, and they said a child was cradled in his arms and he was down on the floor, and there was a lot of devastation to the adult body from the effects of fire. I guess he was cradling the baby. It was difficult trying to find him. We were looking through the room, and one of the guys had seen something similar before and he recognized it as being human remains.

I don't know if this is appropriate, but I grew up around death, so it wasn't as foreign to me as it was to some of the others. My father was an undertaker, and we lived upstairs over the funeral home. But I certainly was upset over the death of these children. At that point, we had a child of our own, so it certainly cuts right to your heart when you see anybody's kids suffer. It's funny, I'll sit here at night and I'll see something on the TV news about a child and I'll come to tears. And I'll just sit here quietly, but it does, it breaks my heart. Some of the other guys, though, they were terribly affected by it, and this wasn't even a routine death. This was a horrible tragedy, and to go from — some of those guys have probably never seen any kind of death — to something like this, it was just like getting hit with a pallet of bricks.

As bad as I felt about the whole thing, I always learned from the incident with McMahon, because that was something that I could control, or did control. That has always bothered me. I learned a lesson there. There comes a point in a situation where you have to recognize there's nothing more that is humanly possible, and you're almost sending someone into gravest danger at that point. But luckily McMahon is a streetwise kid, he's an intelligent guy. He knew enough to get out. Here's a guy who gave 100 percent and more, and could have lost his own life in this situation, but I know that he was deeply upset after the fire. He had hoped he could have been able to do more. Truthfully, the threshold of survivability, I think we had passed that when we arrived from headquarters.

And since that time, I've made it a point to learn as much as I could about flashover. That's something that occurs at most fires, all right. I've become a student of flashover since then, because the last thing I want to do is send somebody into his death, you know what I mean? For years, firemen just opened the front door and went in, okay? If a fire has gotten to a stage where it's going to flash, you have to be very careful that you're not in the room when it does flash. They describe flashover as the total consumption of the room and contents by fire when the heat level reaches a certain point. That's what they call a flashover. It doesn't always flash all the way to the floor. Sometimes you'll see a line of demarcation on the wall, you know? You usually have a room that isn't totally enclosed, but there isn't a significant air-flow through it. The smoke rises, the heat build-up occurs, it hits the ceiling and it has nowhere to go, so the level of heat is greatest at the ceiling but now it's starting to come down. That's why firemen go in on their hands and knees, because it's certainly hotter the higher you are in the room. But there comes a point at which everything in the room will burst into flame. And when it explodes, you don't want to be there, because they say if you're about three seconds away from the door, that's it. If you're any more than three seconds into the room, you won't survive.

Fire departments have this macho attitude, this can-do attitude, and it's great to have that. But as I learn about all these deaths in New York City, or in other big cities, what I find is that it's human error on the part of the fire department when firefighters die a lot of the time. This is a business where people get killed, and where fire-

fighters get killed. I realize it's going to happen, but anything we can do as a group to minimize that, all right? Proper ventilation, recognizing the stage that the fire is at when you arrive, and having a unified plan to put the fire out, that's all part of doing it in a safe and efficient manner.

Because fire is an element of nature. I don't know if that's the right phrase or not. But man hasn't totally figured out how to deal with nature. In a scientific sense, in a laboratory, they can remove one aspect or one element and control things, but out in the real world, in a burning building, with so many other significant factors — the construction of the building, the weather conditions, broken windows, a strong breeze will affect how a fire is going to play out within any type of building — so I certainly learned something that day.

I didn't go to the funeral, because what I was afraid of . . . well, there was a lot of talk about how we should handle it. The fire department offered to be bearers for these children. What I was afraid of was that the fire department would grieve. If the guys who were actually at the fire went and acted as bearers, they would be as grief-stricken as the family, and it wouldn't be a comforting situation for the family, you know. So as I remember it was a lot of the off-duty guys came forward and acted as bearers, and they tried to keep it low-key. I don't believe they wore their uniforms, because the last thing you need is something . . . you should give some comfort to the family. The reason I didn't go is I was afraid it would have exactly the opposite effect of what it was supposed to do. I watched it on the news that night, and I saw some off-duty guys. I know Jack Stinson went up to be a bearer, with Don Kimmey and Tommy Miter and some others.

Heroic firefighter feels only anguish
By George Pawlaczyk
The Record

TROY - Eric J. McMahon faced the core of an inferno with the following equipment: Helmet, Nomex fire resistant hood, "bunker" pants and boots, also of Nomex, a fireax, a Scott Air Pak breathing apparatus, and heavy gloves. But this gear could not protect his heart.

The 26-year-old Rescue Squad member had burst into the blazing, smoke-filled hell that was the second floor of 73 116th Street just after 1 a.m. Friday. His only direction had been the cries of an anguished father.

McMahon kept his head. His training told him to make a primary search. In flames, all he could do was to reach and hope to touch a child. McMahon caught on fire, jumped out a window, rolled in snow, and went back up.

Other firemen stopped him. They knew he would die in there. They told McMahon it was too late. The children were dead.

Hours after the fire McMahon sat in a physician's waiting room, his burned hand reddened. The look on his face might easily have been the look of a battle veteran or a Vietnam ambush survivor. It could have been the look of Khe Sanh, Pork Chop Hill or D-Day. McMahon did not want to talk. It would have been unwise to have said to McMahon, "You're a hero."

"People work for the city and they get paid. They plow snow. They get paid. I work for the city. I get paid," he said, evenly trying to control his anguish. "This is not a good thing to write about," he said. "Five people died. The firemen put the fire out. End of story."

McMahon would leave the doctor's office a little over an hour later. He might have gone straight home, or if he remembered, might have picked up his paycheck. Like clerks, city managers, snow plow drivers, most city workers, Friday is payday for the men who work in the flames.

Charley Willson
New lieutenant, joining 3rd Platoon

Actually, what happened was, I just got promoted, and the next day I was going to be at that firehouse, up in the Burgh, on the 3rd Platoon, assigned to the truck up there. So I was still on the 1st Platoon when they had the fatal fire. That was just when I made lieutenant and I was going to the 3rd Platoon. So I just missed that fire by one work day. And I was thinking, "Oh, boy, if I just got promoted and that was my first night, on that thing." That wouldn't have been good at all. I don't care how many years you were on the job. That wouldn't have been good at all.

So, anyway, that's why I agreed to be a bearer, so I could do my part. I felt kind of obligated, too, and I wanted to get in the good graces of the guys on the platoon I was going to, because they all felt so bad, you know. The 3rd Platoon had all volunteered themselves, because they felt such remorse at the kids all dying and everything. The chiefs thought it had been stressful enough, with the fire and all, that those guys had already been through so much, that they shouldn't be put through that, too. Which was good, because I never even saw those kids and it was probably one of the worst days of my life, sitting through that funeral.

One of the kids was an invalid, I think he had cerebral palsy, but he was handicapped, anyway. He was the one that we carried, the nine year old. The minister, whoever he was, I mean, we've never had a day as bad as the one he had. I can't imagine trying to go through that and talk. I knew the woman who was the fiancee of the adult that died, and the mother of the baby that they found under him, that girl there, I had worked with her up at the Sunset. We had coffee every morning, so I knew her through that. And I knew her first family, her husband and her two children from before that. I didn't even know it was her until I heard the news afterwards and saw her on it.

But when the minister started talking about how the handicapped child was "walking in heaven," and "he's up out of his chair," and all these other things, I'll tell you, it was brutal, absolutely brutal. All I could think of was what the families were going through. I couldn't believe they were able to sit through all of it, could survive it. It was that bad. It was terrible.

And I'm the kind of guy, I can't make it through "Touched By An Angel" without crying, so that was not a good place for me to be. Boy, did that hit home. Of course, all of us had young kids that we were relating this to, you know, and then the severity of the fire and the damage and the burns to the bodies and everything. It wasn't just like they went to sleep, so that made it that much worse, too. It was an awful day. It was as bad as any day on the job, and I wasn't even on the job that day. Here we were just in suitcoats and ties, we just volunteered to do that, but it was devastating.

At the funeral, I just remember the emotions, because I knew Janice, and then all of a sudden, she walked by. And I couldn't even say hello. I opened my mouth to say, "Hi, Janice," and nothing would come out. And I'm never lost for words, you know, but I didn't know what to say to her. You're trying to make her feel better, but you're thinking that nothing's going to make her feel better. So she got by me, and then we had to bring the caskets in from the funeral home.

Just these white caskets, and they're so small and everything else, you know, that's part of the emotion. I had never been to a child's funeral before. I've been to a lot of funerals, and I've been at deaths from fires, but I'd never been to a child's funeral before. When you're caught up in the emotion of a fire, something like that, that's one thing, because you have so many distractions, but when you actually get time to sit there and think about it, you know, that was the worst part of it.

And then listening to the minister, who was doing a beautiful job, but I even felt sorry for him. I had no idea how he could get through it. How good can you be to get through something like that? Talk about somebody at the height of their profession. The worst part of the funeral service was about the handicapped kid. I was thinking, "How much more could this kid go through?" He spent his whole life without the privileges of so many other people, and then to have to die like this. He didn't even have an honorable death, you know, of going out peacefully. It had to be a tragic end like that. I think the minister was reading letters from his friends at school, ones his classmates had written to him. That was heartwrenching.

And then we came out and the news media was all over the place. You knew they were fighting for the story and everything, because it was a regional thing. It wasn't just like something for a neighborhood or something, because of the amount of deaths. And then you could just see how people react to the cameras. They were good enough that they were across the street and doing long shots, there was a distance, it wasn't like they were in your face or anything, but you could still see how impersonal it gets. You could see how people would get bitter about that.

And then we went to the cemetery, and it was still so cold. I remember that day, it was really freezing. Everybody kind of lined up, and then the realization of how final it was hit us. That those people were leaving, and they had nothing any more. Their family, their kids are gone. And then they had another funeral to go to, too, because they had to go to Janice's fiancee and baby, out in Canajoharie. I don't know if they went or not, but I was thinking, "Here, these people aren't even done yet. We're going home and they've got another grieving procedure to go through yet."

If they were that close that they were all living together, I'm sure they showed support for each other, because Janice was at this funeral, of course. I remember the mother of the kids trying to throw herself on the coffins, calling out, "My babies, my babies," and we were in the back, and I couldn't even look then. I was trying to think about anything else at that point, where I had to be the next day, or anything, just to get myself through it.

Fire victims laid to rest
By Carmen Napolitano
The Record

TROY - The bodies of 9-year-old Sam Rizzo and his younger half sisters were buried in a clearing in St. John's Cemetery overlooking Lansingburgh Tuesday.

Tears were shed as the three caskets, one not much bigger than a child's toy box, were carried by Troy firefighters into the Faith Lutheran Church on Route 40. And once inside with her children she hadn't been with since the night they died in that terrible Lansingburgh fire five days ago, Susan Mason collapsed in her family's arms.

Relatives, friends and strangers with only emotional ties wept. The healing for all, though still far away, began.

"A lot of tears are being shed by people who are not even in this room; strangers, people we do not know, but who hurt with you, who, like you, don't understand what has happened," Pastor Stephen Cordes told those who filled his church. "But there is one in this world who does understand and who will take these children to a place where there are no more tears, where the hurt is gone."

A letter written by Rizzo's friends at the school he attended in Chatham was read aloud.

"You're out of your chair now, Sam — run and play and sing," his friends wrote. Rizzo had cerebral palsy and had been confined to a wheelchair all of his life.

Mason and her husband wept aloud as he held her in his arms. Classmates and teachers from Rizzo's school cried too as the letter was read.

About 100 people attended the service.

Rizzo and his sisters, Heather Mason, 2, and 3-month-old Jennifer Mason, died early Friday after the fire broke out in the family's 116th Street home in Lansingburgh.

A family friend, William Sims, 30, and his 1 1/2-year-old son, James, also perished in the blaze.

Sims and his son were to be buried Tuesday afternoon in Canajoharie.

The fire broke out shortly after midnight. Susan Mason telephoned 911, but the emergency number does not work in Rensselaer County. Mason jumped from the second floor of the burning residence and ran barefoot to a nearby fire station for help.

Her husband, Thomas, escaped unharmed and raised a ladder to the second floor to save baby James's mother, Janice Trent. She and Sims planned to marry, friends said.

Spiritual hymns bearing messages of healing and peace for both the grieving and dead were sung. Cordes told biblical stories of heartache, despair and new beginnings, and for a short time, a sense of peace replaced the weeping.

While difficult to see beyond the sadness and hurt, Cordes said, there will come a time when the crying will stop and good memories will replace the bad.

"We look for a new day when the tears are wiped clean, when we don't cry anymore," Cordes said. "There will be another day."

Red and pink flowers covered the caskets that were laid end-to-end at the front of the church.

Dolls and favorite toys had been placed in the children's hands earlier in the week. It was part of getting them ready for their trip to heaven, a family friend said.

Tears filled the eyes of firefighters as they carried the caskets out of the church and placed them in the hearse. Many of them have children, too. At the cemetery, in a spot cleared of snow and ice, the caskets containing the bodies of Sam and his sisters, Heather and Jennifer, were placed beside the graves. Susan Mason, her husband, family and friends said goodbye.

"Today is a matter of broken hearts," Cordes said. "We look to God to mend these wounds and send us on our way."

In the photo that runs alongside the article in *The Record*, Don Kimmey and Tom Miter are two of the six pallbearers carrying a small, white coffin down the steps of the church. Today is the day after the funeral, another workday for the 1st Platoon, and Don and Tom sit side by side at the table in the common room of Central Station, and read different sections of the paper.

"They called and said they needed people down there, to help out, and I said I'd be available if they needed me," Don says, without looking up from the paper.

"I'm not sure if they asked us or if we offered, I don't know. I figured it was something I should do," Tom says. "I've got kids of my own that age."

"Fourteen of us went down, all together," Don says, but it's clear he doesn't much want to talk about it. "The church was bad enough, but the cemetery, Jesus, with the grieving and things like that. Boy, was that bad."

Tom folds his section of the paper and throws it into the center of the table. "It was packed. We, the pallbearers, had to stand in the back of the church until we went up to carry the coffins. There were three coffins — the nine year old, the three year old, and the three month old. The other two victims were being buried out in Canajoharie. The family was incredibly upset. They cried at the funeral home. They cried at the funeral. They cried at the cemetery. At the cemetery, the mom, at the end of the ceremony, she screamed that she wanted her babies and that was the hardest part for me, and for all of us. She tried to grab the coffins, but her mother held her back. But that was her own private hell, and we didn't feel like we should be part of that, so we all just hustled out of there.

"We wanted the emphasis taken away from us, which is why we did not go in uniform. We thought too much emphasis was being placed on how we felt, and we didn't think that was right. It wasn't about us. We just do our jobs.

"I carried the nine year old's coffin, the boy with cerebral palsy, and it was extremely light. There was six of us carrying the coffin. If any one of us let go, you never would have felt the extra weight. The whole thing, even with the coffin, probably only weighed 50 pounds. I don't know. He could have been a small kid for his age, and, after a fire, there's not a whole lot of moisture left in the body. I don't know. I never had it by myself. There were six guys on it. I just know it felt extremely light to me. It was really weird carrying something that had hardly any weight to it.

"We got through it and went down to Sidelines to have a drink and, I'll tell you, I would have given anything to just stay there at Sidelines and get ossified. But my choices were do that or go home and see my own kids. I wanted to do both, but I wanted to see my kids more. I took all of them down to my father's house, but he wasn't home, so the three of us just hung around there. It was nice. It's a terrible thing, but something like this sure made me pay more attention to my own children. You just don't know. Sometimes it scares me to think that I'm down here working and they're fourteen miles away. If anything goes wrong, the fastest I'm going to get there is fifteen to twenty minutes, no matter what it is.

"The only thing that would have helped those kids is if their father had either learned how to use a fire extinguisher properly, or if the mother had known they didn't have 911 service and had gotten the kids out of the goddamned house before she called. The only other thing they could have done is close the door to the rooms. That's it. Maybe a rope ladder. They sell them. But the best thing about a fire, if you can talk about a best thing, is that most people die of smoke inhalation. They die before they feel the heat. The vast majority die of carbon monoxide poisoning.

"That fire free-burned before we even got called, before we could even get a chance to straighten out what was going on.

And we'll never know what really happened in there. The family is so distraught that they'll never be able to clearly know exactly what they did. I'll tell you, though, the best thing in the world for me is to be back in here, right away. When I have a bad day, I need to get back here, because the next day is going to be better. We have a little fire today, and we put it out quick and nobody gets hurt. That will make it a little better. Maybe next time we'll get the kids out.

"The third platoon did nothing wrong in there. That's the worst part. They did everything anybody could do. Nobody on this shift or any shift could have done better than they did. My dad used to tell me that being a fireman is like being a doctor, but there are two rules. Rule number one is that people are going to die. Rule number two is that firemen aren't going to change rule number one. He told me that when I became a fireman, and then again when I became a paramedic. 'Do everything you can,' he said, 'but if their number's up, it's not your fault.'

"We're not always going to win. That's the bad thing about these TV shows like *Rescue 911*. They only show the good side. A fire like this is never going to be on that. William Shatner isn't going to show this. It's bad for ratings."

Mike Harrison

I remember a similar fire where we had three children die in 1978, down in an apartment building in South Troy. That was one that I was in on initially. I don't know if that was the worst, though. To tell you the truth, the worst fire that I remember was down on First Street. It was only three or four years ago. We had heavy fire on the first floor, and we had voice contact. It's the only fire I ever had where I had voice contact with the victim and we didn't save her.

She was screaming for help and we just couldn't get to her. We couldn't find her, number one. We didn't know where she was, with all the smoke and fire. That's one where I would have retired if I didn't get the copies of the tape from the dispatcher's office to make sure that I gave the orders that should have been given. Fortunately — I can't say fortunately, or I say fortunately maybe for my own emotional comfort — I did give the right orders, but they weren't followed the way I hoped they'd be.

I told a company to go in through the front and search. "Ladder and search the front of the building," I shouted to them. They said the message was received and they were en route. At any rate, you've got to remember, there are eight million other things going on, with the terrible noise from the pumpers and the hoses and everybody yelling, and we had a heavy fire condition on the first floor that had already taken control of the stairway, so an interior search was impossible, and we could hardly see the front of the building.

Anyway, they said, "Message received," and then the next thing I knew, they were on the roof. They went to the roof to ventilate, and they never really did the search. I thought they understood what I told them to do. Then afterwards, when I asked them about it, they said that ventilating the roof was what they thought I wanted.

So I blame myself. Number one, I would have retired if I hadn't found the tape where I told them to do that, to search the front, but maybe I should have retired then and there, because I didn't stay in and watch and make sure that they did do it. That's just a rationalization and an excuse. I feel responsible for that person. It's the only person in my twenty-six plus years where, number one, we had voice contact with somebody and couldn't save them and, number two, no matter how you cut it, I am still responsible, because I was the officer in charge at the scene.

She was saying, "God help me. Please help me." I remember it all as if it was yesterday. I mean, I don't still hear her voice in the night calling to me and all that kind of stuff, but I certainly remember it. I remember her, and I also remember she was pregnant — so it was two people I lost.

I've been at fires with local deaths, unfortunately many of them, but never one like that. And I still feel to this day that we should have saved her. I've had lots of situations where we heard people screaming and we've gotten to them, but never one like that. She wasn't even that far away. She was jammed up against the window. We found her body pressed there under the windowsill, right in the front of the house. But we couldn't see her. There was too much smoke, and I remember screaming, "Where are you? Where are you?" This fire up in the Burgh with these kids will probably be like this, like mine, for Eric McMahon, with him getting so close to finding one or two of those kids. He'll probably think of it every day, right up to the day he retires, and after that, too.

Another thing about that night on First Street. I was extremely hoarse, much more so than usual, from the radiation treatments for my cancer. I'm still hoarse from those radiation treatments. I always had a gravelly voice, but when I had radiation I couldn't talk at all for a month to five weeks. So I'm sure that pregnant woman didn't hear me screaming back to her. It would have been hard to hear it anyway over all the noise, and whatever was happening inside with the fire. And I thought she was on the second floor. I kept yelling to a window I could see on the second floor. As it turned out, she was actually on the third floor, which was even more tragic, because we had more time to reach her up there. There was less heat there on the third floor, but once again we never got to search the front of the building, because of that communication problem, so we didn't get to her until it was too late. I wish I didn't have that one to remember.

7

The floggings will continue until morale improves.

— Note taped to Medic 2's sun visor

7:58 a.m.

It's the last Friday in February, it's very cold, and everything feels a little out of joint already. Through the line of scratched garage-door windows at Central Station and against a sky the color of curing concrete, you can barely make out that it's spitting snow. Carl Campbell and Mike Murnane, the last two members of the 4th Platoon still here at Central Station at the end of their shift, hold the side door open as they chat with Matt Magill in the watch area. Matt was on the 4th before he bid over to the 1st to be captain on the Rescue Squad last year.

When Carl opens the outer door, a frigid gust swirls past him and spills a half-filled cup of coffee onto the watch table. Mike laughs and follows Carl out. "Good luck," he calls over his shoulder to Matt and they both laugh.

A morning radio jock on the oldies station is shouting over the opening bars of "Papa's Got a Brand New Bag," *Bundle up, snowmobilers. It hit 22 below in good old Grafton last night.*

"24 below," Tom Miter hurls back at the radio as he loads the defibrillator into one of Medic 2's side compartments and slams the door. Tom lives just past Grafton Lakes State Park, and he commutes the 15 or so miles to downtown Troy for every workday. He's working with Jeff Gordon on the Medic rig until 8:00 tonight, when Don Kimmey comes back in.

On the other side of the Rescue Squad truck, which is parked second-in-line behind Medic 2, Ric Moreno is yelling at Jeff Gordon.

"What did you say?"

"I said I know this isn't your headache," Jeff answers, walking to the Medic rig and throwing a purse-shaped, purple bag inside another of its side compartments.

"I don't what? What did you say? Wait a minute, what did you say? I didn't catch all that," Ric says with a mixture of mild animosity and weary sarcasm as he advances slowly toward Jeff. Jeff's been on the shift for almost two months now, and Ric still hasn't forgiven him for making Charley Willson bid onto the 3rd Platoon.

"I said that some people are hesitant to carry this bag, based on their feelings of what somebody else's perception might be and their own insecurities, and I said you don't hold any of those, do you? How do you feel about that, Ric?"

"Do I have to pay you, Jeff, if I answer that question, like 65 dollars or 90 dollars for a talk and lay down on a couch or something?" Ric's tone is quickly edging away from sarcasm and into pure animosity.

Jeff spots Chief Schultz coming in the front door. "No, you don't, Ric," he says, and walks over to intercept him before he can reach the spiral staircase in the back corner of the apparatus floor. Once the Chief makes it up those stairs, he'll disappear into his office for the day unless there's a major catastrophe.

Dave Stevens is kneeling in the watch area, going through his drug box checklist, checking epinephrine and atropine and magnesium sulfate and all the other drugs he hopes he won't have to inject into somebody today. He looks up as Jeff tries to collar the Chief.

"Here we go," Dave says, nodding toward Jeff and the Chief. "Watch this. I just got finished arguing with Schultzie last workday about a new turnout coat."

"I didn't sign anything," Jeff says, loud enough that the Chief himself looks around to see who can hear them arguing.

Dave is more concerned with his problem, though. "My turnout equipment weighs about 75 pounds, and that's dry," he says. "That's with your turnouts, your helmet, your gloves, Halligan bar, the flashlight, and with your Scott pack on. That's how much over your normal weight you weigh going into a fire. So if you've got a chance to cut fifteen pounds off of it, it's a big difference. The new coats have Gore-tex liners and they're shorter, that's why they weigh so much less.

"I asked Chief Schultz if I could get a new coat," Dave continues, "because mine's all ripped and the reflective stripes are falling off. Mine is worse than Eric McMahon's, and Eric's caught on fire up in Lansingburgh where those little kids died. In the ten years I've been on the job, this is the first coat I ever asked for. You've got to fight tooth and nail for everything you get around here. We get a 300 dollar a year clothing allowance, but it's impossible to support everything we have to buy and also afford turnout gear. The money goes quick when a pair of fire gloves costs 40 bucks."

Dave stands up now and checks to see if his hands are clean. He frowns, either in frustration or concentration as he rubs at a dark spot on his left palm.

"There are 13 or so old coats upstairs, and the Chief said I could go pick through them, but they're from guys who are deceased or have retired, and there are no records on them. You don't know what kinds of toxins they've been in or anything, all that they've been exposed to. Plus there's a pride kind of thing. A guy likes his own turnout gear. Personally, I believe if a man died on the job, I don't think anybody else should wear his coat. I think it's fitting to retire the coat, but they don't."

Apparently, Chief Schultz has had enough of Jeff's complaints for today, because he turns suddenly and starts down along the side of the Medic rig, holding his briefcase in front of him like a shield, but Jeff follows right behind him. Jeff is wearing his characteristic smirk, the one that always pisses Ric off so much.

"Well, thanks for your help, I really appreciate it, Chief," Jeff says to the Chief's back.

Now Schultz whips around abruptly and puts his briefcase down. "Look, Jeff, your shirt had blood on it from a shooting. You're required to turn it in for cleaning. The shirt came back. Somebody signed for the shirt. We don't have it."

Firefighters can't wear shirts that have blood spots on them. The Troy Fire Department Clothing Specifications stipulate that *Each garment shall be clean and free from any defects which may affect appearance or serviceability.*

"If somebody signed for it, then why can't I get it back," Jeff wants to know.

"I told you. We don't have the shirt. Somebody signed for it."

"Well, it wasn't me."

"If you have the receipt for the shirt, you can get it."

"The receipt was in your office," Jeff says.

"Whoever signed for the shirt must have had the receipt," the Chief answers.

Catch-22.

The Assistant Chief, Dick Thompson, is standing in the door of the Battalion Chief's office, listening and scowling and looking at me. He isn't happy that any civilian is allowed to be in the firehouse so much and is permitted to ride along to fires and emergency medical calls and use a tape recorder and take photographs, let alone be around to hear arguments like this one between the Chief and one of his men. Mike Harrison is on a Kelly day, so Chief Thompson is filling in for him as Battalion Chief and collecting a nice overtime check in the bargain. Given the way Dick and the 1st Platoon feel about each other, Dick working for 24 hours on this shift is, at best, an accident waiting to happen.

"I didn't want to turn it in in the first place," Jeff says. "So just give me the 24 dollars for my shirt and I'll buy another one. How about that?"

"Now if somebody takes your underwear on the job, am I responsible?" Schultz asks, trying to hide his mounting anger.

"I don't wear underwear when I'm working," Jeff answers, and at that Schultz turns and heads for the spiral stairs. Apart from Jeff being a wise guy, here is a second affront to the Chief, another violation of the Clothing Specifications, which state under the heading:

UNDERWEAR

#2. Shorts - white, Fruit of the Loom or equal.

Clearly, wearing no underwear can hardly be equal to a pair of Fruit of the Loom, briefs or boxers, take your pick.

"Jesus Christ," Ric snorts, and heads for the kitchen. This winter is starting to get on everyone's nerves.

9:23 a.m.

"She take any other pills?" Tom Miter asks impatiently.

A woman in her late 20's with short, red hair is splayed unconscious on the bed in a faded nightgown. Apparently, she took ten Motrins and three extra-strength Tylenol capsules and some other prescription drug and washed them all down with a can of Budweiser over an hour ago, but her twin sister doesn't tell us much more than that. She is staring at the empty pill container. "She get these pills yesterday. They was some pink ones, up to here," she says, pointing above the label.

Tom has no patience with suicide attempts. He climbs up onto the bed and bellows impatiently down into the woman's face. "Come on, wake up, can you hear me? Come on. Let's go."

"She don't wake up, no matter what I do," the sister says twice in between her sobs.

We're on the fifth floor of the Taylor Apartments, Building B, and even though it's about 90 degrees in this bedroom, the two young kids standing next to the sister and watching us from the doorway have parkas on, zipped to the top and tied at the neck, with the hoods up. Engine 5 answered this overdose call with Medic 2, so Terry Fox is the officer in charge, and he shoos the kids out of the doorway and into the living room.

Jeff Gordon lifts the woman's arm above her face and lets it drop, hard, right onto her nose.

"She's not faking it," he says.

"Nope, she's out," Tom agrees.

Except for the bed that she is sprawled on, there is nothing in the room but one painting hanging on the side wall. No dressers. No chairs. No rug to cover the scuffed, yellowing linoleum on the floor. Just a bed, an unconscious woman, and a painting. In the upper portion of this painting, a woman's somber face emerges out of the black background as her hand, near the bottom, lifts away a mask that resembles her. But the mask is smiling and has a small heart under its left eye. The woman's motionless face is turned toward the painting.

"Can you hear me?" Tom yells at her again.

"She won't answer you. I been picking her up and shaking her and everything. She don't move," her sister says quietly, as if she is reminding herself of it. Foxy is trying to get her to answer questions for his Pre-hospital Care Report, but she keeps hurrying away from him and sticking her hands under the mattress, even though Tom and Jeff are both now kneeling on it, assessing the woman's condition. A radio, with Smoky Robinson singing *My love is so fine, baby, My love is so fine*, plays somewhere, too loudly.

Foxy is getting agitated, and starts slapping his clipboard against his leg. A tall guy with a huge, light brown afro appears in the doorway now and watches the sister search.

Jeff is holding the woman's wrist. "Okay, she's got a radial pulse," he says. He feels movement behind him and turns: The sister is lifting a corner of the bed and feeling underneath again. "Can you give us all room to work here, please?" Jeff says to her. "If you could just stand back." So the sister moves to the other corner of the bed and lifts that.

"BP's okay, 120 over 78," Tom says.

"What's her breathing like?" Foxy asks. "What's she got for respiration?"

"Hang on, Foxy. Let me listen to her lungs. She's moving air, but not much," Tom answers.

Jeff has finished tying off a constricting band and he's slapping her left arm to raise the vein more. "Don't move your arm there, okay," he calls down at her, although the woman hasn't even twitched since we arrived. He pops the needle into her arm, but there's no flashback of blood. "Okay, negative IV times 1 here," he says. "Trying number 2."

"Lungs," Tom breaks in. "Moving some air all around. Minimal amount, but no rales or anything like that."

Rales are abnormal breath sounds that sound like fine crackling, as if you were rolling strands of hair between your fingers, and they indicate fluid deposits and minor obstructions in the smaller airways of the lungs.

Jeff's in with his second IV attempt. "Okay, I got it. Open it up wide," he tells Dave Paul, who is the new firefighter on Engine 5.

"You got a drip?" Foxy wants to know.

"Yeah. It's slow, but we got one," Jeff answers. "Let's give her a little cocktail. Narcan first, then the D 50."

Narcan, or Naloxone, is a drug which works pretty well to reverse narcotic overdoses, and sometimes it even pulls people out of alcohol-induced comas. The D 50, which is a solution of fifty percent dextrose in water, will provide a rapid infusion of glucose — the energy source that could make sure this woman's brain and other tissues don't suffer any further from possible hypoglycemia.

"Foxy, can you mark the time for this?" Tom asks.

"Yeah, it's 9:33. Yup, I've got it down," he answers, writing.

"Hey, she's coming around," Jeff says and looks over at Tom.

"Well, she's getting some fluids in her." Tom has a sardonic grin on his face, as if there was something else he'd rather say. He moves back a little on the bed and looks down at the woman. "Hey, how you doing there? What's your name?"

She moves her head a little, squinting her eyes against the light, and Tom shouts at her.

"Come on. Open your eyes. Tell us your name."

"Tina," she mumbles.

"Tina?" Tom heard the name, but he wants to make sure she has to think about her answers and use her fogged-up brain. "Tina, can you hear me? Is that your name? Tina? . . . Tina, open your eyes and look at me. Come on. There you go. Do you know where you are? Answer me, now. You've got to talk. Where are you? Do you know what day it is? Do you know what you took? What did you take? . . . Tina, you've got to answer me now. We're trying to help you. What did you take? . . . It was something, what? . . . There was somebody else here? What?"

Now the sister begins to talk excitedly in Spanish to Tina, and the tall guy with the afro hurries into the room and stands next to the bed. He reaches down for Tina, and Jeff blocks his arm and covers the IV in Tina's arm.

"Hey, buddy, how are you?" Jeff says to him. "Can you step into the other room, please? We're trying to give her some medication here."

When Tina recognizes the tall guy, she furrows her brow suddenly and she tries to get up, but she's too fuzzy from the drugs and beer.

"Whoa, hold on there, Tina," Jeff says.

Tina's sister is still searching under the mattress, jabbering at Tina, and Tom is getting fed up. "Okay, ma'am, what are you doing there? What are you looking for?"

"Money," she says, throwing a quick glance over at the guy with the afro. "For her money. She have her money under here, if he don't take it. One hundred thirty dollars."

"All right. Don't worry about it," Jeff says. "It's only money. We're more worried about your sister right now. She's alive, and she appears to not be getting any worse. Money is just, just an object. Don't worry about it."

Tina is starting to swing her right arm around to get at her IV, trying to rip it out, trying to struggle up and get off the bed, and the tall guy is pointing down at her, talking softly to her in Spanish, using words like *corazon* and *amor*.

"I get you," Tina is saying. "I get you, bastard."

"Did he take her money?" Foxy wants to know.

"Sure, he take her money, one hundred thirty dollars," Tina's sister shoots back, "and he give her what she no want."

"Don't you touch me," Tina is sputtering now, and Jeff is fighting to keep her IV intact. "You kill me, you son of a bitch, I got four kids, you got AIDS you fucking pig and you give me that, you wait, you fucker, I get you," Tina is yelling at the tall guy, not seeming fuzzy at all now, and he is backing out of the room, looking at Tom and then Jeff as he goes.

"Anybody got blood on their gloves," Jeff shouts. "Check for open cuts. Make sure you're careful. Pull them off and get rid of them when we're done with this."

"Let's get her packaged up and out of here," Tom says. "Tina, we're going up to the hospital now," he tells her, but she's still screaming and swearing at the tall guy, who is inching down the far wall in the hallway, staring back at all of us.

Tina's sister is shouting at him, too. "Where you put her money, filthy bastard? You know it's no your money."

"I get you, son of a bitch, you screwed me," Tina is sobbing. "I don't ask for no AIDS from you, I get you bad for this."

"Jesus, it's heartbreak hotel in here," Foxy says.

11:15 a.m.

The Rescue Squad takes a left off of Congress Street onto 1st Avenue, its Federal siren blaring as it heads toward a fire call at Fane Asphalt Company.

Ric Moreno and Dave Stevens are pulling on their turnout gear in the back when the dispatcher's voice comes over the radio.

ENGINE 3 AND MEDIC 2, TROY TOWERS AT FEDERAL AND FIFTH, BUILDING B, APARTMENT . . . FOR A WOMAN . . .

"What apartment number was that?" Ric yells up to Matt Magill, who is sitting in the front closest to the radio.

"I couldn't hear it all. Something 07," Matt shouts back.

Dave begins to laugh. "Pandemonium in the streets," he says.

"Did you hear the apartment number?" Ric shouts to Dave.

"We're not going to it, so I wouldn't worry about it," he answers.

"My mother's apartment is 607, and they said something 07."

The dispatcher repeats the call, and Matt turns up the radio.

THAT'S TROY TOWERS APARTMENTS, BUILDING B AS IN BRAVO, APARTMENT 407, ELEVEN HUNDRED SEVENTEEN HOURS.

Ric looks relieved. "Oh, 407," he says.

"What's your mom in?" Dave asks, looking repentant.

"She's in 607."

"Sorry, Ric. I didn't even know where it was. If it was 607, we'd be doing a drop-off. A fly-by. How's she like it down there?"

"She loves it," Ric says.

The dispatcher announces that the fire at Fane Asphalt is a Signal 20 — a false alarm — and Ric and Dave take off their turnout coats. The siren winds down, and I ask Ric what the call was.

"Something about a woman falling out of her bed, I guess. That wouldn't be my mother, anyway. My mother was out of bed a long time ago. She's up pretty early," he answers. "I worry about her a lot more now since my dad died."

Ric stares out the window at the buildings on 1st Street as we roll by them, but he keeps talking.

"My father had a heart attack when we were all on vacation in Maine. Him and I were having a catch, playing ball. It was quick and sudden. He died with a baseball glove in his hand. He never went *anywhere* without his glove and a hardball stuck in it. He was a real good baseball player.

"It was right after dinner. He said, 'Come on, let's go out and have a catch.' We opened the trunk, we got our gloves, we played for about 15 minutes, I threw him the ball, he caught the ball and wham, down he went, dropped just like that, dropped right in front of me. We were in Wells, Maine, and it was a 15-minute ride to the hospital. We did CPR for 20 minutes.

"This was in '82. We waited for the ambulance for about, I'd say, 10 or 12 minutes. They weren't that far away, and I think, during the summer, they have paid — they're like Green Island is here — they have a couple of paid men. So I did CPR with the guy in the back the whole way. The hospital was in York. He vomited, you know, the whole nine yards, right there in front of us. We had just finished eating dinner a half an hour before. Luckily, I had a bystander who came over, who said she was a nurse, and she helped do the compressions. For the vomit, I ripped my shirt off to clean it up. That's what I did. I took my T-shirt off and I wiped out his mouth, you know.

"Sometimes in the hospital now when we're bringing a guy with a heart attack in and a family member is there, waiting, I'll remember myself sitting there in the ER without my T-shirt on, and my swim trunks on, and them bringing me into my father, you know.

"Afterwards, I got to ride back in the ambulance, back to where we were staying. My mother was there, oh, Jesus. But at least my dad got his last request. He was with his family. He was in Maine for the first time. He loved it up there. My mother said the whole ride up he went over Rt. 2, over the Mohawk Trail. You know, he remembers, he used to, when we were little, we used to go take rides out that way, up over the mountain there. My mother said the whole way up, he just talked about how nice the ride was and all that. He was real peaceful, in a real good mood. I had been there in Maine for a week. They were coming to take our place for another week, but then we all had to leave that next morning.

"I came back and I was so busy with work here, you know. A therapist told me that I didn't have a chance to ever really get through the grieving process. I'll bet you it was years, years, before I actually let it settle. It was a long time before I could smile about it, the thought of him, instead of feeling sad."

Ric is staring out the side window as Kennedy Towers, a low-income high-rise for seniors whizzes by, and then at the vacant, snow-covered lots on Sixth Avenue that used to be three-story brick or frame houses with families before the fires caved them in and took them off the tax rolls, and now we're turning right onto Hoosick Street to shop for lunch.

"My father and I worked together. He was a plumber, so we, we worked together. We worked together every single day, and he was grumpy a lot of the time. Guys used to love to take bets at construction jobs, when we showed up, as to how soon it would be until we had our first fight, me and my father. Usually it was him, throwing his tools down. 'Okay, that's it,' he'd yell. 'You know it fucking better. I've only been doing it for 40 years. You tell me how to do it.' Then he'd take off and make it back in time for lunch. Or I'd get pissed off and start yelling at him. 'Yeah, you never give me any goddamn respect. Jesus Christ, I ain't a kid anymore,' I'd holler at him, and then I'd take off. He was like, not only my father, you know, he was a real good friend. But I'm glad he went like that, playing baseball."

11:38 a.m.

At the Price Chopper Market in the Troy Plaza, two doors away from the liquor store where Mike Kelleher was stabbed almost to death a few months ago, the Squad is halfway through its shopping. Frank, as driver for the Squad and chief cook and bottle washer for the 1st Platoon at Central, is also in charge of food shopping. He walks with focused determination down the aisles, swinging his arms and swiveling his head from side to side as he abruptly grabs stuff off the shelves. Matt Magill dutifully pushes the cart behind him. Ric and Dave make wisecracks and yell at Frank when he picks up the wrong brands of bread or pasta, and then they keep changing the weights on the cold cut order at the deli counter to really piss Frank off.

Suddenly a boy about ten, without his winter coat on, runs in and shouts from the end of the baked goods aisle that some-one has collapsed in the Ames discount store, two doors away.

No big deal: Shopping gets interrupted all the time, and the market staff at Price Chopper knows to slide firefighters' shopping carts into a walk-in cooler until they come back from their calls.

A teenage girl who knows Matt grabs him as they all hurry into Ames and tells him it's Ward Reardon, but he doesn't believe her. Ward had been Matt's Battalion Chief on the 4th. He had undergone a triple bypass operation just last Tuesday, and Matt doubts he'd feel well enough to be out shopping today.

But it is Ward. He's slumped in a fetal position on the floor, his burly 6 feet 4 inches accordioned between the cash register counter and the arched, steel lane divider. His wife, Judy, is clutching his collar, holding his face above the linoleum that's cold and wet from shoppers' winter boots. Ward's face looks as ashen and speckled as the dropped register receipt curling up near his head. At first glance, Matt figures he's already gone.

Matt and Ric pull Ward out from the cramped space and carry him out into the main aisle so they can work on him. Dave gets the monitor hooked up and runs a tape. It shows a sinus rhythm, but that's the only hopeful sign. Electrically, his heart is still working, and he isn't clutching his chest or arm, but he's got every other sign of a heart attack: His color has drained out; his clothes are soaked with sweat; his chest swells and falls too fast, again and again, as he tries to take a deep breath. Matt doesn't care what the monitor says; he can tell something is wrong with Ward's heart, something mechanical — it isn't pumping right.

None of the Squad members talk much. They want to get Ward out of there. A cold discount store is the last place he should be in his condition. Besides being one of their own, Ward also needs equipment and expertise that pre-hospital emergency care can't deliver. So everyone is hurrying. The manager at Ames has already called for an ambulance and, luckily, there was one available nearby. It's idling now outside the automatic doors, and the ambo guys are wheeling in their stretcher. Frank quickly slips an oxygen mask on Ward as Dave sets up an IV line for drugs en route to Albany Medical Center.

In a blur of motion, they get Ward packaged and in the ambulance. Matt is Ward's good friend, and he opts to accompany Dave Stevens on this ride. He helps Judy up into the back next to Ward, climbs in, and slams the side door closed.

12:57 p.m.

"What? How do you want it?" Frank asks.

Everybody is starving, and they're bitching at Frank. Because of the call with Ward, Frank and Ric finished the shopping on their own, and lunch is later than usual. Frank planned the quick but quintessential firehouse lunch — hot dogs and beans— and they're almost ready. But almost isn't good enough for Don Kimmey, who isn't even on duty yet. He's just between errands, stopping at Central Station to check on the menu, even though he won't be back in until 8:00, and he's already started complaining about the chicken and vegetable dish that Frank has planned for tonight's dinner.

"I don't want it. Period. It's like last week with the pasta. You said, 'Fuck Donny, he didn't like it the last time so I'll make it again.'"

"Did you have it the last time?" Frank asks.

"No, but it's just like with the Pasta Fagioli."

"Well, then," Frank says, justified. "Number 1, you weren't here to confer with and, number 2, you didn't have any ideas."

"That's fine. I like it all. But I don't like it mixed," Donny spits back, taking his characteristic Rottweiler stance.

"So I'll keep it separate then. I was just trying to explain to you that even if it was mixed in, you could just go and put the red sauce on it."

"I don't want the red sauce on the chicken and the vegetables. I like the chicken and the vegetables all cooked in the broth. Are you going to have extra chicken broth on the side?"

"I don't know. Why?" Frank moans.

"That's what I'm saying. Well, then, I won't have any broth to put on my pasta."

Frank is waving his arms in wide circles now. "But that's how it gets mixed in."

Donny is pointing at him, menacingly. "I saw the way you made fucking pasta the other day when it came out in clumps."

A small crowd is gathering — Ric, Jeff Gordon, Tom Miter, Gary Hanna — and Don is warming to his performance.

"Wait a minute. Wait a minute. That was not particularly my doing," Frank says, and starts to jerk one shoulder forward and twist his hand out. When Frank starts to twitch like that, Don knows he's got him.

"Did you see that pasta the other day?" Don says. "It looked like we were up at Frear Park golf course and they let me do the swinging. I had divets. It came out in clumps. Four pounds, we had four pounds the other day and we got four pounds again and we're going to cook it in the same bucket. That was the day they left the meat balls on the counter. I said, 'Why don't we let these meat balls soften up in the sauce', and they said, 'What are you, crazy?' 'They're a little hard', I said. 'Put them in the sauce, let them cook for an hour and a half, they'll soften up. How come they're not in the sauce?'"

Frank's shoulder and hand are firing erratically now. He's shouting over the rising laughter.

"I was not the cook. Gary was the cook. That's their standing orders with the meatballs, that they don't want the meatballs in the sauce until close to the end because it sucks up too much sauce. There wasn't enough sauce made for that volume of meatballs. That's not my way of doing it. I would have put them in."

"Yeah, so what happened with the pasta?" Don demands.

"What happened with the pasta? He got angel hair pasta, and you cannot cook angel hair pasta in the firehouse, unless you're only cooking one pound. There was so much in there and even in all that water it just does not cook well. It just gets too starchy and it clumps together. I didn't realize it was angel hair until I was dumping it in. We don't get angel hair pasta here. Whoever bought the pasta that day bought angel hair."

"That pasta was made for people with arthritis, where they couldn't twirl it on their fork." Don bends his arm into an arthritic crook and exaggerates a pathetic twirl. "You just stuck the fork in and got a big clump."

"All I know is Gary prepared a Captain Matt Magill meal — a totally fucked up meal. I was not the cook."

Perfect timing. Matt and Dave have just gotten back from Albany Med, and Matt has walked in just as his name is being taken in vain. Frank is spooning baked beans into a bowl and doesn't even notice.

"What do you want?" he continues. "I made Reubens for lunch the other day, and pork chops with Pepperidge Farm apple and raisin stuffing for dinner, and people hollered they were shitting their brains out for days."

"What's the matter with that?" Don calls back as he walks out of the kitchen.

"Nothing. It's good for them." Frank is talking to himself now, jabbing the hot dogs with a fork and slapping them inside the split hot dog rolls. "You can't please any of you."

* * *

Matt wants to talk about the call with Ward, and we go sit on the couches in the common room for some quiet.

"I always do my best on a call, but seeing the friendship I have with Ward, it really bothered me to have to treat him as a patient. At the time, you're into it, but when you step back and look at it afterwards, you get really upset.

"Like last Christmas, we had a call for a little girl with AIDS, and she was having difficulty breathing. It was up on Douw Street, a really run-down place in a crappy neighborhood. I wasn't feeling anything until I got in the house. It turned out to be this really well-kept place inside, and the little 4 year old girl was cute as anything, and the call bothered me the whole next day. It wasn't like there was much we could do for her anyway, except give her some oxygen and make her a little more comfortable, but there she was, scared to death and standing next to her Christmas tree, and that really bothered me, too. It just hit home. I've had to pick up kids who had died in fires, and they didn't bother me as much as this one did. I don't know why. Kids almost identical in age to my kids, kids I did mouth-to-mouth on to try and bring them back, so I don't get it."

Engine 5's crew is still out on a BLS call, but everybody else, including Chief Thompson, is bustling into the common room to eat now. Ric likes to watch *All My Children* during lunch, so he turns on the TV, loud enough to hear it over the lunchtime banter, and I follow Matt out onto the quieter apparatus floor.

"Sometimes I guess I'm able to close myself off," Matt continues, "and other times I can't. Maybe I went in expecting not to care too much, because of the bad neighborhood or the house, I don't know. I let some circumstances like poverty color the way I feel sometimes, I guess, not that I'm proud of it, but it just naturally happens on the job. I didn't think I'd care, but when I got there, I *did* care, and that hit me, that I did care, and I *should* care. None of that changes how I do the job, but we're just human, you know. We have ways to try to protect ourselves from what we see all the time. It's not good. It's not right. But we run into things so often that you do start to not care as much at times. So sometimes it takes something like that, that you don't expect, to get to you.

"Maybe that's what happened with Ward. I've heard other people say this, too. At different times in your career, you're more susceptible. Things that didn't used to bother you, all of a sudden, they do. Or, the other way, things that used to bother you a lot, you build up a brick wall, and now they don't. Maybe it's that I'm doing a lot more calls on the Rescue Squad now. We see a lot all the time. I don't, as I say, have problems on the call. It's after the call. But that's me. I have to learn to not take this stuff home with me. There's nothing you can do about it. You do your best on the call, you do all you can there on the scene, and then you go to the next call.

"But I was scared on this call with Ward today. When I initially saw him, I thought we were going to be doing CPR on him, and I didn't want to be doing CPR on a friend of mine. I don't want something bad to happen to that close a friend. Death's going to happen to us all, but if it's somebody I know, I want it happening in the next room so I don't have to be there."

3:18 p.m.

Imagine your name is James Hack. You're 54. A hospice patient. End-stage lung cancer. You're at home now. Home is 597 5th Avenue, in Lansingburgh. North Troy. A white, 2-story house, with stained aluminum siding. Double-hung windows, painted green, the paint peeling and hanging in limp strips. It's three hours after lunchtime, but you didn't eat anything. Your girlfriend is in the kitchen, making a sandwich for herself. You're lying on the couch in the living room, watching her. You try not to cough, to ruin her eating, but you can't stop. You turn and stare out the bay window. Even with the shades three-quarters down, the pale, winter light hurts your eyes. It's snowing again. Right now, you'd like to hear that snow falling, whatever that sound would be. It would be better than the sound of your coughing. What you can see past the snow are the obelisk monuments up on the hill in Oakwood Cemetery.

You don't want to see them, so you pretend you're standing across the street, outside Neudecker's Hunting & Shooting Supplies, beside their red SPECIAL sign that announces, WE BUY GUNS, in yellow-green reflective lettering, looking back at your own house. You can't see a man lying on a couch, coughing. You can't see a woman preparing food inside a kitchen. You can just see what's outside, and what the dirty windows reflect. Nothing but stained white siding, and green peelings on the windows, and faded window shades, and snow falling, and the wide, opaque sky behind all of it. Those green peelings give the only color.

But it's hard to forget yourself, and you wonder if your lungs look like that, peeling, hanging in strips, but they must be red, of course. You spit again, into the wadded kleenex. It's white and clean, but then the red appears on top, like snow when a cardinal lands. What you could really use right now is one breath. One good, deep breath. That would help a lot. But each time you try for air, your mind jumps in, remembering, showing you pictures of what it thinks is going on inside you, scaring you, chasing you down and making you choke. The air wants to push through, but it can't. You can feel it, catching there inside you. Right there. Under your sternum. Deep, beneath the chest skin you massage raw, where the ripping always happens. It feels as if some small animal has nested in there while you were sleeping. God damn it. It's all blocked up and full and moving around. That little bastard's stealing whatever air you send down, clawing, shredding your insides up to use for his bedding. Go on. Get him. Scrape at your chest. You'll find the little squatter. Blood backs up into your mouth now. Jesus, don't swallow it. It's too much for the kleenex. Grab the plastic thing. Spit. Get it out. Christ, come on. Get some more air down there. Hurry up. Spit it out. Breathe. Spit. A little more. Breathe. Breathe.

ENGINE 1 AND MEDIC 2, THE ADDRESS IS 597 5TH AVENUE. FIRST FLOOR, FOR AN UNCONSCIOUS PERSON. CROSS STREETS ARE 118TH AND 119TH. FIFTEEN HUNDRED TWENTY-ONE HOURS.

When Tom Miter and Jeff Gordon walk into James Hack's living room, they can barely see.

"Yeah, nice and bright. Is this all the light they got?" Jeff asks.

"This is it," Reinhart answers. Reinhart is a hoseman on Engine 1 in Lansingburgh, the station where Mike Kelleher works, and the closest station to James Hack's house.

"Down time?"

"Unknown," Reinhart answers.

A short woman walks out from the kitchen. "He has lung cancer," she says.

"How old is he, ma'am?" Jeff asks her.

"54," she answers, and looks away.

Reinhart and Bill McLaughlin, the captain on Engine 1, have pulled the patient off the couch and onto a braided, oval rug that covers most of the wooden floor, and Reinhart is doing CPR on him.

Jeff Gordon stares down at the scene and tries not to grimace. The guy's hands are covered with blood; his mouth and chest are soaked with it, and more is gurgling out with each chest compression; and next to the couch, there's a round, tupperware quart container that's at least half filled with blood, too. Above his mouth, though, the man's face and head are gunmetal grey. He only has a few ashen wisps of hair left over his ears. He looks 80 if he looks a day.

"54," Jeff repeats quietly. "Okay, ma'am, is this your father or your uncle or . . ."

At this, the woman bursts out crying. "He's my boyfriend. He's not my father. He's only 54 years old," she sobs.

"Oh, God, I'm sorry," Jeff says now. "I didn't look at you, or look at him enough to make that determination. This is, who now? He's a hospice patient?"

"Yes, he's in hospice. His name is James Hack."

"When was the last time he was seen?" Tom asks.

"He's been here, lying right here, on this couch. I've been here, and he was coughing and coughing, with the blood, and then I heard him stop, and I called you guys," she says.

"Tommy, we found a lot of blood around him and in that container that was sitting on his lap. It's all full of blood," Reinhart says.

Tom opens Hack's shirt and attaches the monitor leads to his red, scraped-up chest. "Okay, he was probably puking blood before he went down," Tom says.

"There's no lividity, Tommy, none at all," Reinhart says. "We're gonna start suctioning here."

"No, wait a minute," Tom says, reading the heart monitor. "Hold it. Stop CPR there for a second. It's asystole. No, wait a minute. It's an idioventricular rhythm, Jeff."

"Oh, yeah. Has he got a pulse?"

"I don't think so," Tom answers.

"No. He didn't have any pulse when we got here at all," Bill McLaughlin says.

"Go ahead, start to suction him now," Tom tells Reinhart.

"Is his airway clear?" Jeff asks.

"We cleaned it out the best we could. We've got an airway sort of, yeah, but there's a lot of junk in the way," Reinhart answers.

"All right, hang on," Jeff says, "I'll be there in a minute. Hyperventilate him a little bit."

"I have an oral airway into him now, but the problem is that it's really not clear, and his throat is very small," Reinhart is telling Jeff, who is leaning down to get a closer look at James Hack's mouth and saying, "Oh, yeah, why is that?" when suddenly blood explodes all over everybody, onto their clothes and in their faces, as if there was some Bouncing Betty mine loaded with human lung tissue hidden in the patient's throat and the suctioning triggered the initial firing mechanism.

Reinhart is blinking rapidly, wiping the blood off his face with his shirt sleeve. "Oh, he got me. He got me all right," he sputters.

"Jesus Christ," Jeff says, jumping back. "What the hell is this?"

"We got a problem here. There's a clot, a big one," Reinhart tells him.

"See if you can get it out before I try and tube him," Jeff says, knocking bloody hunks of lung tissue off his arms and shirt-front, and Reinhart goes back to suctioning.

"Check yourself there," Tom breaks in. "Watch your eyes."

Red is everywhere in here. The blood and the saturated tissue that keeps spraying out of the suction tube are red, of course, but the furnishings and the paintings and the rug and even James Hack's girlfriend's sweatshirt all suddenly pulse with the same vivid, demanding color. Who knows? Maybe the people who live here chose it to undercut the gloom of the place, or to remind them they were still alive. Maybe they just liked the color red.

Just past the patient's outstretched body, over Jeff's right shoulder, a garish painting of a clown on velvet is propped against the wall. The clown has a red collar, red lips, and clown hair the exact color of James's blood, but that isn't the most striking connection. Both James and the clown present the same gray-white faces, the same strangely fixed, noncommittal expressions.

The ceramic Seven Dwarf figurines that march across the top of the china closet, sporting their pointy red caps, seem to look down as they pass the gold, 18-inch Statue of Liberty that is surrounded by prescription bottles and laugh at all of us here on the rug trying to save their owner.

A loud crash from outside, and then another, rattle one of

the loose windows, and James's girlfriend hurries over and snaps up the shade to look. She turns and says to Tom, "There's a car accident at the corner." In the light now, you can see her eyes are swollen and red.

"We're busy. Call the cops," Tom says. "We can only do one call at a time." An attempted suicide this morning, and now a full arrest — today isn't getting any better for Tom.

The suction machine is humming now, making a steady whirr like a model airplane engine, vacuuming out James's mouth, but it's still packed solid. Jeff is trying to work an intubation tube down through the deep scarlet mass of blood and clots and tissue, and he finally gives up and sits back on his heels. "Okay, let's hook up the bag without the tube and check for breath sounds," he says. "I think this guy might be completely filled up, though."

Tom has been having his troubles locating a decent vein. "We've got no IV here, we'll have to go with an external, because there's just nothing available," he says.

Over Jeff's radio, we can hear the dispatcher asking Engine 4 what their location is, and then we hear his instructions. ATTENTION ALL UNITS. ENGINE 4, RESCUE SQUAD AND CAR 4 RESPONDING TO 118TH AND 5TH FOR AN AUTO ACCIDENT. EMS. INJURY REPORTED.

Jeff is saying, "I can't keep this bag on with the pressure. Somebody give me a roll of tape," and Reinhart fishes a roll of white adhesive tape out of his pants pocket.

Tom is staring at the monitor again. "Look at this rhythm here that comes and goes. Wait a minute on the CPR," he says. "No, it's got to be something electrical in the house that's doing this, because that's nothing I've ever seen before. Gotta be. Go ahead, start pumping again."

Jeff asks Tommy if he can listen to the lungs again with his stethoscope. Reinhart takes over pumping the bag to simulate breathing.

"Do it," Tom says. "Breathe . . . breathe . . . breathe. . . breathe. Well, I can hear sounds, but god, his stomach is rock hard. That's probably from you guys bagging without the tube. Something's going on in there, but his stomach's way too hard."

"I'd say he's got an aortic bleed. He bled out. He's filled right up. We need another adult bag valve mask, because this one is shot," Jeff says.

We can hear raised voices from outside, people crying and arguing, and now the sirens approaching from down 5th Avenue.

"I've got to figure out this rhythm," Tom is muttering, peering at the green monitor screen. "Whatever the interference is, that's asystole for sure."

All of a sudden, the girlfriend hands a piece of paper to Tom and says, "I don't know if you need this or what."

Tom looks at it and stands up fast. "Guys, we've got a DNR order here."

DNR is the acronym for Do Not Resuscitate, an order signed by a doctor which instructs any emergency care professional to avoid resuscitating a specific patient. That's also a paper she should have handed Tom ten minutes ago, before her boyfriend's lungs exploded onto everyone, because paramedics are legally obligated to resuscitate an unconscious patient when they're called.

"Okay, Tom, get on the radio, if they do, and call a doc," Jeff tells him. "2713424 is Samaritan's number. That's the way to go. You'll get the best service there."

"Keep working until I straighten this out," Tom says, and calls Samaritan Hospital on the unconscious man's phone.

"This is a mess," Jeff says. "This is a real mess. He bled out. He just burst. This guy burst." Jeff looks around, disoriented for a second. "Tommy, is that paperwork in order?" he calls out, but Tom is explaining to the doctor in the ER what is going on. The two voices, Jeff's and Tom's, run parallel as the suction machine whirrs on.

"He's got to be filled up with clots, because I'm getting so much resistance here."

"Well, Doc, let me explain what happened here. About ten minutes into this arrest, a woman came forward and produced a DNR, okay?"

"Keep that cover on that valve, or we're all gonna get more of a bath, and that's not what we want at this point."

"This DNR is signed by Dr. Robert Marshall, and our patient is a hospice patient. He's asystolic, completely filled up with blood and clots, and there's an unknown down time. What should we do here?"

"We're not getting any air exchange at all. I can barely squeeze this bag. He blew a gasket in a big way."

"We'll see you in a few minutes. Thanks, Doc."

Tom hangs up the phone and starts to re-pack his bag. "Okay, transport as is. CPR to continue, with the tube. No meds," he says, and Jeff immediately stands up, away from James Hack.

"Jesus, look at the blood. This is really bad. Let's clear away all the equipment and we'll make the move. I don't have any blood on my face, do I?" Jeff asks, and the Mohawk ambulance workers, who have been standing near the front door for the last couple of minutes, staring, transfixed by the scene, move in to transport the patient.

As we move out of James Hack's house toward our ambulance, we see three cars piled into each other in front of a small cafe where they're already hanging up paper Easter eggs that the neighborhood kids have decorated. It seems that a red Jeep Eagle Summit smashed into a white Dodge Spirit, and the white Dodge Spirit then crashed into a Ford Taurus with Texas license plates, although the issue is being hotly debated. Clear headlight glass, hunks of chrome-plated bumper, and bits of red taillight plastic glint like crumpled wrapping paper in the snow around all three vehicles.

A very excited young woman, 20 or so, is pointing and telling a cop what she saw. "She did it on purpose. Her, in the Jeep. I saw her. I was staring dead at her face. She got mad because the traffic was going so slow with the snow and all. And then I was standing there. She almost hit me. The old man. It's the old man. She hit him. I saw the whole thing. I was standing right where that lady is now, and I was waiting for the traffic to go this way. I seen her coming toward me and then she went over and hit that car and then that car hit that car and then she was like maybe about an inch from hitting me and my son. I'm shaking and I'm like in shock, I'm in shock. I had my baby in the carriage and the tire marks are right over there somewhere, like two inches from where I was standing. I saw her face and the expression. She was like really mad and so she stepped on her gas."

The last one in this line, driving the Taurus with the Texas plates, is a thin blonde woman with stringy hair. She is explaining to the police why she doesn't have a license and why her two and a half year old daughter wasn't in a car seat.

"Chelsea just won't sit in one, that's all," she says, sobbing.

Chelsea, in back, wears Barney pajamas underneath a floral multicolored parka, with a pair of shiny white snow boots. She's waving around a bag of Cheetos as her mother cries and talks to the police.

Frank Ryan is trying to determine if Chelsea is injured. "How you doin', Chelsea? Can you squeeze my finger? Huh? This one here. Can you squeeze this finger and not your mommy's necklace? This one here. This one here with your hand. Okay. Did you hurt your neck or anything? Does your neck hurt you?"

Ric Moreno has already strapped the impatient woman who was driving the Jeep to a long board and is loading her into a second ambulance.

The old man who owns the Dodge Spirit, the one who ended up in the middle, is standing alone, off to the left, smiling strangely. He's wearing a brown vinyl jacket with a fur collar, and a kleenex is hanging out of his coat pocket. His plaid cap is tilted over his left ear, and a hearing aid is hanging halfway out of it. He's mostly bald, with some white hair peeking out from the sides of the cap, and he's swiping at one of his bifocals with another kleenex. He's standing in front of James Hack's front steps, not turning to notice that James is leaving his house for the last time. The old man is watching the tow truck guy try to pry the crinkled fender away from his tire so he can tow the car, and he's breathing heavily, even though he's slight, and his breaths are turning into a string of small clouds that drift away from him and disappear against the stained aluminum siding.

6:40 p.m.

It's after dinner, and Dave Paul is quizzing Ric Moreno and Terry Fox about the pros and cons of being a paramedic. Dave is an FNG, a fuckin' new guy, but he isn't green. He's been around firefighting for a while. He was one of the eighteen new men the Troy Fire Department hired back in December, and he spent the last couple of months in training with the 4th Platoon. But he was also a firefighter in the Air Force Reserve with Tom Miter.

Dave lives up in the Burgh, not too far from Ric, and a few things are already clear: He knows a lot about Troy and its firefighting history; he's competent and serious; he's aggressive at fires; and he's competitive. In other words, he's a lot like Ric. He even has a blonde wife, like Ric. Except that he's younger and more ambitious, and Ric is continually chastising him, upbraiding him every chance he gets for acting like a know-it-all on the job.

"Try it. Why not?" Ric says. "Walking a tightrope is living. Everything else is just waiting. There used to be more of a lack of respect from the guys toward the paramedics."

"A definite animosity," Foxy chimes in.

Okay," Ric agrees. "Used to be. You were trained to do more shit and you were more vocal about it and guys didn't want to hear that. Paramedics were starting to complain about how much more they had to do, so they wanted more money, and that takes us back to the animosity from the other guys. They started to call paramedics 'the killer elite' and 'the golden sandal crew.'

"That and the fact the city wanted to give us more money, and the membership voted it down," Ric continues. "This was back around 1984, just a few years after the start of the program. Nobody was getting any more than regular firefighters back then.

"But it wasn't all bad. When we came on, we both started on this shift. Some of the old guys who were here, they were tremendous. Some of them would tell you straight out, 'We hate this shit. We don't want to do EMS, and we wish it would fucking go away. But since we got to do it, get your asses up here and show us what we have to do, because we want to know what to do so we don't look stupid. We're gonna do it right.' They were traditional firefighters, and they didn't believe EMS belonged in the fire service. They didn't want to handle blood and guts and peoples' vomit. They wanted to go out and fight a fire and cough for three hours after."

"They just wanted to put wet stuff on the red stuff, that's all," Foxy says.

"Finally, the city offered a lump sum to EMTs and paramedics and things changed. Now it's about 1800 more for paramedics and 600 more for EMTs, over base pay."

"For the new guys who are coming on, we were never exposed to the fire department without EMS," Dave says, "so we're going to be less combative than other guys."

"Yeah, you say that," Ric counters, "but you take a new guy and put him in a certain house with a certain couple of firefighters and I don't care what his attitude coming in is or what the fire service is like now, you stick him with a certain group and he'll start to think like them."

Foxy agrees. "A young guy comes on and thinks, 'Well, maybe I'd like to go to paramedic school,' but he's got to live in that house for 24 hours with those guys, and they'll warn him off it pretty fast."

"Even now, there's no real impetus or focus from the top two spots in the department on the absolute importance of EMS," Ric says. Mostly he's talking about Chief Thompson, who isn't shy about expressing his opinions. "I won't mention names, but there are people who even complain when there are two paramedics on the Rescue Squad."

"I'm asking this because I *am* thinking seriously about going to paramedic school," Dave says.

"Well, you'll get up more for calls than most people here," Ric says.

"I recognize that already, but that's no big deal and I'm ready to work. It's not the money, either. I wouldn't have taken this job for the money, because in three years here I'll be making 35,000 a year. In three years where I was working, I would have been making 55,000 a year. So I'm not here for the money. It's whether you want the job or not."

"So, okay, those are the negatives," Ric says, "but there's also the personal gratification."

"You have a sense of accomplishment," Foxy says. "When you go out and affect someone's life on a one to one basis, and you see the look on a kid's face when you finish your work and his dad's feeling better and he's able to talk, where you see you had a positive effect on a human life, nothing can ever pay you for that. When you walk back into your station house, you know you did the job. You did the right thing."

"How long have you been a paramedic?" Dave asks Ric.

"Let's see. It's my fifth re-cert, so that's a little over ten years, or eleven, maybe. A long time, yeah."

"Do you actually feel that the younger guys on the job should go to paramedic school, because you've done your time?"

"No, not because I've done my time," Ric answers. "They should go because it's a big part of the job, and they're crazy if they don't, from the standpoint of opportunity. The downside is, from a firefighting standpoint, you're getting to do less and less of that. You'll be tied up on ALS calls. You get to a fire and they're gonna get you out of there faster to handle some ALS call somewhere else. And paramedics go out the door more. There's no doubt, there's more stress involved, but you do go to every call. You go to all the fires. And you've got more freedom riding in Medic 2. You've got a radio, so you can listen to music. That's the big thing."

9:25 p.m.

The snow has finally stopped, but now the cold has set in again — 9 below zero and dropping fast. Nowhere near the record for the end of February in Troy, but it's still bone-chilling in the parking lot outside the emergency entrance at Samaritan Hospital.

Don Kimmey made it back in time to go on the call we just finished, what the firefighters term a bullshit call, and he's crouching next to Medic 2 now, doubled-over and howling, pretending to vomit, coughing in the cold and aping the various contortions of their last patient to needle Jeff Gordon.

"You didn't have to listen to her in close quarters all the way up, and you didn't have to smell her," Jeff says, blowing on his hands to warm them as he climbs into the truck. Don usually makes Jeff ride up in the ambulance with the patients, even though Jeff is the senior officer.

Mary, the patient they're talking about, had downed at least one full quart of Mr. Boston vodka before someone concerned about her called for us. We could hear Mary vomiting violently as we walked up the stairs to her apartment, and she was still heaving uncontrollably and thrashing around a half an hour later, when she arrived in the ambulance at Samaritan Hospital. Watching Don bend and bellow in imitation of her now, it's paradoxical to remember how professional and compassionate he was in her apartment.

"Okay, Mary, how much booze did you drink?" Don said. "There's a quart of vodka here. How much did you drink?"

Mary wouldn't answer.

"Did you take any pills, sweetheart?" Don asked her.

Mary wasn't answering.

"Mary, can you sit up for us, please?" Jeff broke in impatiently. "We want to try to get an idea of what's going on here."

Mary, who was lying on the floor propped against a green, corduroy couch and covering her head with a pillow, suddenly threw up on herself and on Don's shoes.

"Here, sit up. Let me get a cloth and wipe your face for you," Don said to her.

"Oh, Jesus," Jeff said. "Look, I know you're not feeling well, but we have to talk to you. Come on, now. Sit up."

Mary didn't move.

"What the hell's that?" Jeff wanted to know, pointing at a three-foot iguana slamming around in a chicken-wire cage probably four feet high but only a little longer than itself.

Tom Miter, who was back on Engine 5 but on his second attempted-suicide call of the day, just stared sullenly at the reptile in the cage. "Hey, Mary, you want us to leave?" Tom asked.

After a few seconds, Mary grunted a kind of approval.

"Okay, then, talk to us and we'll leave."

At that, Mary threw up again.

It continued like that for about fifteen minutes, until they packaged and transported her, and she cursed and grabbed stuff and vomited all the way up to Samaritan in the ambulance with Jeff and a female ambulance worker who was hitting on Jeff and then got sick herself when she smelled Mary's vomit. Pretty much a quintessential bullshit call.

"That's the first call where I actually saw people laughing," I mention to Don, and he says, "Aw, what are you going to do?"

"It's tough after a while," Jeff says. "It's just like the doctor was saying today with that lung cancer guy. You give all your compassion, but there comes a point where you just cut it off. You can't do it anymore."

"Yeah, it wears out," Don says.

11:40 p.m.

For the first time since Jeff Gordon argued with Chief Schultz about his blood-stained shirt, just before 8:00 this morning, all the men and vehicles are back in quarters. The call registry on the watch area desk shows there have been 22 calls in the city so far for this shift — that's about one and a half calls every hour since the 1st Platoon started the day at Troy's six fire stations. If we can assume it will slow down overnight, we may only have half that number — perhaps 7 more calls before 8:00 a.m. tomorrow. That would be 29 calls for the shift, and if we multiply that by 365 days, we get 10,585 calls for one year. That seems too high. Last year's total run chart said they only answered 8042 alarms, so this particular tour of duty must be an exceptionally busy one. 8042 divided by 365 comes out to 22 calls a day. That's more like it. 22 calls is the average. We've already done that number, and there are over eight hours left. Maybe that means we'll get to sleep straight through the night.

Foxy is sitting in the watch area, too, smoking his corncob pipe and drinking his customary strong, black coffee from his 2-quart thermos. Hearing about Jeff's fragrant ride up in the ambulance with Mary, one of Engine 5's well-known regulars, Foxy begins to bow and wave the white towel he usually wears around his neck at Jeff.

"You have helped another human being to find a pathway through her depression and misery. You are the light to which they have to go. You are the light," Foxy says.

All of a sudden, Frank Ryan, with his hair slick from the shower and wearing only a green bath towel, comes through the door from the bunkroom and starts across the apparatus floor. Frank is on watch tonight, so he's sleeping in the small room next to the watch desk.

"Take it all off," Jeff yells, and Frank whips off the towel and swings it in a circle around his head.

"Here we go. Look at this," Jeff hoots.

"Hey, nice skid mark," Tom Miter yells.

"He does a little parade every night when he comes out of there. He takes all his clothes off and walks over to the watch quarters, buck naked. He's fucking wild," Jeff says, laughing.

Dave Paul jumps in now. "He turned around one night and said to me, 'Hah, made you look,' and winked.

"I'm letting my body breathe," Frank calls out as he goes by. "It hasn't breathed all day."

"He's a pisser, he really is," Jeff says.

2:14 a.m.

If the sudden wail of the alarm doesn't wake you, or the shock of the lights slamming on, then the dispatcher's voice booming out of the station speakers like some extraterrestrial ultimatum will certainly do the trick.

ATTENTION ALL FIRE UNITS: ENGINE 3 AND MEDIC 2 ARE RESPONDING TO 10 TERRACE PLACE FOR A MAN DOWN. REPEAT: ENGINE 3, MEDIC 2 RESPONDING TO 10 TERRACE PLACE FOR AN

UNKNOWN UNCONSCIOUS. TIME IS ZERO 214. DIS-
PATCHER 9.

Your heart, resting at 56 beats per minute as you sleep, cranks up to probably double that number in the minute it takes you to pull on your pants, push into your shoes, and stumble through the bunkroom and out to the Medic rig. Whatever you were dreaming about feels like it's still going on, even after the cold outside smacks you again.

"I thought it was between Sheldon and that other one," Don says, leaning over the steering wheel and peering into the darkness as we drive up Pawling Avenue, heading east.

"Whitman Court," Jeff answers. "It's the one after Whitman. Should run off of Pawling. Sheldon will be at the lights, then Whitman, then Terrace Place. They're all cross streets here."

Pawling Avenue, and many of its cross streets, hold some of Troy's largest and most expensive houses, and this area is one of the few glittering reminders of Troy's golden era.

"I almost bought a house on Terrace Place last year," Jeff says. "Good thing I didn't. It would have been a financial disaster."

We pass Whitman Court and see the side of a 2-story, yellow-brick Federalist mansion at the corner of Terrace and Pawling. Black ground lights illuminate the whole place, and we can see the curved side portico, supported by white wood columns, repeated and enlarged in the front of the building as we come around the corner. Wide, marble steps lead up to a deep, marble railing and balustrade that ring the building. We can see now that the house and its parking lot take up almost half the dead-end street.

"Jesus, look at this," Don says. "This is where the rich people live."

"Yeah, this is an expensive street."

"What was the number, do you know?" Don asks.

"10," Jeff answers. "There's the engine down the street."

"Where the hell are they?" Don wants to know.

"What's that, that's 8," Jeff says, straining to read the house numbers. "There, 10, yeah, it's the gray one."

10 Terrace Place is modest by comparison with what we've just passed. It's a tall and brooding frame house with several steeply-pitched rooves, eerie rows of scalloped, grey wood shingles, and a narrow, unpretentious porch that looks almost like an afterthought. Behind it, silhouetted in the left bay of the lit-up garage, is a woman screaming.

"Medic 2 arriving," Jeff says quickly into the radio and jumps out.

It's so cold that the snow crunches like broken glass as we walk toward the garage.

Over here, a voice is saying. *I'm over here.*

"I know he's dead," the woman is howling. "Oh, God, I know he's dead." She's standing there in her nightdress, keening, swaying back and forth with her arms wrapped across her chest and her hands clutching her shoulders.

Engine 2's crew is already on the scene, standing near a body on the ground: A hoseman who is acting as captain tonight because no one else took the out-of-grade vacancy, and two FNGs.

The man on the ground is staring straight up at the stars.

That one is Sirius, he says. *Follow the three that nestle together, they're Orion's belt. Follow them to the right, to the bright one there, that's Sirius.*

"Oh, God, look at his eyes." The woman is sobbing now. "I don't believe it. I know he's dead."

The frozen man's eyes are wide open, glazed over and fixed in place. L.L. Bean boots, jeans, a red and grey plaid shirt, a lined Carhartt jacket, black leather gloves — all of it looks normal, as if he finished work and simply lay down for a minute to rest and appreciate the winter constellations before going in to bed.

Shussh, he says, *too loud. Listen to that music.*

Jeff goes in through the back door of the house to clear a spot to work, and Don stares down at the frozen man.

"What time was he due home?" Don asks.

"I don't know," she says. "He was out shoveling. At 10:30, I went upstairs, and I just woke up. It was 2:00 in the morning and I couldn't believe he wasn't in." She is crying again now. "I don't want to believe this."

It snowed all day, honey. I had to get the driveway clear before morning.

"Okay, we're set. Let's get him inside," Jeff is saying as he walks back from the house.

"He's been down for about two hours," the acting captain/hoseman suddenly volunteers, as if that will solve the whole issue.

"Let's go, inside, right now," Jeff says firmly, raising his voice a notch and looking incredulously at the hoseman. Don, who has already started inside with the monitor, is scowling.

The FNGs hurry to lift the frozen man, but he's too heavy.

"Two on each side if we have to," Jeff says, and then he and the hoseman bend to help.

"Oh, God," the woman keeps repeating. "I don't want him to be dead. Oh, God, oh," and her last oh rides up into a continuing, high-pitched moan.

Pull harder, my coat's stuck to the ground, the frozen man whispers to the firefighters.

When all four strain to lift, the man's body does come up and, perhaps because it doesn't bend, seems to float in the freezing darkness as they move him back inside. Even his arms stay locked in position at his sides, his gloved hands rigidly curled.

I bend over to pick the frozen man's glasses out of the snow. "Come on inside," I say to his wife. "It's too cold to be out here."

She takes a few steps, and then stoops to retrieve her husband's tan Yankees cap before she starts in.

In the kitchen, Jeff is talking into his portable radio. "302 to Fire Alarm."

GO AHEAD, THREE ZERO TWO.

"Police officer to this scene right away," Jeff says.

RECEIVED, TWO TWENTY-FOUR.

The frozen man's wife leans heavily onto her kitchen island for support. "Oh, Bobby, I don't know what to do," she says, staring down at her husband. "Bobby, please, don't do this."

It's cold. You need a robe, he says to her.

Suddenly, the dispatcher's voice breaks in. THREE ZERO TWO, POLICE ARE REQUESTING WHAT THE NATURE OF THE CALL IS.

"It's an unattended 12-30," Jeff says.

MESSAGE RECEIVED.

Two of Jeff's brothers are Troy cops, and 12-30 is the police code for a death. The frozen man's wife, still sobbing, walks out of the kitchen.

I never repainted that stained panel, he says, staring at the water-stain on the kitchen ceiling.

He's down to his undershirt now, and the wires attached to his chest curl across his blue-grey arm and lead to the green line that moves flat and straight across the dark monitor screen.

"Call up and see what they want to do," Don says to Jeff, and Jeff grabs the regional emergency medical radio.

"What, is he asystole still?" Jeff asks, and then speaks into the radio. "REMAC, Troy Fire, Med 4, how do you read this unit?"

LOUD AND CLEAR, REMAC responds.

I'm forgetting my name, the frozen man says. *Where am I now?*

"Paramedic 369, Troy Fire, we're going to Samaritan with a full cardiac arrest, 69 year old white male, over."

Don already has an IV line in for fluids and medications, and now he is trying to intubate the frozen man, trying to insert an endotracheal tube that will manage this patient's airway, but the mouth is so rigid he can't get the laryngoscope blade and light down into his throat.

"Hold his arm up straight there, will you?" Don asks. The fluid is barely moving in the line, and his arm is too cold to hold onto without a glove.

GO AHEAD 369, THIS IS MD 562.

"Be advised, MD 562, we're operating on a full cardiac arrest. Patient was found lying outside the house on the driveway, asystolic from the outset. He may have been there as long as two hours. Very difficult intubation being attempted at this time. Patient is very frozen and not very pliable. We're doing CPR. IV access is established, with a lactated ringer solution. What's your pleasure on medication therapy, over?"

369, JUST FOLLOW PROTOCOL AND TRANSPORT PATIENT WHEN YOU CAN, OVER.

"Okay, we'll follow the asystole protocol and update you as needed," Jeff finishes. "The fact that he's so cold might be in his favor," he says to Don. "When he starts to thaw, he's going to need a lot of help."

The fingers on the frozen man's left hand are stuck together in a rigid crescent, as if he's trying to begin one final word in some new sign language, to leave one last message.

*　*　*

An hour and a half later, in the nurses' lounge at Samaritan's Emergency Room, Don is checking through the drug box to see what cardiac drugs have to be replaced. Jeff steps into the room, leans back out to look around for a second, then turns to Don.

"You'll never believe this," he says.

"What now? The frozen guy woke up?" Don asks.

"Jesus, no. Not that," Jeff answers. "I just came past the nurses' desk, and this Robert's wife, the frozen guy's wife, is standing there talking to the admitting nurse, and she says, 'They're working on my husband in that room over there, and I need to know if it costs the same if the patient dies.'"

"Get out of here," Don says. "She didn't say that."

"I shit you not. She was saying it when I walked by her."

Jeff flops down in a plastic chair and starts to fill in the patient report.

"Well, you never know. He might surprise her and come out of it yet," Don says. "You have no idea what will happen. That's like with the kids, the one there in Chicago, he went down and forty five minutes to an hour he was submerged in the lake, and they brought him back, no brain damage no nothing, but that's a little kid. This guy's got cardiac problems. He was admitted here in December for atrial fib. He shouldn't have been out shoveling at ten-thirty at night in this weather."

"I mean, somebody spits at you tonight it'll freeze in the air," Jeff says. "We went straight through the protocol. We didn't do anything extraordinary, right?" Jeff wants to know.

"No. But we could have just tubed him and gotten out of there for the good we did. They've been working on him here for an hour. What's his temperature now?"

"He's officially still alive," Jeff says. "It's down to 81 degrees internal." Jeff is filling in the blanks on the form. "We were there a half hour, right?"

"That ain't bad," Don says, "but I mean did you put down that he was outside and had to be picked up and brought in from the cold?"

"Yeah, I've got, 'Patient moved inside immediately. CPR promptly initiated after clothing removed. Patient extremely stiff and cold. His face purple and reddish in color from the cold.'"

"Hang on for a sec. Did somebody say he didn't come home from work?" Don asks.

"No, he went outside, either to fuck around with the snow or to play with the car or something around 10:30. He didn't come back inside. I truly thought we were going to go up and find a young guy outside that had been drinking and had passed out behind the house. That's the way my mind was thinking. That's why I was surprised when I saw her standing out there. From the street, looking in, it looked like a young woman in her twenties, with blonde hair, standing back there, you know."

"You're nearsighted," Don says.

"And how come you disappeared?" Jeff asks.

"I went in to start to move the kitchen chairs. I wanted to see what kind of kitchen we were getting ourselves into there."

"I wondered where the hell you were. Oh, and when you came back out, did you believe that jerk said, 'Aw, he's been dead for a couple of hours,' right in front of the wife? I couldn't believe it. I go, 'We're bringing him in.'"

"I just assumed the body would be coming in behind me," Don says. "Can you believe that guy's in fucking charge on that call? We can't legally say, 'Uh, he's dead.'"

"One of the first things they tell you about hypothermia is that people aren't dead until they're warm and dead," Jeff says. "Nobody is cold and dead. It's like with a cold water drowning we may have: We work on somebody, because all the water around here is considered cold year round, and until you get them back to regular temperature, they're not dead."

"The guy sure as hell looked dead, but who knows what could happen," Don says.

Jeff agrees. "Yeah, he was too cold to be dead."

7:07 a.m.

Chief Thompson isn't happy. His constant friction with Jeff and Ric and a few other members of the 1st Platoon made this tour as their acting Battalion Chief even harder than usual, and at about 5 a.m. he had to chew out Jeff Gordon for calling the cops to that house where the rich guy was frozen on the ground.

Gordon just isn't a team player. He doesn't respect the chain of command. It doesn't matter if a hoseman was acting as a captain. On that particular call, he outranks a paramedic lieutenant and becomes the incident commander on site. The hoseman's in charge there. It's as simple as that. It also doesn't matter how high an opinion Gordon holds of himself, and that seems to be pretty goddamned high. He wasn't the one authorized to call the cops up there. End of story.

And now this. In the 24th hour of their busiest day so far this year, the 1st finally gets a working fire, one that's blowing out the windows when they pull up. It's in a 2-story, brick triplex that's half a block from the Hudson River and just around the corner from Bella Napoli bakery. There are nine windows across the front of its second floor, and four on the left side are spouting flames. Thick smoke is already tumbling out of the eaves under the roof on the right side, so the fire is communicating somehow — common roof, common ceilings, the walls, who the hell knows? Telephone and power lines are strung low across the front of the building, so laddering the face looks too dangerous. It's fifteen below zero, and the wind shooting off the frozen river isn't helping any. The cops are here, and some concerned citizens of Troy munching Bella Napoli doughnuts can watch every move their fire department makes. Oh, yeah, the hydrants are frozen, too.

Terry Fox is the captain on Engine 5, and Engine 5 is the second due engine. His job is to get water to Engine 4, the first due engine. Engine 4 is parked right in front of the building, and its driver is feeding water from its 500-gallon tank to the hosemen inside the building. With judicious use of their 2 and 1/2 inch lines, those hosemen in there will probably get 5 to 7 minutes of water out of Engine 4's water tank, and then they'll need back-up water from the hydrants. Usually, that isn't a problem, but this morning Engine 5's crew can't even get the hydrant cap unscrewed.

Several minutes into the attack, Chief Thompson has arrived to find hose lays of 5 inch, yellow LDH (large diameter hose) going in three different directions, and all of it is flat. The ladder truck had to park in the alley because they couldn't ladder the face of the building, and that's where Engine 5 is, hemmed in. He can see Captain Fox hammering away now with the blunt end of a flathead axe, trying to crack the cap and coax water out of the frozen hydrant.

Everything is happening at once, of course — it's a fire ground. The radio is crackling with messages. Guys are popping out of trucks and doors and windows like jack rabbits. Even the cops, who usually just keep citizens back from the fire building, are dragging hose lines this morning.

Jack Sheehan, another fire chief, is telling Dick this is a crack house, that it's been under surveillance for a while, that the guys better stay on their feet inside. Crawling around on hands and knees through rooms that may have discarded hypodermic needles on the floor would be a bad idea, he tells Dick.

The heat and smoke from the fire is churning into the street, punctuated by waves of deflected spray and steam that rain down from the shattered windows. Firefighters rush in and out, dragging hose lines, changing air tanks, shouting, punching out window panes with their Halligan bars, and coughing.

Engine 4, pumping right in front of the building, sounds like a prop plane that's too close, racing its engines up and down. Dick, pointing madly, has to scream "Use the gun," four times before Dale, the gun operator on the truck, hears him and trains it on the west end's flaming cornice.

One of the LDH lines is finally charged, and they're getting enough water now, but for Dick this fire should have been out five minutes ago, especially with these people watching. Don't they see the reporters hanging around, digging up the dirt? They torpedoed the police department last month for overtime costs, and now they're working on the fire department. They're gonna name names in the paper. You wait and see. The men on the roof are venting the wrong spot, drawing the fire. Tom Miter shouldn't be on a line, for Christ's sake. He should be back with the crew on Engine 5, getting water out of that damn hydrant. What the hell is Foxy doing, splitting up his team like that? The Troy Fire Department has had standard operating procedures for years, SOPs, that Dick helped to write. These guys know what their jobs are. First due engine needs a continuous supply of water. What part of "continuous supply" does Engine 5 not understand? Hey, look out over there. The fire buffs are pushing in too close to the building along 5th Avenue. 3-alarm fire, the stem-whackers all turn out, even if it is 15 below this morning. Dick wants those people held back away from there. What if that wall comes down? Jesus. Wait until he gets the 1st Platoon back to the station. He's been telling them, week after week. They can make all the fun they want — either you're ready or you're not. No excuses this time. What kind of Mickey Mouse crap is this, anyway?

Dick Thompson

Chief of Operations — that's my job. I'm responsible for the fire ground. I'm responsible for every fire. Absolutely. For every firefighter that's in trouble. I feel it is my responsibility to see that these guys get to and from a fire without getting hurt. Seriously hurt. I feel that if somebody is getting seriously hurt, there's something wrong. My goal is to make sure nobody gets seriously hurt, but that's not reality. It's a dangerous occupation. I understand that, but the Labor Department doesn't understand that. I'm convinced that firefighting is a dangerous occupation. We are going to lose firefighters. Firefighters are going to be injured and going to be killed, doing their job, and doing it safely. But every time a firefighter gets killed, they blame everybody. If you look at the last ten, fifteen, twenty-five times firefighters were killed in New York State, they sued the Chiefs. They accused them of not caring about people. In other words, everything was done wrong. Always. And that can't be, in the last 25 times firefighters were killed, in an occupation as dangerous as ours, you can't convince me that every time it was somebody's fault.

I think of the Syracuse fire, four firefighters, seasoned firefighters were trapped in a building and they died. And all we saw in all the journals and everything was what everybody did wrong. I don't think

anybody did anything wrong. They were four aggressive firefighters,
that were dedicated, and may have overextended themselves a little
bit, I don't know, but they were trying to do a good job, and they were
trying to extinguish a fire. That's dangerous. Every once in a while,
something goes wrong and people are lost. It doesn't mean that any-
body did anything wrong. Those firefighters were probably doing
something right. They were doing what they had to do. The fire we
had on 11th Street, the similarities were unbelievable. Student hous-
ing, four firefighters trapped, Rescue Squad, same thing, same com-
pany, same set-up, they were on the third floor, our people were on the
second floor. They became trapped. I like to think we had some of the
newer technology advancements in place. We had better communica-
tions, I think. Our people had radios. We had Standard Operating
Procedures. We knew exactly who was where. I think we had a better
chance of getting them out, is what I'm trying to say. But most of the
reason they got out is luck, I think. I think that they got out was damn
lucky. I think they got themselves out, but they got themselves out
because they were lucky. They finally found a window. They were just
disoriented and lost. People don't believe you can get lost in a closet, but
you can. You start going the wrong way, you panic, you turn around
and go the other way, you panic again, pretty soon you're going in cir-
cles. Those people were in a dangerous situation. They got out. They
were lucky. The gases were rich enough in there that they were ignit-
ing when they exited the window. The situation was bad. The heat
and smoke was so intense that the engine company couldn't advance. I
don't think the Squad got out of there any too soon. It's amazing to me
that the four of them survived. I've been going to fires for thirty years,
and if you had asked me at the time, were those people going to sur-
vive, I would have said they cannot survive in that situation.

But yes I feel extremely responsible. That's why I make sure I'm
there and I'm reinforcing the safety procedures. I'm reinforcing the
SOPs. I'm quick enough, I hope, to recognize when we have problems
and get additional help there. I'm not bashful. I don't worry about

what other people are going to think. If I need 500 firemen, I'll call 500 firemen. If I need super-firemen from New York City, I'll call them. If they think I over-react or under-react, I'm not worried about it. I've been in the business a pretty long time and I've got a pretty good handle on it. I'm confident.

Here's my concern. I think the City of Troy is like a keg of dynamite. The fire potential in this city is tremendous. I know that. I'm not guessing. It's tremendous. Because of the type of construction, and the people living in this city. The buildings aren't just old. They're multiple dwellings, with people living over people living over people. That's dangerous. They're old buildings. They don't have stairwells that are fire-rated. If a fire starts on the first floor of a three-story brick down in South Troy, we're going to lose fifteen or twenty people. I just told the City Council last November not to let their guard down, that we're going to have multiple fatal fires, we're going to lose families, and they looked at me like I was nuts. Three months later, we lose five people in Lansingburgh on the second floor, just what I warned them about. We have hundreds of three-story brick buildings, thousands probably, families living over families living over families. Open stairwells. We're going to have large loss of life unless we're on the scene in a minute or two. We have to be on the scene with at least enough people to get a line in place to keep that fire from getting up the stairwell. If we're not on the scene within two minutes or three minutes with at least three or four people to get that line in place, it's going to be disastrous.

When I come on the job thirty years ago, almost every home in South Troy was owner-occupied. What that meant was that the guy on the first floor cared about the second and third floor, okay? What that meant is that everything was like it should be. Nothing's owner-occupied in this city anymore. Everything's cut up into flats, cut up into apartments. Buildings that used to house three families now are cut up into six apartments and might have twelve families in them. We've got multiple families living in apartments. There's no question about it: When a building is owner-occupied, there's less chance of a fire. We have a high percentage of senior citizens in this city. People move out of town, they buy the single-family homes, the kids grow up, they get older, they don't want to take care of the house, they move back into the city. Those people need an extra level of care, all right? We have property that's close to property. We have the chance of a fire going down the street and taking out a block. That's devastating to people — they lose their homes, lose their apartments, lose their belongings. It's not right to let it happen.

My job is operations, which is the emergency end of the job. I coordinate the four platoons, make sure they're following the SOPs — the Standard Operating Procedures that we put in place to make sure the job is done as efficiently as it can be done. When I took over, we were running at least four, if not eight different fire departments. Something would happen and if you called it in on a Monday, one thing would happen. If you called it in on a Tuesday, another thing would happen. It wasn't just the written SOPs, but it was somebody out there making sure that they're being followed. Because they just had this idea that we'll all do our own little thing. If you went to a dentist and you needed to get a filling, and you were down on vacation in Florida, you'd expect a dentist down in Florida to fill your tooth the same way the dentist in Troy would fill your tooth. You don't expect somebody down there to say, "Oh, no, down here we use sand." Now, wait a minute, something's wrong here.

So what I try to do is to make sure that everybody's performing the same way, following the accepted standards that are out there. We didn't make our SOPs up. We didn't invent the wheel. We took the standard, accepted procedures that are being used throughout the country, especially in the Northeast, and just, you know, reinforced it and put it out there and told our people what was expected of them and this was the way we wanted to handle the job. Most of it I put together, but I didn't invent nothing. I used stuff that was being used for fifty years. Nothing new, maybe, but I coordinated it and showed everybody what we should be doing, and made sure everybody was doing it. So I'm responsible for emergency operations.

I guess you could say I'm responsible for the pragmatic running of the department.

I'd like to believe that 95% of our people are as dedicated as I would want them to be. Realistically, maybe it's only 70%, but for those 70%, I would want to make sure that people realized that the level of dedication for the majority of people in our department is extremely high. I don't know, but I don't think you get that in most occupations.

We're here to fight fires. Most of the people saying that you don't do that many fire calls don't know what they're talking about. We're doing more fire calls now than we ever did. We're handling them better. We're handling them quicker. We're containing them. We're like an army. You have to have an army. You need it for defense. They're not going to have an army around to once in a great while when there's a flood help out with sandbags. But if you have an army, and you got a flood and you need somebody for sandbags, well, go ahead and use them. They're being utilized.

Cutting back. Cutting back. They want to cut back all the time. If you tell them that we're not having fires, then obviously what are they going to say? "We don't need as many men." And if we don't need as many men, then we don't have the men to send on the EMS calls, which are life-threatening at times. Like I said, 90% of the time they're just basic life support calls, but every day there's one serious call, and if we don't have somebody to cover that call, somebody could die. So that's the importance of having these people. Do we need them for fires? Absolutely. The City Council here, if they start to get their information from people who really don't understand the problem, rather than taking it from the people who do it for a living and have the background in it, you start to run into the problems.

There's no question, when people are in need of help, we're the only service that shows up, and normally it doesn't cost them a dime. I don't even think money is the issue. When people are in trouble, they want help and they want it then. And traditionally, anyplace in this country, when you need help and you need it quick, you call the fire department and they'll be there in 3 to 5 minutes. In the City of Troy, I'd say we'll be there in 3 minutes. It doesn't matter if it's winter. You see, there was a show on TV last night, which I got a kick out of. It was about emergency rooms, and I've seen this stuff going on lately. I think it's a fad, but I'm not familiar with the big city. They were showing how different hospitals when they get too many patients, they close the emergency room and turn people away. Now what if the fire department said, "No, we've got just too many calls. We're not going to take it."

I don't care if we get 10 calls, or 50 calls, or 100 calls, we're set up to answer every call. There's no such thing as turning a call down. You call the police department, they'll tell you they're backlogged. They'll tell you they can't get a car to you for a couple of hours. You call the ambulance — before we got in the business and the private ambulance services realized we were going to be a threat to them — you would call an ambulance and wait a half hour, forty-five minutes, an hour. No other organization will provide a three-minute service like we do in an emergency. And an emergency is in the eyes of the beholder. If your little girl is hit by a car, you don't care what else in this world is going on. You want somebody there, and you want them there then, and we're the only service that does that.

8

The logic of suicide is different. It is like the unanswerable logic of a nightmare, or like the science-fiction fantasy of being projected suddenly into another dimension: everything makes sense and follows its own strict rules; yet, at the same time, everything is also different, perverted, upside down . . . In nineteenth-century Vienna, a man of seventy drove seven three-inch nails into the top of his head with a heavy blacksmith's hammer. For some reason he did not die immediately, so he changed his mind and walked to the hospital, streaming blood . . . There is also the case of a Polish girl, unhappily in love, who in five months swallowed four spoons, three knives, nineteen coins, twenty nails, seven window bolts, a brass cross, one hundred and one pins, a stone, three pieces of glass, and two beads from her rosary.

— Alfred Alvarez
The Savage God

"Right to life?" Don Kimmey asks.

"Oh, God, it was horrible," Jeff Gordon answers. "Right-to-lifers." He rests his forehead on the passenger window and stares at the dark houses flashing by.

"You need fucking help," Don says, and leans forward so he can see better.

It's raining like crazy, and Medic 2 is hydroplaning along 9th Street, tossing sheets of water over the discarded piles of junk that punctuate the narrow sidewalks. Our windshield wipers can't keep up, even set on high.

Thwap. Thwap. Thwap. Thwap. The wipers have established a sloshy rhythm section, and the staccato melody of our siren punches out into the blackness and echoes back to us off the dark, beat-up houses that sit so close to the street.

"'Off the porch,' I was yelling. Randall Terry and a bunch of right-to life, Operation Rescue people were on my porch, trying to save the babies inside my house. When I woke up, I was yelling, 'Off the porch.'"

"Most guys dream about banging women," Don says.

Don's remark doesn't register for a few seconds, and then Jeff sits up straight and looks over at him. "What'd you say? Most guys what?"

Don doesn't answer.

Jeff sinks down again and leans against the window. "I was sleeping like a dog," he says.

That provokes a yawn from Don. "Me, too," he says.

On Medic 2's radio, the fire dispatcher announces that Engine 4 is arriving at the scene. It's 3:32 a.m., the very heart of an insomniac's relentless night, and Don and Jeff have reached the wee hours of another shift long on calls and short on sleep. It's the morning after Easter Sunday, and we are screaming up along 9th Street toward 75 Middleburgh Street, which allegedly lies between 9th and 10th. A woman has apparently locked herself in her bathroom with a razor. The dispatcher tells us the police are already on the scene.

Thwap. Thwap. Thwap. Thwap.

We pass a burned-out storefront with white, melted

aluminum siding that must have buckled and peeled away during the blaze. The sheets of particle board that cover the empty doors and windows are alive with graffiti, spray-painted vertically:

LIL JUNE	SMOKE PT	CASH
SLIM	BLACK	MONEY
MO	HOT	BOYS ARMY

and under all those, the usual

FUCK YOU

over the graphic of a simple, smiling face with several lines of curly hair adorning each side.

This is one of the oldest sections of Troy. The workers who gave the world Arrow detachable collars and Lion Brand shirts a hundred years ago lived in these three-story brick row houses and raised their kids and tried to make it a decent neighborhood. But in the last ten years, gangbangers and dealers from downstate have turned many of the dingy apartments in this area into temporary business locations. They have what they consider safe houses in maybe five or six upstate cities — Newburgh, Poughkeepsie, Kingston, Hudson, Albany, Troy — all towns relatively close to the Thruway, where they can hightail it back to the more populous avenues of the Bronx or Brooklyn or Queens when it gets too hot for them upstate.

So on streets like 9th Street, it's always somebody's moving day. Soaked heaps of mattresses, paint cans, shipping crates, tires, couches, chairs, loose cushions with the stuffing leaking out, headboards, braided rugs, bent pipes, empty drawers, carpet remnants, skeletal Xmas trees, bent shopping carts, and toys — always the primary, plastic colors of broken toys — come to life for an instant in our headlights and just as quickly disappear.

Thwap. Thwap. Thwap. Thwap.

"This better be real or I'm going to kick some ass," Jeff blurts out.

Don is still confused. "Right-to-lifers were WHAT on your porch?"

"They were holding a rescue on my front porch, trying to save all the babies, and I'm screaming, 'Off the porch, off the porch.' Oh, God," Jeff says, and starts to laugh.

Don raises his eyebrows, but he keeps his eyes trained on the near-flooded street ahead. "This better not be an unfounded call," he says.

* * *

About eighteen hours ago, halfway through chowing down on Frank Ryan's famous mushroom and cheese holiday brunch omelets, nobody on the 1st Platoon at Central Station figured Chief Thompson would show up and bust their balls on Easter Sunday. They were too busy eating and making jokes about Don and Jeff's first call of the day (where a pregnant woman had gone into premature labor at 24 weeks) and about childbirth smells, to even think about Dick.

"Hey, remember the day we delivered the premature baby up on River Street," Don said, "and it stunk to high heaven?"

"Absolutely stunk. It was horrible," Jeff agreed. "That's the nasty baby smell I was talking about."

"The doctor asked us over the phone if she had an infection. You remember?" Don asked. "That's the one where Miter stood there and said, 'I'm just so glad you're here,' and I said, 'I would have been glad you were here, too, if you were kneeling in front of her, Tom.' Jesus, I got covered. This was like her fifth kid. Green and brown all over me. The doctor said she must have had some kind of infection when he saw her."

"Umm, muconium and eggs," Ric Moreno chimed in. "My favorite."

They needed some humor, even the weak kind like this. Chief Thompson had been riding the 1st Platoon at Central relentlessly for the last few weeks, yelling at Jeff for every minor infraction and ragging on Battalion Chief Mike Harrison at least once every shift. He even ordered the Rescue Squad crew to unpack all the equipment on their rig, scrub the tools and the truck and all the compartments clean, and then put the whole shebang back together. Picking on the Rescue Squad crew was unusual for Dick, because he had once been a captain on that rig and he was usually protective of the crews that were assigned to it. The Rescue Squad was Dick's baby, that's what everybody always said, anyway.

Plus, it was Easter. A day to celebrate. Most of the guys on the 1st were practicing Catholics. Only Terry Fox and Jeff Gordon weren't. So no more giving up the foods they really liked or attending mass every day during Lent. Frank's omelets tasted better than ever, and so did the sausage, the home fries, and the toast that accompanied them. The flood of holiday calls they knew would be streaming in, simply because most people were at home with their families, hadn't started yet. All the rigs were still parked on the apparatus floor, and eleven guys were eating and laughing and bitching about the local politics. Why should they be worried about Dick coming in on a holiday?

Forget the fact that Dick supposedly trolled for fires or rescue calls when he was off duty. Even if that was true, it was still understandable. In one sense, that kind of dedication could be seen as commendable. He was, after all, Car 2, second in command, and in charge of operations for the department. As the Assistant Chief, he was certainly performing his job when he showed up at all the significant fires. No problem there. Everyone agreed that the guy was an extremely knowledgeable, competent fireman. Always had been. And besides, it was Easter

Sunday morning, when his least favorite platoon was working. Come on. Even Dick gave himself a rest every once in a while.

After he finished his omelet, Dave Stevens began to piss and moan about having to work on a high holy day, and how he missed going to church with his kids. Then he got everybody complaining about George Pawlaczyk and *The Record*. George Pawlaczyk was one of *The Record's* investigative reporters. He had been researching overtime abuses by Troy's police and fire departments for months, skulking around and hurling combative questions at Chief Schultz and at Gary Favro, the president of the firefighter's union.

Ever since the paper published several front-page articles about the police a few weeks ago, naming names and amounts of overtime pay that each police officer had earned over and above his salary, the cops had been stewing. Rumor had it that one of them had tried to slow Pawlaczyk down, or pay him back, by faxing around his criminal record, but not much had come from that. And for several weeks now, the firefighters had been waiting for the other investigative shoe to drop.

"That guy George from *The Record* was here the other day with Gary," Dave said, "and he started getting offensive. He told Gary right to his face that he lied to him."

"Yeah," Dave Paul jumped in, "he told Gary that our job was the twentieth most dangerous job in the world, not the second or third the way Gary had told him." On Saturday, just the day before this shift, Dave Paul had traveled to Manhattan to attend the funerals of two New York City firefighters who were trapped and literally cremated in a flashover like the one that almost killed the 4th Platoon's Rescue Squad members back in December, so as today's tour began he was feeling pretty sure that firefighting was a dangerous occupation.

"That's bullshit," Dave Stevens said. "The problem is they compute it by deaths on the job. They don't consider a man who's 48 and dies of cancer as a death on the job. None of those figures are in there anymore. With all the toxic chemicals we breathe in at fires, they may not kill you right away, but they get you 15 or 20 years down the line, and they're not reflected in the figures.

"'You guys told me you have the most dangerous job, and I did some research, and you're number twenty on the list in terms of danger. You're behind taxicab drivers and truckers,' this clown said to him, and Gary started to get a little hot. 'Hey, this is our livelihood that you're attacking,' Gary told him, and this George guy shoots back, 'Are you threatening me? I better get out of here before I get assaulted.'"

"I told you guys what was coming with that reporter," a voice from the doorway said suddenly.

Nobody had seen Dick Thompson standing there. Nobody had heard a sound from the apparatus floor. He walked over now and stood behind Don at the end of the table. "You didn't believe me, and I told you what was going on. You see what happened with the cops. And we're —"

Before he could finish, Jeff started to sing the Mighty Mouse theme song — *Here he comes to save the day, Mighty Mouse is on his way!* — and then somebody laughed. Whoa, bad move.

Jeff had pissed Dick off plenty of times before. When Jeff came on the job, he was assigned to the 4th Platoon, where Dick was battalion chief, and they hated each other from the get go. Dick got his officer friends on that shift to harass Jeff at every opportunity, and that harassment was the main reason Jeff bid onto the 1st Platoon as soon as he could. Jeff knew the 1st's reputation — they were the rebels and the outcasts, but they also boasted some of the strongest individuals on the job, and they certainly weren't kowtowing to Dick Thompson like some guys on the other shifts.

Jeff will also tell you he's shy, but most everyone else will say he's aloof. If they're that polite. Many guys think he's downright arrogant and elitist. What is true is that Jeff has a business administration degree from Siena College and a Master's Degree from the Sage Colleges in Albany, and that he worked for a couple of years as a case worker for adult protective services in a social service agency before he became a firefighter. So in a fairly strong blue-collar environment like the fire department, somebody with a couple of college degrees and a social work background was a little suspect before he even started on the job.

On top of that, Jeff likes to write letters. Once, when he was still on the 4th Platoon, he was involved in the dramatic conversion of a cardiac patient. The guy was dead, lying on the floor of a pizza parlor when Jeff and Mo Catel walked in. A few minutes later, the dead guy was alive and breathing on his own again, and Jeff thought that he and Mo should get an award for that.

Dick didn't agree. In Jeff's opinion, Dick thought awards were for a dangerous rescue in the Poestenkill Gorge, perhaps, or for saving a child during a fire — some more traditional firefighter deed — but not for something that might have occurred during an advanced life support call. Paramedics, after all, weren't really under fire on these medical calls.

To top it all off, Jeff had sent a copy of his letter to everyone except Dick, so that definitely got under Dick's skin. After the Assistant Chief went up one side of Jeff and down the other, he told him in no uncertain terms that they didn't give out awards to people for simply doing their jobs. Oh, and by the way, don't write any more fucking letters — that was the gist of it. And since Jeff had bid over onto the 1st Platoon, absence had not made either of their hearts grow fonder either. The subtle war had continued and expanded.

But singing about Dick when he could hear you, and referring to him as Mighty Mouse, especially when Dick wasn't exactly the tallest guy in the world and might just have a slight Napoleonic complex? For a guy with a couple of advanced degrees, Jeff's current behavior wasn't so bright. Or maybe he was simply self-destructive.

In any case, Dick damn near exploded right there. He looked at Jeff as if he had finally driven him around the bend, as if his own little elevator had suddenly bucked and jammed and screeched to a halt before it could reach his top floor. Job or no job, lawsuit be damned, he was going to kill this kid Gordon on the spot. Then, perhaps realizing how many witnesses there would be, he turned abruptly and told Mike Harrison to follow him, and both of them went out.

From the apparatus floor, the first volleys of their argument ricocheted into the common room.

We could hear Mike Harrison saying, "I don't have a clue what you're talking about."

"You don't, huh?" Dick shot back at him. "I'll show you what a goddamn clue is."

Then the voices died down. Dick must have moved the battle into Mike's office, out of earshot.

"With Jeff trying this shit on Dick, we should figure from now on every day will be fuck-the-first-platoon day, right?" Dave said.

"Why do you think Jeff and I argue in the rig about when he's going to be accepted?" Don asked, laughing.

"I don't know," Dave answered, "maybe it's not just Jeff. Maybe it's because of this writer riding along with us. We got a monkey on our back. I think we're finished."

* * *

We can't find 75 Middleburgh Street. There is a 71, which is a well-kept, two-story brick half covered with ivy. Going up Middleburgh, the next building has just a 7- on it, and there's a vacant lot in the adjacent space up the hill that leads quickly to Elementary School 2 and then Oakwood Avenue and the St. Mary's Hospital complex. But Engine 4 is idling in front of this 7-, and the wooden front door is partly open, so this must be the spot.

These few houses here on Middleburgh look a lot better than the places we just passed on 9th Street. This one with half a number is only two-stories high, and it's a grey frame house with intact composition shingles, a small portico with unpeeling white columns framing the front door, and elaborate door and window trim and cornice, all of which is painted white and blue. Somebody has definitely been keeping this place up.

Two police cars are angled against the curb. Their spinning roof lights splash an insistent pattern against the first-floor windows and make the rain look red as we climb the steps.

When we walk inside, two small blonde girls in pajamas with feet are sitting side-by-side in a grey, overstuffed chair near the foyer, and they are crying. A scruffy, thin guy in a Metallica t-shirt and black jeans is passed out on a couch set off to the left along the wall. Asleep sitting up, his long legs are stretched out under a coffee table covered with State Line potato chip bags, empty Coke cans, and ripped pages from a TV guide. An older woman in a pink bathrobe is sitting next to him, looking up at a policeman who stands over her, writing on his pad. Another woman, heavy and short, wearing a blue parka with a New York Giants logo on it, stands next to the policeman. For the first few seconds in this front room, it seems almost calm. The only sounds are these two small girls crying and the rain smacking the concrete front steps behind us.

"TOM!" a woman screams suddenly. It's so loud that the two girls jump. In the next room back, the dining room, two policemen are wrestling a slight woman with filthy blonde hair into a straight-backed, dining room chair.

"Tom, help me," she yells.

"Shut up," the small cop behind her says. Her hands are cuffed behind her back, and he is holding onto the handcuffs, pulling her backwards while the taller, heavier cop, who is wearing tight black gloves, pushes down on her shoulders from the front. There is blood on her neck, and a dark patch of it on the shoulder of her flannel shirt. Her hands and her arms down to her elbows are streaked with red, too, underneath the rolled-up sleeves of the shirt. Her wrists are wrapped in gauze and taped, but the blood is seeping through the bandages.

One of the little girls stands up. "Please don't hurt my mommy," she cries.

"Look, I am not under arrest," the woman says.

George Badgely, a hoseman on Engine 4, tries to reason with her. "Look at your children," he is saying. "You got beautiful kids here. We can get you some help. We can tell you who to call for some help."

Past the woman, in the far corner of the dark dining room, there is an infant asleep in a playpen.

"Tom, wake up and help me," she pleads, and then, as the two cops force her down onto the chair, the small one behind her yanking her cuffed hands up and then over the chair-back, she arches her neck and launches a bloodcurdling scream toward the ceiling. At that, the infant shifts and starts to wail.

The two cops restraining the woman are also keeping Jeff from getting close enough to examine her. George Badgely steps in and lifts back the 4 x 4 bandages so Jeff can see the cuts on the woman's wrists.

"They don't know what she took, do they?" Jeff asks Donny, nodding at the two women who are talking to the cop still taking notes.

"We don't know," Don says. "This one lady here just says she cut her wrists is all."

Somebody has turned up the television, and a commercial is telling us, *This is the best 70s rock collection you've ever heard. Just send it back for a complete* — until the taller cop shuts it off with his foot.

The woman in the pink bathrobe gets up off the couch now and says, "Tranquilizers, maybe. I don't know."

"Nothing over the counter?" Don asks.

She picks up a prescription bottle from the end table next to her, reads the label, and puts it back down. "Opiates, I think. No, not opiates."

"TOM!" the woman shouts again.

Don is trying to ignore all the crying and screaming while he assesses the situation. "Do you have the container?" he continues.

"No," she says. "I don't have it here. They're all prescription. She had a toothache. The doctor give her something for her toothache."

"Non-narcotic," the big woman in the Giants jacket adds.

"One she got was narcotic," the older woman disagrees. "Valium or Xanex or something. I don't have no bottles, though."

"No, it isn't," the big woman insists. "It's penicillin. They're all non-narcotic."

Don is pulling on latex gloves. "Go to sleep." he tells the two girls, and walks over toward their mother. "Two pills, ten pills, what?" he says to Jeff.

"What do you take?" Jeff asks her.

"I take Valium," the woman answers, twisting in the chair and kicking at the cop in front of her.

"All right, she's out of here," he barks, and yanks her up out of the chair.

"Please, come on, take it easy," she says, but the two cops are hauling her now toward a stretcher lying in the corner of the front room.

"Ma . . . Ma," she screams at the woman in the pink bathrobe.

Standing off to the side, Don tries to reason with the cops. "Do you have to put her on the stretcher? Let me just look at her, okay?"

The small cop behind her, hoisting her arms up by the handcuffs, glances down at her bandaged wrists. "They don't look that deep," he says. "They're more like just scratches."

"I am not under arrest for anything, so don't fucking restrain me," she is hollering. "Tom, Jesus, wake up and help me."

"Okay, no intense bleeding though, right?" Don wants to know.

"No, no," the cop assures him.

"Can I just take another look at her while you're doing that?" Jeff asks.

Now she plants her feet and stands up straight. "Hey, I'm talking, right?" she says to the cop in front of her, making eye contact with him and trying to look as calm and reasonable as possible. "I'm okay. Can't you see I'm talking here? I'm okay, really."

"You going to put her face down or what?" Don asks.

"You got it," the cop fires back. "Face down. We're taking you up to the hospital," he says to her.

"No, you let me wake my husband up first," she wails, leaning back and pulling away from him again.

"We'll notify your husband," the small cop says.

"He looks comfortable," the one in front says. "We'll talk to him."

"Yeah, I'll comfortable him," she says, and she starts screaming his name again. "TOM! TOM! . . . Wake him up, Doris," she yells at the big woman. "Wake the fucker up. Wake —"

But the cops bend her over and slam her face-down on the stretcher before she can finish, and the two small girls in the grey chair begin to howl even louder.

"She's only going to the hospital. She's not under arrest," Doris tells the two girls, and she takes off her Giants jacket and wraps it around them.

"What hospital?" the woman's mother wants to know.

"Samaritan," Don and Jeff answer at the same time.

"I can refuse to go," the woman is screaming now, but her

words are muffled by the stretcher. "I can refuse to go to Samaritan."

"You can refuse anything you want, but you don't have any choice right now," the small cop tells her, cinching the restraining straps firmly in place. The other one wipes her blood off his black gloves with a white towel.

"TOM! TOM!"

"Where's the razor blade she used?" Don asks.

"It's gone," her mother says.

"She threw it away," Doris chimes in. "She really didn't mean to hurt herself. She's all right, you know."

"Okay, as long as she doesn't have it on her," Don says.

Doris steps into the middle of the room now and raises her voice so we can hear her above the din. "She's upset. She's not gonna hurt anybody. She just needs a rest. She does. She's got eight kids."

"How many kids?" Don asks.

"She's only 29, and she's got eight kids."

"Holy cow," Don says.

"She takes good care of her house," Doris goes on. "I live over here and I seen her with these kids a lot. She's a good mother. She does the best she can with the eight kids. She does keep her house nice. Her husband just got home, too, and he's tired. He worked until 8:30 tonight."

"Somebody ought to tie some tubes, you know what I mean," the taller cop says.

"They did tie her tubes," Doris says. "She's a little flippy today, because she just had her eighth child. They tied her tubes, and it didn't work. The baby's like two months old, and it didn't work. She found out she's pregnant again."

Here the woman's mother piles on. "It didn't work. It didn't work. She is pregnant again." She leans over and shakes the sleeping husband by the arm. "Tom, open your eyes, for one minute. Open them." He doesn't move. Turning to us, she explains, "He's really tired."

The Mohawk ambulance workers, who have stayed out of the way until now, pick up the stretcher and start past the couch.

"Which school do you go to?" Don asks one of the girls.

"It's right up the hill, but it's closed right now," she answers.

"Tom, wake up." The mother is shaking him again, and he begins to stir. "Tom, the cops are taking your wife," she warns him.

At that, Tom bolts straight up off the couch, lifts his t-shirt, and pulls a black pistol with a long barrel out of his pants.

"Gun," the two cops yell as one, and reach for their holstered weapons. The ambulance workers duck and slam their way out the front door. Suddenly, the policeman who had been taking notes earlier dives over the end table and knocks Tom backwards into the corner behind the couch, punching him and grabbing for his pistol. The girls run toward the dining room, shrieking, and the other cops train their weapons on Tom.

"Please don't take him, too," the mother pleads. "He's okay. Please don't take him. It's only a BB gun."

"What was he doing with the gun in his pants?" the small cop shouts at her.

The mother is backing away from all this into the dining room, clutching her pink bathrobe, pulling it tight at her throat. "He was showing it to me earlier. He passed out and that was that. I didn't even realize he had it with him still."

Tom comes up off the floor in the corner now, with his arms pinned behind him. His face is red, he's panting, and he bends slightly forward in pain as the policeman who wrestled him down jams his wrists together. The taller cop re-holsters his pistol and helps to cuff Tom while the other keeps his gun trained squarely on Tom's chest.

"You knew he had this with him all the time we been in here?" the small cop asks the mother.

"No," she says, "Oh, no. You think I wouldn't have told you earlier if I knew he had that? I just don't want him to go, too. Believe me, he's okay. You know, he's a baby. I could knock him out with one hit."

"Relax, all right," the cop says. "We don't want to knock anybody out. Do you have any other guns in this house?"

"No, no, we don't. That's all there is." She gestures vaguely toward the dining room, where the two crying girls are crouched next to the playpen. "These kids don't need to see any of this. He's a good worker and a good father," she says. "He's been out cold for hours."

"He came close to being out cold forever," the taller cop says, shaking his head.

* * *

This tour of duty has been all about mothers and babies, which would be more appropriate for Christmas, but what the hell. It's Easter. First we had that premature labor call before Frank's brunch. Then, late yesterday afternoon, a couple of hours after the 29 pounds of turkey and giblet gravy and Dave Paul's mother's famous stuffing plus a pile of other holiday fixings, just when everybody was starting to doze on the couches in the common room, another woman-in-labor call came in.

From the moment we pulled up and saw the stained sheets covering up the 2nd-floor windows, we knew it would be a messy call. Her name was Jessica. She was 19, and this was her third pregnancy. She was lying on a bare twin mattress in a narrow bedroom next to the kitchen. She was wearing some kind of t-shirt, but the grimy blanket she was clutching covered most of it. The floor was so covered with dirty clothes and crumpled newspapers and Burger King cups with the straws still in and Kentucky Fried Chicken boxes half-filled with bones and balled-up french fry bags that you couldn't tell where to step or what was underneath, so we just walked on all of it.

As soon as Don and Jeff began to examine her, Jessica started to hyperventilate. Jeff began to lift the blanket off her legs, and she pushed herself up onto her elbows and tried to inch back, crablike, away from him.

"Let me see if you're crowning, all right?" Jeff said. "Just pick up your butt."

"I've got to pee," she said.

"Just relax," Jeff told her.

"I've got to pee."

"Do you feel like you've got to move your bowels?" Don asked.

"No, I've got to pee," she said again, moaning then and swinging her head side to side on the discolored mattress. Jessica's face was contorted and she tried to roll toward the wall, so Jeff had to kneel on the mattress and lift one of her legs up so he could peer in.

"Are you having contractions now, dear?" Don wanted to know, but Jessica wouldn't answer him.

"No crowning yet," Jeff said, "but I think her water's going to break soon."

Don raised his voice a notch, and bent closer to her. "Look at me here, Jessica," he said, but she turned her face toward the wall. "Are you having contractions, or is it that you've just got to pee?"

At that, Jessica closed her eyes.

"Well, I can't get an answer," Don said.

He straightened up and stepped back from the bed, and the call went further downhill from there. In the kitchen, Jessica's mother started to complain loudly about her daughter being a slut, and Jessica wouldn't talk to anybody, so they let her go to the bathroom and pee. Then the ambulance crew refused to carry her down the stairs on the stretcher. They said the stairway to the street was too crammed with junk, and she just hoofed it to the can, so why should they get hurt carrying her over all that crap when she could walk down. That didn't fly with Jeff, so we compromised. We moved the metal twin bed frame, and the broken baby carriage, and the eleven bags of empty beer bottles, and the stack of blue recycling bins, and the soggy newspaper bundles, and all the garbage bags with the rips where the dogs or cats or whatevers chewed through to get at the smelly scraps inside, and then they carried her down to the ambulance.

After the call, as we were leaving the Samaritan emergency room, Don saw a guy he knew from working out at the Troy YMCA. He waved to him, and asked Jeff if he knew the guy.

"I don't know. What's his last name?" Jeff answered.

"Jesus, I don't know. Ralph . . . Ralph somebody. I don't know. His wife was the one who said she had the baby and buried it in the back yard."

"Burns. Margaret Burns.

"Right," Don said. "Ralph Burns."

"Has she since died?" Jeff wanted to know.

"No," Don said. "We had a call with her where she set the house on fire. You remember that?"

"Yeah, vaguely," Jeff said. "She was the one where they dug up her baby like 40 years later. He was in a war or something. He went away, and she had a little affair and got pregnant."

"Right, in Korea." Don was trying to remember the whole story, too. "But then he come home. He was home when she was supposed to have been pregnant, and I think he never knew about it."

"She buried the baby, and her conscience got the best of her after 40 some years, and she told somebody," Jeff said.

Don didn't remember that part. "No, I don't think they ever found the baby, though, because she's a nutcase."

"They did find the baby," Jeff insisted. "They dug up a strongbox and it was inside."

"Are you sure?" Don asked. "Because she's a loony tune."

"No, I'm dead sure, they absolutely dug up a baby in her backyard."

"Okay, maybe you're right about that," Don conceded. "But I'm telling you that she's a mental health patient, too, because she set the house on fire with herself sitting in the bedroom. When we got there, her hair was all singed and everything else."

Jeff was standing there, staring at him, and Don finally got frustrated. "Look, I'm telling you that Ralph was gone overseas and this thing happened with his wife. She went along for all those years carrying that with her, what she had done. Then maybe three years ago, she called up one day and reported it. They dug up her backyard and she wasn't lying. That's what I'm trying to tell you."

It all came clear for Jeff then. "Yeah, right. Little metal box. Brand new baby. Newborn. Buried it the first day it was born, I guess. She must have. I mean, she was never right after that. She snapped because of it. They never even charged her with manslaughter or anything like that. That was just the end of it, except she ended up as a mental health patient for the rest of her life."

"Okay, exactly," Don agreed. "*The Record* did a big report on it."

Don stowed the defibrillator in the side compartment, Jeff climbed into the passenger side and slammed the door, and with that, they figured the baby portion of the shift was over.

"Let's go there, Big Cat," Jeff yelled. "Get us home. That's it. I'm thinking only about turkey sandwiches for the rest of the day. Don't talk to me about anything else."

* * *

Outside on Middleburgh Street, as the cops guide a hand-cuffed Tom down his front steps, the rain has quieted to a light drizzle. It's almost 4 in the morning now. A group of eight or nine teenagers has gathered at the Eagle Food Market just a few doors down, where 9th Street meets Middleburgh. The red, neon OPEN sign in the convenience store window buzzes and silhouettes them in an eerie, cinematic glow. They laugh and point at Tom as the police stuff him into the back of their patrol car.

George Badgely and Tommy Blake, the new guy assigned to Engine 4, are telling Don and Jeff how the call began.

"The call didn't come in as a possible suicide," Blake says. "It came in as an unknown EMS call, and when we got there, the cops said, 'She's locked in the bathroom, she has a knife, and she's taken some pills.' So that's when we called it in as a possible suicide."

"I was the first one in the door," George breaks in, "and I said, 'Where is she?' and they said, 'In the bathroom.' So I went right over and I kept saying to her, 'Come on. Let us in. We're only here to help you. We're the fire department.' She had a hasp on the door hooked on the inside. I looked in and I could see a little blood on the sink, not a lot, and she was complaining of 'welfare this and welfare that.' She was a little disoriented, but she was saying how she had eight kids. I was getting ready to kick the door in, but then she opened it."

"We tried to get in the door and she wouldn't let us in. She was talking a lot," Blake says. "She kept saying, 'Go away. Leave me alone.' And her mother's screaming, 'Kick the door in. I give you permission. Kick the door in.' Then she just came out. She went over and got a flannel shirt and poured herself a cup of coffee, but by that time, that's when the cops came flying in."

George is shaking his head. "No, wait, what actually happened was when she first come out of the bathroom, she went over by the crib to see her little baby. I was trying to tell her that things couldn't be that bad. We could try to find some help for her, and we tried to talk her out of it. She was fine. I was talking to her. After we helped her out into the living room, she did get kind of belligerent. She started throwing her arms around, and we were trying to restrain her to see how bad she was bleeding. She had blood on both wrists, and she had real minor cuts. It looked a lot worse than what it was. I took a 4 x 4 and I was trying to clean her off, and then she really started thrashing. That's when the police came in and handcuffed her. When the cops snuck around to the back of her, that's when she got agitated, when she really started to lose control and —"

"They didn't like really jump her," Blake interrupts. "She brought her hand back like this and she had her back to the cops and he slapped the cuffs on her, and she went berserk, which I guess anybody would. Her kids were sitting there."

"She was trying to hit me," George agrees. "The cops didn't lump her, but they used a little force to get her in the chair."

"Well, they escalate everything," Don says. "Maybe they're still pissed off about *The Record's* articles." Don's father was a policeman, and he harbors some affection for the cops.

"Naturally this woman was going to resist. She was being treated like a dog," Jeff says. "You'll see the same call handled any number of ways, either depending on the disposition of the cops you're with or depending on how much they know about what to do. Even with our guys, everybody knows what to do with a heart attack — start CPR. But on somebody who is having a behavioral problem like this, we don't really get a lot of training on this job in how to handle people and how to defuse them. I don't know what you just got in that EMT course for new guys," Jeff says to Blake.

"We didn't get much," Blake answers.

George is getting all worked up over this. "Another thing is, like, I think she more just wanted attention. Did you see the wounds on her? They were just superficial. I've had them where they really . . . well, you know. There was a guy up in Lansingburgh that Jimmy Martin and I had. This guy went into a brand new building, a building that was under construction, right? He took razor blades and put them inside where the railing starts as you come up the cellar stairs."

George holds his arms up over his head now, with his wrists out, and slices them away from each other in a quick arc against the overcast night sky. "He put the razors inside the wood there and he went whack whack, and he just bled right out. In fact, that still sticks out in my mind, because I can still picture the guy. The guy was an older man, maybe in his late 50s or early 60s. His eyes were wide open like this. He was laying there on the cellar floor, like this, just pointing at us. He was deader than a shoe lace. Apparently, the guy found out that he had a terminal illness and he couldn't cope with it."

One of the pack of guys in front of the Eagle Food Market turns on his boom box now, and two of his friends strut back and forth under the streetlight at the corner, shouting and styling, pointing at us, jeering at this crowd of white guys in blue uniforms huddled together by their trucks and cars with the usual flashing lights. Don't we know this is their neighborhood? They hold their clenched fists up to their mouths, singing along as if they had wireless microphones, or as if a 29 year old mother with eight kids tried to kill herself while her husband snoozed on the couch every night in most of these old houses, or as if they didn't have parents who were tired out from working so hard themselves and who were maybe still up, worried about their kids not being home, or as if 4 a.m. on a cold, rainy night in early April was the best time in the world to hang on a street corner and laugh at people and sing along to hip hop.

Why the hell not?

Who was going to stop them?

Jeff Gordon

You know, a lot of times, people who are harming themselves don't get all upset and go out of their minds and go crazy until the police show up. The cops just exacerbate the problem by doing exactly what they did tonight. The only reason I think that it happens most of the time is that cops don't want to spend the five or ten minutes that it might take to calm somebody down, and say, you know, "You've got to go to the hospital with us. You've got to get checked out. It's a matter of routine at this point. Let's go out to the ambulance, and we'll get you strapped in out there, and you can go for a ride up to the hospital."

You know, it's as simple as that, but it takes an extra ten minutes to do it, and they don't want to take the time, or they don't have the training to recognize that's all it takes. What if she had been seriously injured on her wrists? How do you treat somebody who's got frigging handcuffs on? It doesn't make our job easy when they do something like that. And once we get there, we all have uniforms on, and we're all equal in the eyes of the people there. We're all the same, and it's very hard to differentiate at 4 in the morning who's who. And all of it happened right in front of her kids. The next time a fire engine drives by that kid's house, he's liable to throw a stone at us, saying, "Look what they did. They beat my mother up last week. Fuck them."

And you know, not every cop is like that, but the vast majority of them are. I saw my brother Peter — who's also a cop with the Troy Department, just like my brother Paul is — I saw him disarm a guy once. This is years ago. I was only on the job a couple of years. We got a call for a guy — attempted suicide — it was in the middle of the day. And he had a small knife, not a switchblade, maybe a 2 or 3-inch blade knife, and he was making superficial attempts at cutting his wrists. My brother Peter went in, and there were a couple of other guys besides myself on the engine company. I don't know if the medics were there yet or whatever. And my brother Peter started talking to him. The guy was very despondent and what not. My brother Peter took out his club, and with the simplest motion, he hit the guy's wrist — not even the wrist — he hit the guy's knife. He never even made contact with the guy. He disarmed the guy just by hitting the weapon, and that was it. It was all over after that. Then he sort of moved in, and it was over. He could have easily taken the club and smacked the guy across the side of the head, like so many of them do. It was just a different approach, and it worked. Nobody got hurt. The situation didn't get any worse. The guy went peaceably up to the hospital, and that was the end of it.

I get along well with Peter, but not so well with Paul. I think Paul's approach would have been more typical — to slam the guy on the side of the head. So not every cop is bad, but a lot of them just don't know any better. That's their tactic for handling a patient like that. They don't realize. That's not a criminal. That's a patient. That's somebody that has a problem going on, a medical problem, or a behavioral problem, which is the same thing. For firefighters, there are only victims and patients. For the police, these people are either scumbags or criminals or somebody they can rough up when they get back to the police station. It's a shame, because that woman didn't commit any crime. She had no reason to be in handcuffs.

And it isn't just the cops. There are guys here, on this job, who aren't so sharp. When I was on the other shift, on the 4th Platoon, I always had to keep track of what my partners were doing. They'd get a phone call and forget to load the drug box onto the rig and I'd have to remember to do it for them, that kind of thing. Their hearts were in the right place, but I always had to watch what they were doing. I never feel that way with Donny, because I know that he's always going to do the right thing. I can focus all my energy on managing my relationship with Donny, rather than trying to manage Donny. It's a great feeling to be on this shift. My worries are over, other than what might happen at a call, which we all worry about.

Like the guy tonight with the gun, I mean, think about it. That didn't cross my mind when it was happening but, in retrospect, wow, we could have all gotten blown away up there. Or got caught in the crossfire of all those cops taking shots, you know. I mean worry in that respect. Or worried that, when we get to a call, it's a cardiac arrest and we're in the third floor bathroom, and that's going to be a drag. Things that we're supposed to worry about, I mean, I have a conscience, and that's when we're supposed to kick into high gear a little bit. But in terms of being prepared and knowing that the guy I'm with is going to do the right thing — I don't worry about that. My worries are over.

Our job is to do the best we can. Not everybody's going to be saved. I'm not of that reality, to think that everybody is going to be saved. You know, I think that Robert Coates overdose is a prime example. Even if he was an absolute fresh kill, even if he dropped the minute we walked in the door, and we did all the right things, which we did, maybe he still wouldn't have lived. And I'm of that reality. That's the way it is.

At least if you do the right thing, and you're prepared to do the right thing, then you don't have to go home kicking yourself. You can go home feeling bad that somebody died, or like that night in February up in Lansingburgh where those kids died in that fire, they did everything humanly possible to get those kids, so no one should go home kick-

ing themselves that they fucked up. A lot of guys went home with sad faces that day, but there's a difference.

Whatever's going to happen is going to happen. It's fate. We do try to intervene a little bit, but if you think about it, when your number's up, your number's up. We do our best, though, and that's something.

9

OT inflates firefighters' budget
By George Pawlaczyk
<u>The Record</u> — Sunday, May 1

TROY — Would you feel confident about how your taxes were being spent if the head of your city's most expensive department was an officer in a labor union — a labor union holding a contract with that same city department?

Or, during a year when overtime broke all records, would you have felt secure knowing that this same top official received $2,457 in overtime?

Well, hold on to your tax bill.

If you live in Troy, you reside in a city where that is exactly what happens: Labor and management mix.

Fire Chief Edward Schultz is secretary/treasurer of the Fire Chiefs Association, an 11-member labor union with a contract nearly identical to that of the rank-and-file's Uniformed Firefighters Association.

The Record could find no other fire department in the state where the chief is paid overtime or belongs to a union.

So perhaps it is no surprise that the union-member chief conceded he has no effective control of overtime in his department.

Last year, the cost of paying for overtime for uniformed firefighters was $890,000. Despite spending hundreds of thousands of dollars to hire new firefighters, the Troy Bureau of Fire is again faced with a significant number of vacancies. And vacancies are the main cause of OT, according to a survey of documents by The Record.

With a contract requirement of a minimum of 28 firefighters per 24-hour duty shift, cuts in overall manpower due to not filling vacancies increases the possibility of OT.

With fewer men to start with, any duty-shift absences due to sick or personal leave, or other factors, directly affect the likelihood that a man from another platoon will be called to fill in at time-and-a-half.

Nine firefighter slots have become vacant since January, when 17 new firefighters completed training and were assigned to on-line platoons in the 146-member firefighting force.

By the end of May, retirements are expected to have created a total of 11 vacancies. Last July, when OT peaked, there were 15 vacancies.

And a jam-packed summer vacation schedule is sure to drive OT near the range of the sky-high daily levels of last year, when overtime hit $5,000 per 24-hour shift.

Since last year, little has changed in the way overtime is handled at the Troy Fire Department.

No studies have been made by department or city officials.

If you're Gary Favro, firefighter and paramedic on the 3rd Platoon and current president of the firefighters union in Troy, you're pretty ticked off that this junior muckraker for *The Record* took all the information you supplied and twisted it to fit his biased purposes. Not that you ever thought he'd come around to your way of seeing the situation. He's a reporter, after all. Dirt sells papers everywhere, and Troy's no exception to that rule. And if there's no real dirt, he can always create the illusion that there is some from a creative shifting of the details. To skew the angle so that the whole story hinged on overtime abuses is one thing — okay, you expected that after the paper slammed the cops a couple of months ago — but to suggest in a sidebar that tug boat operators and window cleaners and taxi drivers and loggers and amusement ride operators all have jobs that are more dangerous than firefighters because of some cooked-up, compensation-insurance, ratings schedule bullshit is really playing dirty. The public's perception of public safety workers, especially firefighters, is pretty damn important. If you're a firefighter, you know that you're going to be out there in a dangerous situation, maybe even on a daily basis, that's a given, and one of those times you're going to need more than the public's cooperation. You're going to need help from somebody, and help relies on good will, and *The Record's* articles are striking directly at the heart of the public's good will. Now that's dangerous.

If you're Charley Willson, wishing you were back with your old friends on the 1st Platoon, you feel guilty just for being on the job now, like you should either walk around with a mask on or be absolutely perfect on every single call so people always see that you're doing a good job, so you can justify being paid with their hard-earned tax dollars.

If you're Ric Moreno or Dave Stevens or Mike Kelleher or Frank Ryan or Don Kimmey or Jeff Gordon or Terry Fox or Tom Miter or Gary Hanna or Mike Harrison or any of the other firefighters or officers on the 1st Platoon working today, you've been reading and talking about these mean-spirited articles all week. The first in the series of four investigative bombs was dropped last Sunday, and one more has exploded every day until today. This morning, though, *The Record* finished up with a diplomatic editorial that tried hard to sound more reasonable, but was really just another slap in the department's face.

If you're any firefighter working today, you probably feel embarrassed or angry or any slippery, hard-to-identify emotion in between those two. What you certainly don't feel is real appreciated. You're not one of the "intent men," retired already and living way past comfortable somewhere far away from Troy. You're just another grunt showing up for work and doing your best and taking the heat, not only for a few guys who got lucky and cashed in on a once-in-a-decade opportunity to pad their retirements, but also for a self-serving, incompetent city administration that can't even keep the damn vacancies in the fire department filled and hold the overtime expenditures in the reasonable range.

You aren't the one who hit the public safety jackpot this time around. After your federal and state withholding and social security are taken out, you don't really make a hell of a lot. You still have to work a side job to pay your mortgage and send your kids through school. You coach local athletic teams. You support your church. You pay your taxes. But apparently you're also the one that *The Record* and the politicians and the public want to blame now for Troy going down the tubes, and there's nothing much you can do about that.

For you, today has been just another tour — May 4, a Thursday — and by noon it had turned into a scorcher of a day, with enough moisture in the air to make it feel as humid as late in July. It was the first hot, sticky day of the year and, except for the standard cleaning, mandatory training, and whatever other punitive maintenance work Chief Thompson could find around Central Station for the 1st Platoon, it stayed pretty quiet until twelve hours into the shift. It was an okay day until night fell.

Now, at 10:30 p.m., with the thermometer still hovering around 80 degrees, when you're really starting to feel tired, right about now is the time when all the street folks have decided to come out and play. All the regulars who have been partying all day and pretending it's summer come a month early are finally ready to rock and roll in a serious way, and what better place than at 3rd and Congress Streets, smack dab in the middle of downtown Troy.

Within spitting distance of just three corners of the intersection here, you can find a bus stop, a Kentucky Fried Chicken, three bars — two of which feature flickering, orange neon Old Milwaukee or Budweiser signs in their grimy front windows — and Barb's Coffee-Tyme, a 24-hour coffee shop that sits directly across Congress Street from a clothing store that has no name, sells Motorola pagers and extra-large clothing with assorted sports logos, and currently has a 39.99 beeper special going on. The fourth corner holds the Rensselaer County Court House and County Clerk complex, and during business hours that corner is busy with prosecutors, lawyers, court personnel, jurors, testifying officers, witnesses, and relatives of a lot of the folks who are hanging out on the other three corners here tonight.

At this moment, Terry Fox and his crew on Engine 5, Tom Miter and Gary Hanna, are trying to separate Isabel and Adam.

At first glance, it wouldn't seem like much of a contest: Adam is tall and thin but he still looks menacing, with a once-white, ripped t-shirt that exposes his surprisingly taut abs and pecs, and he is half-growling, half-slurring most of his words.

Isabel's dark eyes are moving frantically, focusing briefly on one person and then another, and she is wasted-looking inside her faded sweatshirt and jeans, with wiry, black hair that seems to be constantly accelerating away from her head like some interstellar explosion. She's at least a foot shorter than Adam is, but she's also a hellcat, slapping and kicking at him and hollering with an hysterical, high-pitched whine.

"No, I'm all right. Fuck you, Adam. I haven't had no seizure."

"Yeah, you have. You had more than one," he yells back.

"I'm just asking. Have you had any seizures?" Foxy says to Isabel. He steps sideways to stay in between them, holding his arms out to keep them separated, but he's keeping one eye trained on Adam. At a call last week, Adam pitched ass-over-teacups down the interior staircase of the Trojan Hotel and slammed bloody and screaming through the glass door onto the sidewalk in front but still came up swinging a short wooden club when Foxy leaned over to help him. So Foxy isn't taking any chances with Adam tonight.

"No, I haven't," Isabel shouts at Foxy.

"Okay, okay," he says. "But do you have a history of having seizures?"

"Yes. Yes, I do," Isabel admits, and she begins to walk in tight circles, waving her arms back and forth fast, like a power walker imprisoned in a small cell.

Adam starts to chase after her, pointing his finger at her. "Was you drinking all day long?" he carps at her, and then he quickly answers his own question. "Yes, you was drinking."

Gary knows Adam. "Calm down, friend. Give her a break," Gary tells him. Years ago, right out of high school and before he became a firefighter, Gary worked as a mechanic for Troy Public Works. Back then, Adam could occasionally still show up for work there as part of his welfare obligation — riding on one of the city's garbage trucks.

"I want to kill somebody," Isabel says, and suddenly reaches around Foxy to slug Adam in the ribs.

Foxy grabs Isabel's arm and steers her a couple of steps toward Engine 5, which is idling at the corner in front of Barb's Coffee-Tyme. "Let's keep that to a minimum, okay," he tells her.

Adam spins around once and teeters a little, pointing at Isabel, but his unsteadiness seems far more related to how much he has drunk this evening than to the effects of Isabel's punch. "Hey, girl, I'm your friend," he says, and flashes a wide, toothy, cartoonish grin at her.

Tom Miter holds Isabel's left wrist and looks at his watch. "I want to take your pulse, all right?" he asks her.

At this, Isabel rips her hand away and glares at him.

"No pulse. Got you," Tom says, stepping back.

"Stop fighting. Let him take your hand," Adam yells at Isabel.

"Fuck you, Adan," she shoots back.

"Come on. Come on, now," Foxy says quietly. It isn't solely the fact that Foxy is the ranking officer and paramedic on the scene which explains his professional behavior: He also has some hard-won empathy. Not many of Troy's firefighters are teetotalers, but for many years Foxy has struggled with his own serious drinking problems. Late at night, cranked on coffee, he will occasionally still tell one of his juicier Vietnam-era stories — like the one about drinking a full bottle of Aqua Velva aftershave lotion, because they'd drunk all the other liquids containing alcohol that they had, then competing in a palmetto bug-eating contest and, finally, literally trying to bury his head in the sand outside his tent. Apart from that, Foxy on many past occasions has raised a glass at any number of Troy bars with some of the very regulars he is now helping on the streets.

"Look, you need some help, right?" he asks Isabel.

"Yes, I need a lot of help," Isabel says, starting to cry. "I need a lot of fucking help. I want to kill somebody. I want to kill myself. I want to do something."

"Have you been drinking today?" Foxy wants to know.

"Yes, some."

"But you're on medication," he says. "Have you had a seizure?"

At this, Isabel straightens up and tries to seem sober. "No, I'm all right now," she says.

"Did you take your medication today?" he asks her, but before she can answer, she sees Adam.

He is strutting back and forth behind Foxy now, taunting Isabel, angling his arms into his sides, arching like a chicken and clucking at her. "Come on, you want to fight," Adam yells.

"Just get out of my fucking life," Isabel shrieks back.

"Tell him the truth, girl. Tell him how you hit me," Adam chants.

Isabel lunges at Adam now, swinging her fists, and Foxy catches her. "Tell him to get out of my fucking face. Tell him," she cries, and Foxy has had enough.

"Okay, okay. Your behavior here, I know you're angry, but that's it. You can't do this on the street," he tells her.

"You ain't shit, Adam," Isabel screams.

"Thanks, Adam. That's a big help," Tom Miter says.

Foxy is dragging Isabel toward the back of an Empire ambulance that has pulled up in front of Engine 5.

"I'm all right. I don't need no fucking ambulance," she hollers.

"The thing of it is, you can't walk down the street hitting people," Foxy answers. "Listen, you're not giving me many alternatives here."

"I'm not hitting nobody," she says.

"Okay, okay. Your one option here is that you go along with

the folks in the ambulance and go up and get sober. That's it. Are you willing to go along with them?"

"Yeah, I'm trying. I'm not hitting nobody," Isabel insists.

As Foxy lifts her up into the back, Isabel keeps shouting, "I'm not hitting nobody. I don't know what he's talking about. I'm not hitting nobody, and you know I'm not. Tie me up. I need some fucking help. I'm not hitting nobody."

Foxy climbs up into the ambulance behind her and slams the door.

On the sidewalk, Adam is pleading his case to Tom Miter.

"Last time I called y'all, you remember? That's when she kicked me in the nuts," Adam says, and laughs.

"Ouch," Tom says, and grimaces.

A small, rotund woman with two filthy, paisley scarves wrapped around her head and carrying two paper shopping bags stuffed with either rags or clothes walks over to Tom Miter. She has a slight, scoliotic stoop and a giant crook of a nose and a pasty, small-featured face that, framed by the scarves, makes her strongly resemble the Sea Hag from the Popeye cartoons. She is also covered from head to toe in layers of mismatched clothing, but the only hint that she is feeling the heat under all that is a thin line of sweat running down her face in front of her left ear.

"She has to go to the hospital?" she asks Tom.

"Yeah, Mary," Tom says, smiling at her. "As soon as somebody states that they're gonna harm themselves, they've got to go to the hospital."

"I thought maybe they should have kept me up to St. Mary's," she says. "They said I had dropsy or pneumonia. I was coughing, like whooping cough. That was last week, and this week I had a fever, so I may have to get in touch with you if I get sick again."

"Call us up, Mary. We'll take care of you," Tom says.

Inside the ambulance, we can see Isabel yelling and flailing her arms so much that the vehicle actually starts to rock.

Gary starts to laugh and asks Tom, "Jesus, is Foxy getting some in there or what?"

"Don't come a knockin' when the van is rockin'," Tom answers.

"I like Mohawk better than Empire," Mary says.

Tom nods at her. "They got better looking guys," he agrees.

"They keep me good, Mohawk does. I thought your name was Teddy Roosevelt," Mary says.

"No, I'm Don Kimmey," Tom tells her. Tom knows Mary likes Donny. She shows up at Central Station once every couple of weeks with hunks of mashed-up brownie that she fishes out of one of her many pockets for him. She calls him Kimbey. "Here you go, Kimbey, this is for you," she says when she hands him her gift.

Now Foxy walks back, and the ambulance pulls away from the curb with its lights flashing but without any siren. At least Isabel will have a room for tonight in Samaritan Hospital's alcohol rehabilitation unit, or maybe in its psychiatric ward, if they feel she's an imminent threat to herself. Adam is already staggering away down toward The Ruck, a bar with a sign announcing that it's a Four Nations Pub, whatever that means.

Adam has washed out of so many alcohol rehab programs in Troy that he usually isn't welcome in the hospital programs at Samaritan, or Leonard, or St. Mary's any more. The local Department of Social Services denies welfare payments to chronic substance abusers now, too, so if Adam is short on cash he can't get a voucher to stay at Joseph's House and Shelter, and the Bethany Center is a drop-in center that serves meals and offers showers to homeless people only during daylight hours. Adam will probably stumble around until he hurts someone or breaks something and the police pick him up, or he'll get a lift up to Oakwood Cemetery and camp out near one of the neo-classical granite mausoleums, or he'll wander across the Green Island bridge and catch the van that ferries folks to the alcohol crisis center in Albany. But it's a warm night, so he may just eventually collapse into one of the doorways in the Williams Street alley behind Famous Lunch and find Isabel again somewhere tomorrow.

Foxy breaks into an enigmatic smile when he spots Mary. "Don't you have your legs insured for a million dollars?" he asks her.

"No, that was Betty Grable like me," Mary answers.

"I thought you and Cyd Charisse."

"No, that was Ava Gardner like me. Me and her."

"It's those sweaters you keep wearing," Foxy assures her.

"No, that was Marilyn Monroe, the Greek goddess like me," Mary says, and points at Foxy. "That one is my favorite, but I pick and choose," she tells Gary. "He's a troublemaker. He says I'm good-looking. He's a flirt. I don't like any man touching me. Where I live at the Y, there are a lot of women around to protect you. But the fact is women think they own you, and they don't own me. Sometimes I think I got that Christ look. Christ. God. I think I was God in school. I'm not exaggerating, because I'm Catholic."

Mary has been wandering around Troy on and off since 1951. With part of her monthly $600 Social Security Disability check, she rents a room at the local YWCA, which offers rooms and supportive services on site to almost eighty women. Mary will tell you she doesn't like living at the Y, but she will also tell you that Christ gave her blue blood and that she wears all those layers of clothing to retain her vital body fluids which could easily be sapped out by bathing. She may also tell you she played shortstop for the Hoosick Valley baseball team in 1945 or that they took her car away because her grandmother had a bad driving record. What Mary probably won't tell you is that she had ten brothers and sisters, was second in her high school class academically, and has been beaten up several times by local high school kids. She probably won't ever mention her incurable schizophrenia.

"How long have you lived in Troy, Mary?" Tom asks her.

"Well, that's getting kind of personal, isn't it?" she answers. "I don't give out too much information about myself." Mary begins to straighten out and re-pack what could be coiled-up sweaters and socks and gloves inside her shopping bags. "I'm gonna let you go to work now, before we all get in trouble," she says.

"You take care of yourself tonight," Foxy says to her as he starts back toward Engine 5, and Mary looks up at him as he goes, and then points at him.

"These are the old, ancient types. I like these guys here," she says, lifting her bags and trying to straighten her back a little as she waddles away, still talking.

"I'm gonna live out my life the way I want to. My own happiness. I got a family, but none of them own me. I got a room at the Y, but the Y don't own me. I think I'm Christ, like God. It doesn't mean that nobody else in this world is God, if I think I'm the only God there is. But I'm not gonna work a miracle for nobody, because they're not gonna save themselves right in front of me. I think I'll be Christ until Judgment Day. Maybe things will change then. Maybe they'll be better. I think maybe we'll see a sign. You know they sent those things up to Saturn? I don't know if they should go up there and start to destroy Saturn."

Maybe *The Record* should send reporters out to interview a cross-section of homeless folks in Troy about what kind of a job they think the firefighters are doing, and whether the fire department is worth the 9 million dollars or so that taxpayers here spend on it every year. Who knows, the homeless may not be any more grateful for them than the local press and the politicians are, what with all these trips to the hospital emergency rooms and detox units and psychiatric wards that they have to endure when they get out of control. It's possible that the only vote the Troy Fire Department would get so far tonight would be Mary's, and that might change before midnight.

'Intent men' pocket bulk of fire OT

By George Pawlaczyk
The Record — Monday, May 2

TROY — Psssst! Wanna retire and get a weekly check bigger than a regular paycheck? Wanna double your pay during your final two years of work? If you do, then take this advice: Become a city firefighter and join the Troy Uniformed Firefighters Association.

Certain Troy firefighters can earn all the overtime they want, sometimes more than $50,000 per year, through a retirement provision of the Troy Uniformed Firefighters Association contract.

No firefighters anywhere else in the state, except for some New York City firemen, earned OT near the amounts picked up last year by some members of the Troy Bureau of Fire.

Due to years of steady overtime earning, these Troy firefighters have retired at rates higher than their base salary.

"There is nothing illegal about it. It's part of the contract," said Troy Fire Chief Edward Schultz. "But," Schultz added, "it looks bad to the public."

The UFA contract includes a retirement provision that allows almost unlimited overtime for firefighters who have at least 18 years service and have signed an "intent to retire" form. The OT is available during the two years before retirement at 20 years of service.

As a result, 68 percent of last year's record OT total for firefighters of $890,000 went to just 15 individuals. Those "intent men," as they are known in the department, earned $605,964 of the total.

The names of the 15 intent men in the department had been placed on a "retirement wheel" after they signed the necessary papers. They were then offered all available overtime on a seniority basis among "wheel" members.

In some cases these firefighters, who are mostly in their late 40s and early 50s, worked more than 400 hours each per month last year in straight time and overtime — an average of almost 13 hours a day, seven days a week.

Intent men averaged $40,397 in overtime on top of their base pay. Among the seven fire captains in the group, the OT average was $47,274. "We had no idea they would be earning these kinds of amounts," said Chief Schultz.

A few minutes before 11 p.m., as Foxy and Engine 5 are backing into the middle bay at Central Station, the Rescue Squad is answering a call at Troy's northern boundary, one block below the bridge that crosses over the Hudson River to Waterford, for a man experiencing chest pains at the 24-hour Price Chopper supermarket.

Ric Moreno, the only paramedic on the Squad tonight, is starting to worry. A dispatcher's characterization of a call as "chest pains" often leads any responding paramedics to presume a heart attack, and a heart attack around 11 at night in a public place usually spells trouble. First off, Dave Stevens is on a Kelly day, so there are no other paramedics there to help if this guy crashes and burns.

Ric doesn't usually even like medical calls, mostly because he's a self-admitted adrenaline junkie. He feels most alive when his life is on the line, and his own life isn't the one that's in question on a medical call. Give him a fire that's blowing out the windows of a building as he pulls up to start a search, or put him on a rope rescue call where he has to rappel down into the Poestenkill Gorge, with an RPI student trapped halfway up the sheer rock face and screaming for help. Now those are calls that make your heart pound, unlike medical calls — even serious, advanced life support calls like this one. Which isn't to say he's bored. Ric is, if anything, nervous about doing his best, and that will push him to be more than conscientious. Ric cares about people; he just doesn't much care for medical calls.

Secondly, this guy who is maybe having the heart attack is a tall, gangly character who looks dead already. His face is a dull, putty color, at best, and his ears are the size of big yellow peppers split in half and de-seeded. He's slumped on the wooden bench near the supermarket's automatic exit and entrance doors that make that weird buzzing sound when they open. The damned doors are doing just that, right now: They're opening, and buzzing, and letting in a stream of late-night shoppers who stop and gawk and chatter and perhaps even remember the news stories about the fire department they've been reading all week. So they watch what Ric is doing even more closely and basically just get in the way, which makes patient assessment and treatment in front of all these staring eyes and scowling faces even harder than usual.

And finally, no matter what this guy sweating here on this bench can tell Ric, he really does look like garbage, and that's how Ric's father looked in Maine when they were rushing to the emergency room after his dad's heart attack. So heart attacks scare the hell out of him, and this guy's almost definitely having one: He's as clammy and grey as the row of haddock that's laid out on the ice-bed between the live lobsters huddling in their tank and the line of cold cut circles and rectangles jammed together in the deli case.

Ric wants to package this guy and get him into an ER as soon as he can. The quicker he can get him into somebody else's hands — and someplace where there are nurses and sophisticated equipment and bright lights and operating rooms and all the stuff Ric doesn't have out here in the Price Chopper entranceway — the better for everyone concerned. But first he's got to assess him and then stabilize him. That's the job, no matter what else is going through Ric's head.

Assessment is a paramedic's primary task on a call. What has happened to this person? How did it happen? What kind of care does this patient need, and how will he respond to that care? Those are the essential, initial determinations. Find the right answers, act as the ER doctor's eyes and ears and hands at the call site, and you can save somebody's life. Choose the wrong ones, and you might begin a procedure that proves dangerous, or administer a drug that becomes life-threatening.

What's clear from Ric's visual and visceral assessment — the "look test" and his "gut feeling" — is that this guy's got one foot in the grave. Ric takes one look and tells Bill McLaughlin, the Captain of Engine 1, to set up a bag for an IV drip. Ric opens up the monitor/defibrillator and pulls out the leads.

"What have we got?" Ric asks him.

"Walter Dayton's his name," Bill answers. "Truck driver, lives in Waterford, says his chest hurts bad."

At this, Walter Dayton whips his left arm out and smacks the plastic globe of a tall gumball machine as he tries to tear the oxygen mask off. The multicolored gumballs rattle around and the machine teeters for a few seconds but stays upright. Bill repositions the oxygen mask over Walter's mouth.

"My father died of a heart attack when he was 60," Walter

says suddenly, but his words are muffled by his coughing into the oxygen mask, and Ric repeats the statement to be sure.

"Your father was 60, and he died of a heart attack, is that right?"

Walter nods, and his bloodshot eyes, fixed on Ric, seem bigger than the gumballs.

"Okay, that's good to know, " Ric says. "How old are you, Walter?"

"54," he answers, but his thin, greasy hair, plastered flat with sweat, somehow exaggerates the pale skin of his broad forehead and skull, and all of it makes him look easily twenty years older.

"Walter, you might be having a heart attack. Have you had a heart attack before?" Ric asks him.

"Yeah, I figured that," Walter says, looking down. "When I started sweating and all, it was like a month ago, and they took me to the hospital. They said that was a heart attack, and they put this catheter in, but they said they couldn't get my valve all the way open."

"They tried an angioplasty?" Ric says.

"They got one. The other valve they said was plugged too bad. They weren't even going to try, or they were changing it or something. I don't know what the fuck they were doing," Walter answers. "Jesus, it hurts. Right here," he says, poking at the left side of his chest.

"You didn't take any nitro yet, before we got here, did you, Walter?"

The straps of the oxygen mask are pressing against the top of Walter's overlarge ears, flaring them out to make him look even more like *Star Trek's* Dr. Spock, and they flap as he shakes his head — "No." He pushes at the straps with his left hand and then tugs at the mask.

"Okay, okay, hold that mask near your mouth, Walter, even if you don't want it right on you," Ric tells him, reaching up to help him. "Pull it and hold it a couple of inches from your nose, like this, so you're getting the benefit of that oxygen. Are you short of breath?"

"Yeah."

"Besides the heart attack, have you had any other medical problems in the past?"

"I had a brain tumor, and surgery for it."

"When was that?"

"In the 70s. '76, I think. I'm thirsty. I need something to drink."

"Just hang on a minute, okay, Walt?" Matt Magill is frantically trying to write Walter's answers down on the PCR, but Ric knows he doesn't have any time to fool around with this patient, so he's trying to rush through the medical history questions. "Have you had any ulcers before?"

"Yes, I have."

"What medicines do you take?"

"Shit, I don't know. Tagamet. Xantac. My mouth is dry."

"I know it. It's because of the oxygen. Hang in there, buddy."

Ric pulls Walter's t-shirt off and presses the fast patches in place so he can attach the monitor leads, and he hesitates just for a second, looking at the guy's upper body. There are tattoos all over him. His lower right forearm sports the expected heart with the arrow through it, but this one is personalized, with the name *Doreen* scrawled along its wobbly shaft. There's a long cross on his upper right arm, with its vertical line maybe five or six inches long and its bottom almost parallel with his elbow. Another heart, on his lower left forearm, announces the names *Elaine* and *Walter* underneath it, brighter than the Doreen is, and exuding the confidence of a more permanent union, though it does have a slightly faded "2" above it.

On his chest, though, is where the real action is: Under one of the defibrillator patches Ric has pasted on, a mouse dances above Walter's left nipple, its little arms spread wide in delight, and he shakes and shimmies whenever there's movement, whenever Walter sways forward or jolts back upright in pain. Across from the dancing mouse, above his right nipple, a dog shaped like a pit bull is barking over at the mouse, with lines for the barking sounds coming out of his mouth, as if he is shouting, *Dance, dance, dance*, perhaps because he is offering impatient encouragement to the mouse, or maybe *Dance? Dance? Dance?*, because he isn't on the mouse's dance-card this particular night and wants to be.

Ric is staring down at Walter's heart monitor strip as it curls out of the machine. It looks to him like Walt's ST interval is prolonged, but Ric isn't about to eyeball a few inches of monitor strip and bank on a quick analysis about the complex electrical activity of this guy's heart.

Walter is still coughing into his mask, swinging his head from side to side in frustration.

"I think we better take you to the hospital, Walt. Where do you want to go?" Ric asks.

"Albany Medical," Walt says. "That's where I went before."

"Do you smoke?" Ric wants to know.

"Yeah."

"How much?"

"I'm down to about two packs a day."

"Two packs a day," Ric says. "So that's been how long? 20 years. 30 years?"

"I started young, as a kid."

"Okay, over 40 years."

"Yeah," Walter says, coughing again.

"Sorry, Walter," Ric says. "I'm not passing judgment. I'm trying to get a good history. The doctor will need it at the hospital."

"No, I understand," Walter says, nodding, and then he stares up at the long fluorescent lights on the ceiling. "As a young kid, I started out with maybe a pack a month. Then it just got more and more. It got to three packs a day for a long time. I'm cutting back now."

Two packs on average, that's 40 cigarettes, times 365 days, equals 13 or 14 thousand a year, and that times 40 years — probably six hundred thousand, maybe up to three-quarters of a million cigarettes or more that Walter has smoked in his lifetime.

"On a scale of 1 to 10, how would you rate your pain when it first started tonight?" Ric asks.

"Maybe a 7," Walter says.

"And how about now?" Ric presses.

"Jesus, I don't know — 9, okay?"

Walter's head flops back now and he groans loudly into his mask.

"Tell me what's going on there, Walt," Ric says.

"My chest hurts," he gasps, raking the outspread fingers of his right hand across his sternum and shutting his eyes. Suddenly, he springs forward and grabs Ric shoulder with his left hand.

"I don't think I'm gonna make it," he says, pounding his right hand hard against his chest.

That's all Ric needs now, a patient with fear of impending doom. Ric has seen this happen three or four times in his paramedic career — patients who, for whatever mysterious reasons, decided they were about to die, and expressed certainty about their apparently inevitable fates — and, unfortunately, he saw all those other impending doom predictions come true.

At this, Ric drops the monitor tape and grabs a small bottle of nitroglycerin spray from the drug box. Nytroglycerin is a rapid muscle relaxant that is given sublingually, and it usually coaxes the heart into slowing down. It dilates the arteries and veins quickly — opens them up wider — so if Walter's chest pains are from angina and if he's having a heart attack, the nitro should give him some immediate relief.

"Okay, I want to give you medication to take your chest pain away. I'm going to spray it underneath your tongue, all right?" Ric says. "Stick your tongue up on the roof of your mouth. That's perfect. Don't move."

Ric is cradling the back of Walter's head inside his hand as he aims the nitro spray into his mouth, and Walter's dark eyes dart back and forth, narrowing under his ominous brow, as if they're looking for an escape route.

"Don't move," Ric continues. "Open your mouth a little bit wider. There you go. You feel any relief from the pain?"

Walter shifts on the bench and stretches his neck from side to side a little, moving his right hand from his chest to the back of his neck now, working it with his fingers, concentrating hard on this manageable task, as if by repositioning a cervical vertebra that's out of place he can somehow make all the other physical ailments, inner and outer, fall into line.

"Pain's still there, but it's let up some," Walter says.

"Okay, scale of 1 to 10, what is it now?"

"Down to about 2 or 3," Walter tells him, but his face is still contorted, and small drops of sweat pockmark the wide ridge above his eyes.

"I guess we did okay," Ric says. "It's let up a little bit. Good. Let's get going then."

"I need my shirt," Walter says, standing up suddenly, then swaying and coughing, and finally sitting back down.

"Take it easy, we'll get your shirt," Ric tells him. "Don't worry, okay? But I think we'll go over to Leonard Hospital. It's a good place, and it's right around the corner."

"Okay," Walt agrees.

What Ric isn't telling Walter is the rest of the truth, which is that he probably won't need his shirt pretty soon. That his tattooed pit bull can bark all that it wants: If he doesn't get some serious cardiac support, his dancing mouse is going to stop dancing forever; that his blood pressure is dropping and Albany

Medical Center is at least twenty minutes away, and that Walt may not have those twenty minutes to spare; that halfway down Rt. 787, Walt's heart could go, *bingo*, and that would be that; and that it probably won't be some amazing, Fox Channel, reality-show crash of eighteen-wheelers on an interstate highway in Tennessee that will claim trucker Walter Dayton's life, nor will it be some suicide bomber who chose a McDonald's where Walt happened to be eating to catapult himself and everyone else there into the afterlife, leaving behind a shredded jumble of C-4, body parts, designer jeans and Big Mac wrappers that the local news cameras will pan solemnly for the viewers at home. Ric is guessing that the truth about Walter's final moments won't end up on the front page of *The New York Times*, or even inside one of the back pages of its Metro section. His final truth, if this is it, will be unspectacular, and painful, and preventable.

That's what Ric would like to say — that stopping this specific, predictable medical condition has been in Walter's own hands for most of his life — but Ric also knows that for Walter and for all the people who love him, it's still heartbreaking. And Ric also knows it's pointless to say anything now, so all of this just becomes another reason he doesn't like medical calls. Here's one more scared, sorrowful face to hang next to all the others he's seen on this job. How much of a firefighter's pension should be earmarked to deal with each one's unforgettable gallery of dying faces? But now isn't the time to think about that. Now is the time to help Walter pull on his rumpled shirt, and to help him walk toward the waiting ambulance.

> **Firefighters say: "We're worth every penny."**
> By Carmen Napolitano
> The Record — Wednesday, May 4
>
> TROY — Troy firefighters say criticism of the overtime they earn

ignores an important point: They have one of the most dangerous jobs in the world and are worth every dollar they're paid.

Despite their comfortable salary and benefit packages — an average of $38,475 of regular and overtime pay, plus generous vacation and other time-off allowances — firefighters say few people are willing to do what they do.

As firefighters tally the job-related injuries they've suffered and the countless close calls, they defend their contracts — and say they sometimes believe they don't get paid enough. Given the likelihood of injury and the possibility of being killed in the line of duty, they say, it is only right that the city provide them with a liberal sick-leave policy, overtime and annual bonuses.

Troy firefighter Eric McMahon said most people aren't aware of all the services he and fellow firefighters perform and related risks they face.

Last year, McMahon said, firefighters rescued nearly a half-dozen people from the bottom of the Poestenkill Gorge. McMahon said firefighters could easily slip on the sharp ledges, break a leg or, while the chances are slim, fall to their death. And, earlier this spring, firefighters rescued a dog from the icy waters of the Hudson River.

"There is no question that the people of Troy are getting a big bang for their buck," McMahon said.

The dangers stretch beyond falling from a cliff or succumbing to spring flood waters. Firefighters and para-medics are also at risk of contracting HIV, tuberculosis and hepatitis. Such potentially fatal diseases can unknow-ingly be taken home to wives and chil-dren, people who didn't choose to take such risks.

"You go out on a call and there's this heroin addict bleeding all over your gloves. You go home and you're kissing your wife, your kids, then you get this call and it's the doctor telling you the guy was T.B. positive," McMahon said. "Then what do you do? Who is going to compensate me and my family for this?"

During his four years on the job, McMahon said, he had seen several firefighters test positive for tubercu-losis and hepatitis.

On top of all this, McMahon said, firefighters are forced to work in uncomfortable conditions. In the win-ter, McMahon said, ears and fingers freeze; several firefighters have suif-fered frostbite. During the summer months, when temperatures inside their heavy synthetic fire-resistant coats often climb to near 100 degrees, firefighters are sometimes overcome by the heat. Some have collapsed or suffered heart attacks.

The stress of the job takes its toll, too, firefighters say. Firefighter Robert Connolly said he still has "cry-ing fits" when he thinks about the three children who died earlier this year when their 116th Street home in Lansingburgh caught fire. Connolly said he doubts this fatal fire will ever fade from his memory.

"It's very stressful," Connolly said. "You go to call after call, see people hurt and die, and then come back to the station and wait for the next call — and hope it's not as bad as the one before."

Don Kimmey is a worker, and ready to tell you so. When he complains about other guys on the job, it's usually because he thinks they're lazy. The ones who don't immediately pull on their latex gloves and get down on their knees and clamp their hands over a stabbing victim's arterial bleed because they'd rather let the patient's blood spray all over *somebody else* — those guys shouldn't be firefighters, in Kimmey's view. They just don't thrive on chaos the way he does.

When Don runs on the treadmill at the YMCA, he starts at about 6.7 and notches it up incrementally as he runs — 6.8, 6.9, 7.1, 7.3, 7.5 — defiantly pushing himself harder the longer his workout lasts, as if he has to outrun whatever it is that keeps him almost constantly aloof. "Worker" is the term that firefighters usually apply to a working fire, one that's blowing out the windows when they pull up in front of it, the kind of 3-alarm fire the 1st Platoon hasn't really tackled since the night in February when the hydrants froze. But Don Kimmey's like that, too, always volatile and jumpy and self-assured. If he were a cop, he'd definitely make people nervous. He's an in-your-face, spoiling-for-a-fight, know-it-all, aggressive character most of the time, and you can't help but admire the guy's moxie. And tonight has certainly been an opportunity for Don to exercise his moxie.

About 11:15, a teenager pounded on Engine 4's front door at North and River Streets. He told Bob Davis, Engine 4's captain, that there was a white kid lying in the parking lot diagonally across River Street, and he was all cut up. Bob immediately called the dispatcher for a trauma response, and Medic 2 was dispatched to North and River Streets on a stabbing call. The standard operating procedure for serious trauma calls, like stabbings or shootings or car accidents with injuries, is to send the closest engine, along with Medic 2, the Battalion Chief's car, and the Rescue Squad. Tonight, though, with Ric Moreno watching Walter Dayton's blood pressure drop faster and faster inside Leonard Hospital's ER, Don Kimmey and Jeff Gordon were on their own.

By the time Medic 2 arrived, Bob had his right hand clamped over the arterial bleed on the kid's right leg, and thick blood was oozing up between his fingers. Don nodded his approval to Bob, pulled on his white latex gloves, and asked him what he had.

"He's got a severe laceration on his foreleg, right to the bone," Bob told him. "It's about eight inches long, and I think he's got some head injuries. His name is Michael."

Michael was a thin white kid wearing what used to be a white t-shirt and faded blue jeans, but both were so soaked with his blood that they glistened red under the streetlight. He was lying in front of a dilapidated, 3-story brick building with a battered sign that read, *John B. Garrett — Medical Supplies and Equipment*, but most of the windows on the 2nd and 3rd floors had jagged, fist-sized holes in them, and weeds along the edges of the parking lot were waist high.

There were cops everywhere, and not just the uniformed kind. Several guys in levis and stained sweatshirts with rigid bulges on one side stood against the building, out of the light, and talked to each other. Strange as it seemed, they had a vested interest in this kid. He had been theirs, a police informant for the CRASH (Community Resources Against Street Hoodlums) program, at least until tonight.

Ever since New York City became effective in battling their drug problems and those problems flowed out of the boroughs and followed the Hudson River north to Troy, the police here have had their hands more than full. The same crack that sells for 3 to 6 dollars a bump in New York City goes for 17 dollars a bump, or even higher, in Troy, and that's a profit margin hard for freelancers to resist, especially when Troy's only a quick, scenic bus ride away.

So Troy's police department has teamed up with agents from the New York State Police and from the Bureau of Alcohol, Tobacco and Firearms and from the Drug Enforcement Agency, and has recruited some thin white guys like Michael, to keep an eye on neighborhoods like North and River. Then they can bust drug buyers all night long and take down their dealer, flush with cash, on his way home in the early morning.

Unfortunately for Michael, tonight seven or eight guys caught him and exacted some payback. They jumped him in an abandoned lot, sliced him from head to toe with box cutters, and melted back into the night before any of the undercover cops slouching in dark cars or peering out from behind apartment curtains could do a thing.

"Relax," Don began. He loved the intensity of trauma calls. "Relax, pal," he told Michael, and then he started waving his hands and barking orders and directing the show. "Get a towel. Hang on. Relax. Show me the leg. Don't move your head. Relax, Mike, okay? We're going to need a collar here. Take a deep breath, Mike. In . . . in . . . in . . . Quiet. Two more. In . . . in . . . Turn him over. Get the light. Okay, that's superficial. Get a 4 x 4 for this. Watch your hands, buddy, watch your hands, I'm cutting here. We'll get you new pants. Relax, pal, relax. Okay, that's it. Come on, come on, let's get him out of here."

After Mike was packaged and gone, Don scraped a haphazard jumble of bloody clothing and bandages into a pile with his foot, looked over at a Troy cop holding a flashlight, and shook his head. "You want me to take this garbage? I'm not going to take it. If there's any blood on that, I ain't getting my ass in a jam. We'll take the papers, but we're not touching the rest. That's all for evidence. You got gloves with you?" Don asked him, and the cop just stared at him. "We'll leave you some gloves and a red bag," Don said. Then, seeing Mike Harrison walk toward him, Don peeled off his own gloves, dropped them into the pile at his feet, and laughed. "Chief, what did I tell you? As soon as we started up here, I told Jeff, 'Here's our stabbing.' That kid lost a lot of blood. His clothes were saturated."

Mike shook his head. "We'll get no sleep tonight, Donny."

Don laughed again, and bent down to collect the bandage wrappers on the ground. "The night is just beginning," he said, and flashed Mike a knowing smile.

Here it is almost 2 o'clock in the morning, and the temperature has only dropped into the low 70s. Don and Jeff spent most of the last hour with a diabetic, 50-year old man who beat up his elderly mother because he blamed her for his low blood sugar. Now they're approaching a huge man who is lying face down in front of his run-down, shotgun-style apartment on 4th Street in South Troy.

Two black and white taxis are idling, one at the curb and one in the dead end street next to the house. Their drivers, a thin woman in tight jeans with frizzy, platinum hair and a younger, darker guy in an unbuttoned flannel shirt, are both standing over the man down, smoking and gesturing and explaining to the crew of Engine 6 that this guy lives here and he drinks a helluva lot and they've given him rides home, yeah, and they stop every once in a while and help him into his house but tonight he won't wake up and, shit, they're really worried this time he's gone and fucked himself up royally and so they put a blanket over him and stuck an old pillow under his head and they called the fire department because who else would come and help?

"Is he awake? We get any vitals?" Don shouts as he walks over.

Mike Hogan, a hoseman on Engine 6, answers him. "No, we just got here, too."

Don kneels beside the guy's head and peels back a closed eyelid with his finger. "Do we know if he hit his head at all?"

"Nah, when I come by, he was already down," the woman driver tells him.

"So we don't know anything at all about what happened to him, how he got here, or what?" Don asks, and tries to roll the guy up on one side to examine him, but this guy isn't budging. "Was he inside that building?" Don wants to know, jerking his head to indicate the cluttered room that lies beyond the three peeling green steps and the warped wood screen door.

"His name's Bill," the other driver says.

"So we don't know anything," Don says.

Mike Hogan is holding Bill's wrist. "84 on the pulse," he says to Don.

Don leans lower, angling his left ear close to Bill's mouth, and listens to his breathing. Now he grabs his shoulder with both hands and flops him over onto his back. The blanket slides away and Bill's grimy blue t-shirt rides halfway up his stomach, which jiggles side to side for a second and shines suddenly with an eerie, artificial luminescence, as if, transported a few hundred miles south and east, this could be the bloated underbelly of a beached porpoise in the moonlight.

"Hey, Bill, open your mouth," Don suddenly hollers down at him. "Wake up. You've got all your friends here." Don pulls on his chin and looks into his mouth. "You know where you are? You want to go in?"

At this, Bill's eyes pop open.

"You've got to talk to me if you want to go in," Don says. "Can you talk?"

Bill's eyes are still open, but they look glazed over. He's just staring straight up, at the phone wires and past them at the hazy night sky above him.

"Do you want to go to the hospital? Yes or no?" Don asks him.

Bill hears that, and he slowly moves his head back and forth. Nope.

"Well then, you've got to talk," Don insists.

Bill coughs now, and then he grunts — not a pre-conversation, throat-clearing sort of grunt to dislodge some phlegm and make it easier to talk — but a grunt that says grunting is Bill's preferred form of communication, and he keeps shaking his head back and forth.

Jeff Gordon's patience is running out. "He obviously doesn't want to go. Let's help him inside," Jeff says to Don.

"You want to go in the house?" Don asks Bill, and Bill is suddenly and inexplicably on board, nodding his head up and down, vigorously, and shifting his focus from Don to Mike Hogan and back again.

But he's also not trying to get up, so everybody there — Don, Jeff, Mike, Andy Waterman, who is the captain on Engine 6, Pete DeChiaro, another hoseman, and the two taxi drivers — all grab some part of Bill, hoist him onto his feet, and steer his drooping, massive bulk up the steps and into a kitchen chair inside the one long room of his house.

Inside, sitting up, Bill isn't much more cooperative, but he is coughing more. Don is trying to listen to his lungs with a stethoscope, and Bill keeps hacking, clutching his knees with his hands and coughing straight out into the living room, spraying saliva and yellow-tinted mucus in a scattershot pattern on the oval braided rug at his feet. After he coughs, when he flops back upright in the chair, you can see how huge he is: 6 feet 5, maybe taller, at least 300 pounds, with red suspenders that keep his pants within shouting distance of his giant belly. Sitting, he is almost as tall as Don Kimmey is standing next to him.

Bill points to his chest and wheezes.

"You've got asthma, right?" Don asks, and Bill nods.

The woman driver puts a hand on Bill's shoulder and says, "We have to go, okay. Please let them take care of you."

But Bill doesn't want that. He starts to wave his arms in the air, and that makes him wheeze more. He tries to get up, but Mike Hogan and Pete DeChiaro each grab an arm. Bill's eyes begin to roll around in their sockets and he swings his head from side to side again, but wildly this time.

Jeff is preparing a ventilator treatment for Bill's asthma. "Hey, we're here to help, buddy," Jeff says. "Please don't try to hurt us."

"Let me get some oxygen on you," Mike Hogan says, lifting the mask toward Bill's face, but Bill knocks it away.

"Settle down," Don barks at him.

A Mohawk ambulance driver appears outside the screen door, but no one mentions that to Bill.

Bill grabs his head with his hands now and rocks back and forth on the metal chair as if he's autistic. His t-shirt bunches up at his neck, and his giant belly washes up and down like a wave of skin, swelling and receding as he works to get enough air into his lungs.

"Don't lean back, okay," Jeff tells him. "Stop fighting us."

Bill swipes at Jeff now, slowly, like a bear annoyed by a hornet, and Jeff steps out of the way.

"We're trying to help you. Please don't hurt us," Jeff reminds him. "I know you're in pain. We're doing the best we can."

Don is trying to attach heart monitor patches to Bill, and he's swatting at Don's hands.

"Take it easy," Don tells him. "I'm just putting electrodes on you."

Jeff is offering Bill a ventilator with medicine for his asthma, and he finally takes it. As Bill sucks on the tube, and the vapor seeps into his lung sacs and eases his breathing, he visibly relaxes. He drops one hand into his lap and holds the ventilator with the other, breathing deeply and letting his shoulders slump.

"You want to hand me an IV and a tourniquet, Donny," Jeff says. "You're not moving a lot of air here, Bill. I'm going to start an IV on you."

Bill doesn't want to hear that. He rips the ventilator out of his mouth and glares at Jeff, then goes back to violently shaking his head — NO!

"What do you mean, no?" Jeff says. "You need it. You don't look too good, buddy."

Bill reaches out now and clamps his massive left hand on Jeff's chest.

"Whoa, Bill. You're all infected. We've got to take you up to the hospital and get you brushed up, okay?" Don breaks in.

Bill drops his hand, but keeps shaking his head.

"What hospital, buddy, St. Mary's?" Jeff asks. "You've got to go up. You're hurting."

"Let them clean you up. Couple of days, that's all," Don says. "Can you make it to the ambulance?"

Bill is pointing to the couch.

"No, no," Don tells him. "You see that crap you spit up? That's killing you. Let's not argue. We're ready to go. The ambulance is waiting. Let's go."

Bill spots the ambulance driver and reaches for Don.

"I can't go by cab?" Bill demands, startling everyone by actually speaking. His words sound garbled and faraway, like a man yelling underwater.

"No, you can't," Don says.

Now Bill stands up, wavers for a second, and then catches himself. He raises himself to his full height, and he's easily a foot taller than Don, and twice as wide. He waves his fists erratically over Don's head, and takes menacing, stiff-legged steps toward him, acting like some pathetic but still scary imitation of Boris

Karloff's Frankenstein. "Hey, wait a minute. Why can't I go by cab?" Bill shouts down at Don.

Everyone begins to back up now, and the atmosphere in the room feels suddenly electrified, but Don doesn't move an inch. He spreads his feet, plants his hands on his hips, and stares up directly into Bill's face. Don wanted to be a cop once, and he can assume the prototypical cop walk and attitude when he needs to. Don's dad was a cop in Watervliet, and Don took the tests to be both a fireman and a policeman. He didn't care which job he got. When he only passed the firefighter test, his father went nuts, but when Troy hired him as a fireman, his father relented. "Oh, Jesus, you got that job," Don remembers him saying. "You got it."

Now Don counts every person in the room, pivoting at the waist and pointing to each. "One, two, three, four, five, six, seven, eight. Eight to one," Don says to him. "We took a vote. 8 to 1. We win."

"What do you mean," Bill hollers, and swings at Don, but his fist flies over Don's head.

"Relax," Don tells him, still not moving. "We took a vote. It's the democratic way. We all want you to go up to the hospital in the ambulance. I can't let you stay here. Your lungs are killing you. We gave you the medicine. You've got to go up. You can't get the medicine if you go up in a cab."

Bill takes a step back, but keeps glaring down at Don.

"Let's make a deal," Don says. "Your friends from the cab company can go up with you. If you don't want to stay there, you can come home."

"I don't want to stay in the hospital, " Bill says, starting to wheeze again, and he swings his arms behind him to keep the other firefighters away.

Don steps over and grabs Bill's meaty arm to steady him.

"Look, out front you couldn't even breathe and now you're ready to fight," Don tells him, breaking into a grin. "We're making progress."

OPINION
The Record
Thursday, May 5

In the hour before dawn on a Wednesday just a week before Christmas, an awful calamity almost occurred in Troy. Almost, that is, because nobody lost their lives.

On that day, as most of us slept, four Troy firefighters plunged into a burning two-story apartment house, attempting to rescue someone they mistakenly believed was trapped on an upper floor. Three colleagues already had been forced to retreat from the blaze. But these four men did what they promised they would when they joined the ranks of firefighters — they willingly risked their own lives attempting to save another.

Suddenly, as they groped through the thick smoke on the second floor, they found themselves trapped behind a wall of flame. They felt their ears beginning to burn. "It was life or death," recalled one of the men later. Reflexively, they dove through windows to the ground, two stories below, and lived to fight another fire.

This scene is one we dare not forget, even as we evaluate whether Troy has been too generous in its contracts with the fire and police unions. Firefighters don't face such close calls every day, and many cops retire without ever facing a threat of death. But we are lucky these people stand up for us when we need them — and they deserve fair compensation for their fulfillment of that duty.

Recognizing that, however, does not diminish the conclusion that most readers surely will draw from The Record series on firefighter compensation published this week. The newspaper's findings were similar to those of an earlier study of the Troy police pay and benefits package: Troy is generous to a fault with its uniformed services.

The Troy Bureau of Fire is the most expensive branch of city government, costing taxpayers $9.7 million a year. It is a hefty bill, considering that the city is facing a deficit this year that some city officials say could hit $17.9 million.

What should especially concern taxpayers is that nobody in City Hall — until very recently, anyhow — has taken a serious look at alternatives to the huge overtime bills racked up by firefighters and police. Until reporters for The Record began pecking away on their calculators, nobody had even analyzed why overtime had soared in each department. In the last few weeks, a former city public safety commissioner has begun to examine the problem and a city council member has vowed to investigate. But at this point, more than one-third of the way through a year that could leave Troy a financial disaster, nobody has put forward a plan to solve the problem, and the analysis in this newspaper is the only one that exists.

It remains to be seen whether the unions representing those in uniform will cooperate with any effort the city may put forward to trim expenses.

Fortunately, most police and fire union members are Troy taxpayers. Like everybody else in Troy, they have good reason to fear excessive city spending.

As taxpayers pursue solutions to these problems, however, they must be careful that their efforts not harm the effectiveness of those police officers and firefighters whose work is so valuable to this city. That is why it is important to bear in mind that cold morning in December, when we nearly lost four of Troy's bravest men. They and their colleagues deserve our gratitude and our respect — and from them, in turn, the citizens of Troy have a right to expect fair evaluation of what kind of a load taxpayers should be expected to bear.

On a lot of emergency medical calls, it's hard for firefighters to see: In cobblestone alleys where drunks collapse, or in single room occupancy hotels where bugs have begun to swarm under the unshaven men with rigor mortis, or in filthy, three-room apartment bedrooms stinking of piss with bloated women howling as they emerge from their diabetic comas. Somebody always grabs a big flashlight when they jump off the rig for a night call, but a single beam can only illuminate just so much. On the darker calls, paramedics try to keep especially close track of the needles they use.

But in here, in Samaritan Hospital's Treatment Room #1, it's always artificially bright. These lines of overhead fluorescents never get a rest. Here, you're forced to see everything, including this AVOID NEEDLESTICKS! poster on the back of the door, where a doctor is performing CPR on an obese, shirtless man. One of the nurses is applying a bag valve mask and another is starting a second IV line. Halfway down the poster, in orange capital letters, it blares at us: HANDLE SHARPS CAREFULLY — DON'T RECAP BY HAND. And if someone still doesn't want to take it seriously, there's a statistic in the poster's lower left quadrant, informing the reader that, *"More than five health care workers will die this week, and every week this year, as a result of Hepatitis B."*

To the left of the poster, hanging on the wall, there is a red plastic bin for needle disposal. It has a frost-white, hinged lid that holds the sharps until someone shakes them down into the red bottom part, and there are more written warnings, too: *Drop, don't force sharps into container* . . . INFECTIOUS WASTE . . . BIOHAZARD . . . *Forcing could cause puncture!* There's even a graphic of a needle silhouette on the bin, with the word SHARPS printed inside the needle, and under that, a silver lock, so only authorized personnel can remove the bin full of used needles.

How can they make it any safer? If you read the poster and then examine the bin, how can you get hurt? But if you've been answering emergency calls for five hours straight, and you're trying to give the ER doctor accurate information, and if you're saying, "Very diminished in the lower fields, but he was moving some air in the upper ones, though," the way Jeff Gordon is, and you're tired and backing up and talking and turning down your radio so you won't bother the ER patients and reaching to drop your used sharps in the hospital disposal bin, all at once, and somebody left a needle sticking out the top, then you're in trouble.

"Who the hell got stuck with this?" Jeff demands. He yanks the strange needle out of his hand, and stares down at a drop of his blood that is quickly fattening.

Suddenly, neither of the nurses knows anything.

"Who got stuck with this?" Jeff wants to know, scowling now as his blood thins into a line and finds a crease in his palm.

"No idea who. Where was it?"

"In the top of the container," Jeff says, pointing.

"On the top of the container?"

"I haven't given a needle, so I have no idea."

"Ask Diane."

"What happened?"

"He got stuck."

"By a needle?"

"From the container."

The IV nurse walks over to the bin. "Where? This needle?"

"That was laying right on top of the box, uncapped," Jeff tells her.

"I gave a shot in that color syringe to a lady in the hallway, but I don't know if it was the one I used or not, because there are other needles in there, too."

"This has to be written up," the bag valve nurse says.

"Anybody going to find out whose body that was in?" Jeff asks her.

"I hope it wasn't the one that I put in there," the IV nurse says, and walks out toward the nurse's station to ask the rest of the night crew.

The bag valve nurse looks noncommittal, but at least she's looking at Jeff and not avoiding his determined gaze. "I can acknowledge this. It's happened to me, too," she adds.

"You guys given anything tonight at all?"

"I haven't."

"Erin hasn't given anything."

"I gave an IM injection to a lady in the hall, but I didn't think it was sticking out. I wouldn't purposely leave it sticking out. If it was . . . "

Jeff, pressing a gauze pad onto his needle stick, has moved to the hallway now, and his voice comes out louder and testier — still under control, but with a panicky edge to it.

"Bottom line is there were needles sticking out of the box," he says. "Is that standard operating procedure?"

"No, but when we drop them in, we don't know how they're dropping in either," the IV nurse answers.

"Does anybody look?" Jeff shouts. "Somebody fucked up here, I'll say that, without any hesitation."

* * *

For some reason, the unthinkable has occurred: Don Kimmey can't sleep. Usually, he's in the bunkroom, horizontal and unconscious, before Medic 2's motor cools down. Maybe his adrenaline is still pumping from the stabbing call or from facing down Bill the giant. Or maybe he's pissed off about Jeff getting the needle-stick at Samaritan? Who knows? But, in any case, here he is, wide-eyed at 3:50 a.m. on the brown, vinyl couch in the common room at Central Station, watching Paul Newman's character in *The Verdict*, the lawyer Frank Galvin, wearily getting up to give his final speech to the jury.

You know, so much of the time we're lost. We say, "Please God, tell us what is right. Tell us what's true. There is no justice. The rich win, the poor are powerless . . ." We become tired of hearing people lie, Frank Galvin is saying, and Don cuts in over him.

"Look at this here, with this cover-up, just like with them up at St. Mary's. This is why I always say, 'the good Catholic Church.' This typifies what Catholic hospitals are all about. If my dog was sick, I wouldn't take him up there. *I love my dog.* The good Catholic Church — that's bullshit. St. Mary's, the Daughters of Charity."

Whenever Don sees any part of this movie, it reminds him of his father's death. In the movie, a young, healthy woman is admitted to a Catholic hospital to deliver her third child, but the attending doctors negligently over-anesthetize her and she ends up in a coma. In Don's life, his father was anesthetized too, but he wasn't lucky enough to even end up in a coma.

And we become victims, Frank Galvin is pointing out to the jury members. *And we become weak . . . and doubt ourselves, and doubt our institutions . . . and doubt our beliefs . . . we say for example, "The law is a sham — there is no law . . . I was a fool for having believed that there was."*

"That's it," Don says. He hits the power button on the remote and heads toward the bunkroom. "That's enough of that."

It's probably the notion of becoming a victim, or being weak, that pushed Don over the top tonight. If he had just waited a few more minutes, he could have seen movie justice prevail again, in the huge damage settlement that the jury awarded to the comatose woman's family — the fruit of Frank Galvin's *And I believe that there is justice in our hearts* closing line.

But Don has probably seen the end of this movie a few times before. Maybe he's tired of hearing about somebody else's justice.

Don Kimmey

My father was a fireman first, before he was a policeman. For about a year. See, my grandfather on my mother's side, my grandfather and then my uncle, he used to chauffer Dan O'Connell around. O'Connell was the head of the Albany political machine. My grandfather was, he was like the bookie of the area. Oh, yeah, he was a big bookie. He owned the slot machines, the card games in the back. When Dan O'Connell went to the cockfights, my grandfather used to take him. This is going back to the 40's and earlier. Don't forget, bookies then weren't like they are today. People never had a lot of money — if you had a quarter or a buck, that was a lot of money then, back in the 30's and 40's. It wasn't like it is today. You know, he had the slots and all. He had money, but he pissed it away, too. Always a new car, you know?

Well, my dad was a fireman for a year back when they all drank. There were a lot of drunks, years ago, before I came on the job. When they made 4000 bucks a year, you know, you'd go to the meat market and the guy'd give you a break on the steak, or whatever you want. It was just accepted. They drank. Some guys, not everybody. And then when I come on, some of them still drank a lot, in the station. That's just the way it was. It was accepted. You know, you weren't supposed to, but nobody was going to turn you in, you know what I mean?

That was in '73, and then by '75, in two years, it was like the guys that were coming up now, the captains, the older captains were retiring or dying, the new captains told their guys, "It's ended." So what a guy would do, if he wanted to drink, he just bid out of the house that that particular captain was in and went with another one who would accept it. The other captains were all saying, like Dick was coming and being a captain, and Schultzy — they were saying, "Forget about it; it's over," and things like that. They weren't going to put their asses on the line. Stinson was another one. All the guys who are chiefs now. Stinson said, "I'm the captain. If you drink, you're going upstairs. I'm not losing my job. If you want to lose your pension, keep drinking. It's up to you." You know, you knew where you stood right away. It all changed after they moved up.

My father was on the police force when he died. See, he got kicked in the chest on a call, and a couple of weeks later, he developed blood in the eyes, and the doctor he went to told him, "There's nothing wrong with you. You go see an eye doctor." So he went to see one eye doctor, who said his problem wasn't there. So they made another appointment and he went back, and they go, "I told you. Get out of here. There's nothing wrong with you. There is one thing, though," he said. He didn't want to call him fat. "You're obese," he told him. "You got to lose some weight."

So they put him on a diet and he started losing weight. But the blood was still in the eyes. So they made another appointment with this eye doctor at Seton Hall. He said, "Your eyesight is perfect for a man your age." He was about 43 at the time. Then he said, "You got something wrong internally, though. Something's wrong." So they put him in St. Mary's Hospital for a test, and he never came off the table.

So I got a personal thing with St. Mary's. Not just what I see on the job when I'm in there. My father died in that hospital, and I still say they killed him. He went up for a simple test on the operating table and never came out, back in 1973. It was just supposed to be for a bronchoscopy, where they were going to look down his throat. What I actually believe is that they never ever did a cardiogram on him, pre-vious to him going on the table. They never did blood work, and they tried to come up with a story that what he died of was something that less than 1% of all the autopsies in the United States show. In a year, less than 1% of the post mortems done in this country show what they said he had. And so they asked us, "Jeez, were you in the West Indies or Africa or something?" I said, "My father's a policeman. Don't be fucking stupid. We don't make that kind of money to go on these voy-ages. What's wrong with you people?"

So I still say somebody fucked up somewhere and nobody had the balls to admit it. They think, "We don't want any problems, you know. It never happened." Just like right there in The Verdict. *Classic case, because five years later, when my wife was in Lamaze class, I recog-nized the nurse, who said, "Oh, yeah, Kimmey,"— it was longer than that, maybe six years— she come up to me and said, "Did they ever tell you what really happened that day?" I said, "No, why, what hap-pened?" Then she just clammed right up. "I don't really remember all of it," she said. "But," she said then, "let me tell you. The shit hit the fan, and major changes were made."*

So I kind of believe that like they let a nurse anesthetize him, or they practiced and let somebody else do the procedure, because the doc-tor was supposed to be in two places at once, and he couldn't be, okay? He said he left the room, and then they could never find him.

We tried to sue them. We had a firm out of Albany. His death certificate says he died of the anesthesia, a reaction to it or something. See, when I walked into the room, I was just so pissed off with the two doctors, they were fighting amongst themselves. I didn't even hear what they were talking about, but they were arguing back and forth. I took a kleenex box and I hit the one guy in the head with that. He come after me and I go, "Come on. I'll throw you right out the sixth fucking floor window, right out this window." I go, "A guy comes in for a simple test and he can't come off the table?" I go, "Something's wrong with you people."

When we started the litigation against them, my wife worked at St. Mary's, in the ER. They started harassing her. We were in the office there, and I just made a little telephone call, and I told them, "The next time something is done to Mrs. Kimmey, we're going to have another lawsuit of harassment on you people, because of the litigation that's going on." They just left her alone after that. They didn't bother her. It's stupid, what they did. Then, years later, we find out the same doctor, the medical board brought him up on charges for doing needless surgery. The guy's practice is going down the tubes.

But I came this close to exhuming the body, because the lawyers, after they sent tissue samples to like Columbia University, to Berkeley University, all these places, our lawyer said, "They've got all their I's dotted, their T's crossed. It would be nearly impossible to prove. But I don't believe their story," he said, and I go, "Neither do I." I wanted to find out, you know, whatever it was they had done. So me and my mother went to lunch with them, and one of the lawyers said, "We'll take the case and if we get anything, we'll take a third." Well, they didn't make a dime, not one dime, and this was over a year they worked for us on it. They had files and files and files of shit. It was just unbelievable.

Somebody at that hospital did something. They claim nothing was wrong. But somebody did something. They said the anesthesia was . . . I don't know. You always get a death certificate, you know, where you can put "heart attack" or whatever. They put down "anesthesia." So one, maybe somebody didn't document that maybe he was allergic to lydocaine, or whatever anesthesia they did, or two, maybe somebody just gave him too much and weren't watching the machine or what went on. You never know what goes on in that place.

10

The planet is full of hurt people, angry people, lost people, confused people, people who have explored the vast cartography of trouble, and people stunned by a sudden grief. Someone has to help them; and so we become our brothers' allies, if not their keepers. We nourish them, and they inadvertently nourish us. The minute one imagines oneself in the victim's predicament, and moves to save him or her, it becomes an act of self-love.

— Diane Ackerman
A Slender Thread: Rediscovering Hope at the Heart of Crisis

"He had a seizure and I pulled over and I tried to open his mouth so he wouldn't swallow his tongue."

At Samaritan Hospital, in the wide corridor outside Trauma Room #2, Kathy Diamond is telling a nurse what happened. "Then he stopped breathing and I started giving him mouth to mouth."

"This was at CHP?" the nurse asks.

"No, we had started leaving CHP and we were walking down the stairs and he could barely walk. He was in terrible

318

pain. He said, 'Both my arms are going numb.' Oh, God, I should have brought him right back in."

Tears appear in Kathy's eyes and slide down her face so quickly that they fall onto her blue dress with the pale diagonal stripes and raise two darkening slashes there.

"I brought him down and we got in the car. I drove just a little ways and all of a sudden his eyes rolled backwards and he started having a seizure. I pulled over and his arms started doing this."

Kathy throws her arms out in front of her, tightens her fingers into contorted, almost-closed fists, and jerks them spasmodically up and down. Now a watery grunting begins in her throat, and she twists her mouth sideways so the gravelly sound rolls around and turns into an unnerving growl.

"I opened his mouth and he was going like that," Kathy says. "Then he chomped down on his tongue and made a rattling kind of sound. He opened his mouth wider and he was rattling and . . ."

The nurse breaks in now. "Can we get somebody to call someone for you?"

"They called somebody. My mother-in-law," Kathy answers, and shifts back to the growling. "He kept doing that, making that noise, and then he just stopped breathing. I ran out of the car and got on the other side and began giving him mouth to mouth. And this lady, where I was stopped, I yelled at her, 'Call an ambulance. Call an ambulance.'"

The nurse tries to take Kathy's arm, to comfort or calm her, but Kathy steps back, just as another nurse steps out of the trauma room and quickly closes the door behind her.

"Is he gone?" Kathy blurts out. "Oh, God, I'm so scared. Are they still working on him?"

"It's definitely something with his heart," the trauma nurse answers.

"Was it all the back pain that gave it to him?" Kathy wants to know.

"I wish I could give you an answer, but I can't. You did everything you possibly could."

"I know CPR," Kathy says now. "I was breathing into him."

"You did wonderful," the first nurse says, but she doesn't try to touch her.

The trauma nurse joins in. "You did everything right. There's nothing more you could have done."

Suddenly Kathy is sobbing so hard she loses her balance a little, and now the two nurses reach out and steady her.

* * *

Dr. Lundgren

I was told that he had started with pain in the upper back area, but some people actually have heart pain that, rather than in the chest, is felt that way. There's no particular type of heart attack that causes that. But it's also one of the reasons that sometimes heart attacks aren't immediately, clearly heart attacks. They present in a way that sounds more like a back pain or an arm pain.

Basically, the entire thing is that he had a cholesterol plaque in an artery. What causes a heart attack is, well, it's called a plaque rupture. There's a cholesterol plaque narrowing an artery. The plaque develops a sort of fissure or crack in the surface of the plaque. This is not something that you can see in any individual, but this is what's known to be the cause of heart attacks. That triggers a blood clot to form. So, in other words, normally what keeps the blood from clotting in the arteries is that there's this smooth lining, a smooth surface on the inside of the artery. A cholesterol plaque can actually disrupt that surface, so the plaque is there for — well, no one can know with certainty how long it's there — but this crack or fissure develops in the surface of the plaque, so the blood is then exposed to material that's the inside of the artery rather than the smooth lining, and that triggers a sudden blood clot.

* * *

Skip Diamond is a maintenance mechanic for the Rensselaer County Sewer District, at the water treatment plant in South Troy, right next to the Hudson River. It's a little after 8 a.m. on July 12 — just another humid, summer Tuesday for him — and Skip has been working to hide his pain for over an hour. It hurts high up in his back, right in between his shoulder blades, and it grabs him so hard that when he bends over to tighten the lower bolts on the pumps, his eyes water. He's only taking shallow breaths now, but it's still like there's a big fist twisting around inside him, trying to punch its way out.

The pain started a month ago, off and on. It was dull at first, and then last week his left arm started to tingle, and he thought it might be a pinched nerve. But then that went away, too. Only it came back a whole lot worse the last few days, and last night it nagged him until he finally just got up and stayed in the kitchen. He didn't want to ruin the night for his wife, Kathy, or wake up their two kids, so he made some tea and sat at the kitchen table, pushing his back against the ribs of his straight-backed chair, but that didn't help very much. So he ended up pacing around until it was time to get dressed for work. He called in sick yesterday, Monday, so today he had to show up. He couldn't miss two days in a row for something stupid like back pain. They counted on him to keep all the machines running right.

This is crazy, though. He can't breathe; he can't bend; his vision's getting blurry. He can't get anything accomplished like this. Last thing he wants to do is take off work and go down to see a doctor at CHP. Frigging HMOs, they make you wait forever. But what if it's serious? Maybe something's popped in one of his lungs? Maybe it's a heart attack. He's only 39, for chrissakes, and he's in great shape. How could he be having a heart attack? It's probably something simple, like a disc problem or a pinched nerve, because of how it comes and goes. Some days he's been able to run his four miles and feel fine, and then the next day, the simplest movement would stab him right in the back and double him over. That's not what a heart attack acts like. But with the tingling back in his arm and the pain that's not letting up this morning, he's got to do something pretty soon, that's for sure.

* * *

Dr. Lundgren

We did do an echocardiogram on Mr. Diamond in the emergency room, but that's sort of an incidental thing. An echocardiogram is an ultrasound of the heart. It just takes a picture of the heart with ultrasound, so you actually see sort of a two-dimensional image of the heart on the screen. You can see the heart valves and you can see all the walls of the heart and you can see what's contracting and what isn't. So it gives you an impression of how much of the heart is damaged by the heart attack, what the strength of the heart overall is, and if there's any heart valve damage.

I mean, everyone who has a heart attack has an echocardiogram done at some time, and an EKG at some time, also. Basically, we take an ultrasound of the heart to evaluate the strength of the heart's pumping and, in Mr. Diamond's case, his heart did show anterior wall damage. To characterize his as a large heart attack would be appropriate. What we do is we look at the strength of the heart pumping, and try to see what extent of the heart muscle isn't contributing. In other words, with a heart attack like this, where there was an artery that was narrowed, the part of the heart that has had the attack doesn't contract well. So at the very least, Mr. Diamond's heart had a moderate to a severe amount of damage. Really, though, you can't say what percentage it was.

Usually, in these kinds of events, the patient's anterior wall just stops contracting. What happens is that the segment of the heart that is supplied by the blocked artery, because it's not getting any blood flow anymore, the heart muscle doesn't contract. So basically it sits still while the rest of the heart pumps. It's called the left anterior descending artery, and it is the largest individual artery of the heart. That's usually the one that's blocked in anterior heart attacks. Again, because that's the largest artery, anterior heart attacks are usually the most severe. They're the ones that give you the most weakness of the heart muscle.

* * *

"Don't look," the big woman tells Kathy Diamond.

You stay here, Skip.

The big woman in the wrinkled housedress, holding a portable phone, with a sagging row of socks and bras and dresses stretching along the clothesline in the yard behind her, leans over the fence a little more and says, "Don't look anymore, honey."

Don Kimmey puts the medic box down and asks, "How old?"

"39," Andy Waterman answers. Andy is captain on Engine 6 today. Jefferson and First, where Skip Diamond lies motionless on the narrow strip of grass next to the sidewalk, is in Engine 6's district. Pete DeChiaro is one of the 1st Platoon hosemen at Engine 6, and he's pushing rhythmically on Skip's chest.

You can't go yet. Remember the kids. Just hold on, okay? God will help you. Let Him help you see the kids.

"He got a pulse?" Jeff Gordon says to Andy.

"Nothing."

Skip's dark blue pants are unzipped, and the left side lies folded down so a triangle of white underwear gleams in the sun. His white undershirt is pulled up and bunched underneath his armpits, and its folds shake every time Pete presses down.

I drove really fast. We had time, even at CHP, we had time.

There were doctors there. On the other floors, there were doctors, and they wouldn't let him in.

Suddenly Andy says, "No, wait, that felt like something."

"See if you get a pulse," Jeff tells him, and opens the medic bag for intubation tools.

"If you don't get a pulse, just keep doing CPR," Don says to Pete and turns toward Kathy. "Were you with him?" he asks her.

"I took him to CHP," Kathy answers, but she doesn't take her eyes off Skip. She reaches up mindlessly with her left hand to wipe the sweat off her forehead, and then clenches a handful of her red hair and pulls on it. "He was having back pain, and they didn't do anything."

Two prescriptions. That's what we get? A painkiller and a muscle relaxer? What if it's Skip's heart? The heart's a muscle, isn't it? The script, for God's sake, not even the pills, so we had to wait at their pharmacy, too. Three, four, five, six, the minutes kept piling up. Couldn't they see him? How could they not hurry, when a human being hurts so much right in front of them like that?

Jeff presses the fast-patch electrodes into place and attaches the black and white lead wires now. The monitor/defibrillator begins to beep erratically, as if there might be enough electrical activity in Skip's heart to generate a reassuring, repeating spike in its oscilloscope's horizontal green line. But in the machine's small, dark window, turned mercifully away from Kathy's gaze, the green line stays ominously flat.

I rubbed his back. That's what I thought it was, his back. I was rubbing, trying to . . . what? . . . Just rub, touch Skip, keep rubbing, what else could I do until the pills came, finally, and then there was no water. A Coke machine, glowing red in the hallway corner, that's what we had. Skip was digging in his pockets and I had nothing, no change, one ten but no dollars, nothing that would work and Skip couldn't even hold onto the coins. He dug and scooped them out and they fell on the floor and rolled, pennies mostly, all over the floor and the pharmacy people were glaring at us. So what? I didn't care, why should I, I

mean, care for them, or care about their disapproval? They had doc-
tors there, and they wouldn't let us in. So I scooped up the quarters I
needed and got a soda and made him take the pills, one each of the pre-
scriptions, so he swallowed both pills with the soda and I was standing
there, helping, and didn't even know what was happening.

Don moves around to see the screen better. "Nothing," he
tells Jeff.

"Stop CPR," Jeff insists. He pushes his knees firmly into the
grass now, balancing himself, and charges the defibrillator paddles. "Clear . . . clear," he shouts, and delivers the shock.

Don't you leave, Skip. I see you going. God, don't let him leave.
This is how he was in the car, in front of Pusatere's Market, he
pushed my hand away. I put my hand there, on his leg nearest me, to
comfort him, and he shoved it away. I looked at his face then and he
seemed separate, like he wasn't even there, and he was biting his
tongue, biting so hard the spit and blood was pushed out onto his chin
with his face pulled back all tight and his voice a scary rattle in his
throat. That ugly rattle deep in him somewhere, and there was only
that for him. No me, only the biting and the rattle and not even any
him, no Skip.

Like now, he's floating up so slow and peaceful, it's almost like he
wants me to be alone. I can see you, Skip. Get back here. You're not
leaving me and the kids by ourselves. Oh, God, don't you take him
now. I can see what he's doing and You can't let him leave yet. He has
kids here and we can all be home for dinner, all four of us, like always,
at home, but You have to stop him.

"Is there a pulse?" Don wants to know. "Check the pulse.
What do you got?"

"Fib," Jeff answers.

Fib: Ventricular fibrillation. No organized heart rhythm.
No P Waves, no P-R Interval, no QRS Complex. A lethal dys-
rhythmia with no cardiac output. Asystole. Cardiac arrest.

Kathy doesn't understand any of those terms, but she can see
a person she loves lying on the ground, and she knows what

"Clear!" means, and she can see the electrical shock only made Skip's body twitch up into the air for half a second, and now he's splayed out, half-dressed, not moving again. She gets all that.

Kathy stands up and takes a step toward Skip now, but the big woman leans over the fence and gently takes her arm.

"You ain't gonna do any good over there," she tells Kathy. "Try to stay calm, okay, honey. I know it's hard. It's really hard."

"Once more, check the pulse," Don says. "If you got nothing, let's put him on a stretcher and get him over to Samaritan."

Jeff stands up, steps past the monitor and off the curb to call Samaritan on his radio.

"MD 565, this is Troy Fire Paramedic 369. We have a 39-year old white male in full arrest. How do you read this unit?"

* * *

Dr. Lundgren

So what happened to him is that the cholesterol plaque caused a blood clot to form in an artery of the heart that blocked off the blood flow to that section of the heart. Ordinarily, clot-dissolving drugs have been the standard treatment for that type of heart attack. When Mr. Diamond came in, he had what amounts to brain damage from the lack of blood flow to his brain. In that situation, it generally isn't safe to give clot-dissolving medications. So he wasn't eligible to have anything like that, because of the issue of possible brain damage.

Well, in general, if Mr. Diamond had been conscious when he was admitted, and if someone had given him a clot-dissolving medication, that would have been desirable. If the drugs dissolve the clot, they can reduce the extent of a heart attack. In someone who comes in unconscious, though, it's not safe to do it. It's hard to say exactly why, but you need a conscious patient, where you can tell if they're alert or what their symptoms are and so on. His largest problem was, obviously, the heart attack. But because his heart had stopped for some period of time, when he came in he was unconscious. In that situation, clot-dissolving drugs can cause problems. One of the side effects of them is bleeding into the brain. In someone who is already unconscious, you can't tell whether they're having bleeding, or whether they've had a stroke in addition to the heart attack.

He had a heart attack caused by a narrowed artery to the heart, but a large part of his problem in his treatment, really, was his mental status. We couldn't interview him when he came in about when his pain started. It may be that the onset of the pain was the heart attack itself. Or it may also be that he was having pain from a blood clot forming — one that hadn't completely blocked the artery — either way, I mean, it's all the same thing. The pain would have been caused by the blockage of the artery. I think it's most likely that the blod clot had formed a day or two before we saw him, but it didn't completely block the artery, and then the day he came in with the pain being worse, it completely obstructed the artery.

He really benefited from the availability of prompt defibrillation. If he had had this happen somewhere where there wasn't someone available, like the Troy Fire Department, to defibrillate him properly — well, most people don't survive, because they're not treated promptly enough, that's all. It just takes time to summon an ambulance, for it to physically get there, and then to get the treatment administered. It isn't necessarily anybody's fault.

* * *

Four of the five receptionists, or physicians' assistants, or nurses, or whatever they are, or do, here at Community Health Plan, at CHP, are glaring at Kathy Diamond.

"My husband needs to see a doctor now," Kathy tells them.

One of the women, an obese one wearing a rumpled, white doctor's coat with a long brown stain on the left sleeve, steps forward. Kathy knows this one, from another miserable time she had to bring her daughter down to CHP for an ear infection. This one's a physician's assistant.

"I'm sorry. We gave him an appointment," the P.A. says, in a whiny, nasty tone meant to convey fake sorrow and omniscient authority all at once. "We've already talked to him, and that's the best we can do."

At this, Kathy turns to scan the HMO's waiting area. Her husband, Skip, is pale and sweating. Even from ten feet away, she can spot the sickly gloss on his neck and chest. His work shirt and undershirt are both off, his right hand is clamped around his upper left arm, and he's hopping in place, walking in circles, sitting down and then jumping back up, moaning, bending over suddenly, sitting back down, shifting his hand from his arm to clutch and scratch at his chest, all in ten seconds of time, and finally groaning so loudly that his friend, Bob, who drove him to CHP from the water treatment plant where they both work, leaps out of his chair to help but just stands there next to him, not knowing where he could touch Skip that wouldn't make the pain worse. "It's really bad," Skip is gasping, in a frantic, hoarse whisper. "It's really bad."

Besides Skip and Bob, the waiting area is empty.

Kathy turns back and leans on the counter. "Can't you squeeze him in?" she pleads.

"Look, if we try to squeeze him in, he'll only end up waiting longer, and it'll be worse that way," the fat P.A. answers. "Believe me, he's better off if he just goes home and takes the medicine I prescribed for him and comes back later when we can see him."

Kathy looks from one woman to the next, searching their eyes for any softness, for any hint of compassion that might offer an opening. One older woman who might be a nurse, Kathy can't remember right now, returns Kathy's gaze, almost as if to say, *I feel really bad for you, this is horrible, but she's in charge*, and then lowers her eyes. The other four women stare at her with no expressions.

Kathy didn't really expect better treatment at CHP. She just didn't have much choice. She and Skip couldn't afford to go to the emergency room at Samaritan or St. Mary's, and CHP was the HMO her job had chosen, so that was that. They had never treated her family with kindness, or concern, or even common courtesy, any time she could remember, and when she called earlier from her cubicle in the check writing department of the financial counseling firm in Albany where she worked, she told the woman on the phone that her husband had back pain. Excruciating back pain, but back pain, and that's when the woman blew her off. Kathy heard it in her tone.

"Well, he'll have to wait for an appointment," she had said.

"He can't. He's in terrible pain right now," Kathy begged into the phone.

"Where, in his lower back?" she asked, wearily.

"No, in his upper back, right between his shoulder blades, " Kathy had told her. "He's got tingling in his arms. He's talking about calling an ambulance."

"He can't call an ambulance," the woman barked. "We won't pay for that. It has to be an emergency to call for an ambulance, and this is only a back problem. You'll have to wait. A nurse will call you back."

At that point, Kathy had hung up and called Skip back to tell him what happened. He said he couldn't wait. He was going to call an ambulance, and she told him she didn't think they'd pay for that. They wouldn't even give her an appointment for him.

There was silence then on the phone, and Kathy said Skip's name. No answer. She said it again, louder, but then she heard Skip asking Bob to give him a ride to CHP, and then he came back on.

"Bob will drive me," he said. "Just meet me there, okay?"

"Okay, I'll wait a few minutes to see if they call back and then . . ." Kathy was saying, but she realized Skip wasn't there anymore, and she got panicky. A voice inside her said, *You have to go. Now. Right now. Don't wait. You have to go.*

As Kathy walks back to Skip now, he is on one knee, leaning against a chair. He holds out a note for her.

"She gave me this," he tells her. "Two prescriptions. One's a painkiller. The other's a muscle relaxer."

"She gave you these?" Kathy asks. "Did she check you over at all?"

"No. Nothing."

"Did she take your blood pressure, your pulse, anything?"

"No."

Oh, my God, Kathy thinks. No one is going to help us.

"Let's just go downstairs and get the pills," she says to Skip now. "They'll make you feel better, and we'll go home and you can rest. Then I'll bring you back down here and they can see you."

Bob takes Skip's right arm, and Kathy takes his left, and they help him to his feet.

"Now my arms are completely numb," Skip whispers.

Kathy hesitates, looks toward the women behind the counter, and considers going back up one more time.

What good is it going to do. They still won't see him.

* * *

Dr. Lundgren

Honestly, there's not much to this incident. It was basically a life-saving event that the fire department did for him. Mr. Diamond had a heart attack and had a cardiac arrest, and he was defibrillated at the scene. Normally, this is something he would have died of, if it weren't for the availability of EMS services.

You've got to watch the terminology here, because almost everyone with a major heart attack survives. There's a difference between a heart attack and a cardiac arrest. Most people that have a cardiac arrest didn't have a heart attack. It's a different thing. There's a tremendous difference between the two and you've got to be very clear about that. To say that people with heart attacks don't survive is just inaccurate. In the current era, 96% of the people with heart attacks survive the initial hospitalization. So, at any rate, a heart attack strictly means a blood clot forming that obstructs an artery. A cardiac arrest is basically the heart stopping from v-fib — ventricular fibrillation. I mean, some people with heart attacks will have ventricular fibrillation, but it's not necessarily so that everyone with v-fib has a heart attack. It is pretty much the experience, in general, that a patient who experiences a cardiac arrest will not survive. I shouldn't say it's useless to treat them, but most people that are treated for out-of-hospital cardiac arrests don't survive. Most people that fibrillate outside the hospital don't get medical attention immediately. And it's a feature of entirely how soon they're treated, which is why there's this push now for automatic defibrillators to be placed in public buildings and the like. But the biggest factor determining whether they live or not is how soon they are defibrillated.

*   *   *

Don Kimmey's in a bad mood. He came in with his jaw set, swaggered into the kitchen, and immediately started bitching to Mike Harrison about Chief Schultz. What, did he have a fight with his wife, Connie? Drink too much last night? Get out of his car in the station parking lot and realize it's 88 degrees already, at quarter to eight in the morning? With Don, it could be any or all of the above, and nobody will know, because Don isn't about to tell you the real reasons he's pissed off, at least not directly. Those reasons are private. They're just his, for his own perverse enjoyment, and they provide an accessible reservoir that he can draw on in any situation, stressful or not.

But he isn't necessarily wrong a lot of the time. It is hot. It's

July 12th, and it's been unusually hot for the last three weeks. Global warming hot. And everybody's been complaining about Schultz and his obsession with dress codes for this whole heat wave. He insists that all men on duty keep their light blue, fire service shirts on and buttoned. Even on the hottest days, like today. No stripping down to the dark blue, departmental t-shirts, except when the men are washing or working on the fire trucks. Which is Schultzy's other obsession — fire trucks. In his office, on the wall next to his desk, he has thirty framed photographs, and all of them except for one are horizontal shots of fire engines or chief's cars. The one, anomalous vertical picture, poking its white mat above the middle of the top row of photos, directly under the speaker box, shows a Troy firefighter in full turnout gear standing on a frozen rooftop, with rounded layers of ice shrouding any hint of shingle or cornice, surrounded by a ghostly mist and covered with ice himself, pointing skyward in an unearthly pose, his whole body mysteriously haloed in the center of the photo.

So what does that tell Don Kimmey about the Chief? That he likes fire engines? Of course. That he believes firefighters should be deified when they survive horrific conditions and assume heroic poses? Maybe. So what's the big deal? If the guy likes fire engines and thinks firefighters are heroes, why can't he let the good citizens of Troy see his men in their uniform t-shirts on a sweltering summer day? Don doesn't get it.

Or what if it's just that Don hates the job in the summertime? He prides himself on being a worker, and the call volume for the Troy Fire Department plummets during the summer months. If the department's year-round average is about 22 calls a day, it's pretty clear that September to May are the months of heavy lifting, because in the summer, some of the houses will go all day and only answer one or two calls. Central Station does stay relatively busy, but that's because the Medic Truck and the Squad carry the paramedics who respond to all the advanced life support calls. The resulting down-time drives Don crazy, and it also means there's plenty of time to finish all of Assistant Chief Thompson's particular 1st Platoon tasks. Way too much time. For instance, this morning Dick has Frank Ryan, Ric Moreno and Dave Paul cleaning every single tool and piece of rescue equipment, as well as all the storage compartments on the entire Rescue Squad again.

To top it off for Don, when he started his morning check of the Medic rig, he discovered that the paramedics on the 4th Platoon failed to fill up some of the oxygen tanks. That really set him off. He started swearing a blue streak and lambasting one of them in particular — Mo Catel — which Don loves to do, anyway, because he had to work with Mo for a stretch once and he has a long list of personal and professional complaints against him. Jeff Gordon stood up for Mo, and told him that Mo wasn't even working yesterday, but Kimmey didn't care. Having to do somebody else's job for him, whoever it is, always gets Don's goat, and when he makes up his mind about something, no matter how wrong or alone he is in his opinion, that mind sets up like quikcrete.

In any case, Don and Jeff had to drive up to Engine 2 on Bouton Road first thing, right after they finished checking out the drug boxes, to fill up the oxygen bottles. But then a call came in when they were almost there — a pedestrian struck by an auto at Hoosick and 16th Streets.

So here he is, turning around and heading back down 15th toward Hoosick. It's going to be one of those days, he knows it.

"Time to save somebody, Donald," Jeff says, and laughs. He leans his head out the window and lets the warm wind hit him full in the face. Jeff's mood today is diametrically opposite Don's. He absolutely loves summertime. He's got friends in Provincetown that he visits whenever he can, and most of the time he seems to forget how much he hates Dick Thompson. And since Jeff has been working out recently at the Troy YMCA with Don, Jeff has decided that Donny's the MAN. No more arguments, no more condescending remarks, no more pulling rank at calls. Last tour of duty, Jeff even told Don he was turning over a new leaf. Just like that. He even used the cliche without being sarcastic. It also didn't hurt that Jeff learned the results of his bloodwork a couple of weeks ago — no HIV positive, no hepatitis. He's even finally stopped ragging on the Samaritan nurses.

"Probably a kid," Don says, hearing a Federal siren blaring somewhere and glancing quickly in his side mirror.

"Hopefully, it's nothing," Jeff answers. "But that's a tough spot. Everybody's trying to jockey for position as they go up Hoosick."

"That's right by the fried chicken joint, right?" Don is asking as he starts his turn onto Hoosick.

"Watch out for that engine coming up," Jeff shouts, as Engine 2 swerves and shoots by the front of Medic 2.

"This idiot is the guy I'm worried about," Don says, shaking his head. "That asshole. Did you see that fucking guy, not moving over?"

Suddenly the sirens begin to wind down, and the dispatcher's voice comes over the radio: ALL UNITS: FALSE CALL. CAR 4 REPORTS FROM THE POLICE WHO TALKED TO THE ORIGINAL CALLER THAT THIS WAS A FALSE CALL.

Don immediately turns off Hoosick onto 16th, and for some unknown reason, his mood shifts, and he starts talking about Brenda, one of the new nurses at Samaritan Hospital.

"She had this one tight little outfit on last week and I said to her, 'You know, that's the type of outfit where I just lean you over the desk and lift up the tail and go to town on you,' and she said, 'Oh, God,' and started laughing like hell."

"Bend over, Brenda," Jeff mimics, grinning.

Now Don winks conspiratorially and shoots a glance at Jeff.

"If I looked like her, I'd figure every guy was thinking that and I'd want them to think the same thing."

Jeff whoops now and peers out the front window, over toward the back of Samaritan Hospital and the Emergency Room entrance, as Don turns down toward 15th street again. "If you looked like her, I'd be thinking the same thing you're thinking," Jeff says. "Bend over, Donny, and pull up that little skirt of yours."

"I've said it before and I'll say it again, Jeffrey," Don says, giving him a sideways, cautionary glance, "I'll never let you stand behind me." But at least Don seems about to smile as he says it . . . maybe only the hope of a smile, but it's a start.

Jeff Gordon

When was that call? Middle of July, right? Eight weeks ago already. It was a Tuesday, I remember that, because I got my test results the day before Skip had his heart attack. I drove down there on a Monday. Driving down, I was trying to figure out what kind of mindset I had, and I couldn't figure it out. I was totally ambivalent. I figured, whatever it was, I'd deal with it when I knew. There was nothing I could do about it.

I had known a couple of friends who had been tested. One of them, who is gay, had some genuine concerns when he was going through the testing process. He was a fucking wreck for two weeks, but he came back negative, too. He called me that Sunday night, before I went down, and we were talking about it, and I was telling him that I didn't know how to prepare myself emotionally. So I just went down with a completely open mind and I said, "Whatever happens, happens."

They're very meticulous about the testing. All they have is a number, then age, race, and gender – 32-year old, white male. So he verified my age when I walked in. They don't fuck around at all. He had the folder open, he checked the number, and as he handed it to me, he said, "You're HIV negative." And I said, "Okay," and I was looking at the sheet, and I said, "Can I photocopy this?" And he said, "No."

336

I can only imagine if I had gotten the opposite results what would have happened. It wasn't like giving high-fives on the way out or anything. I don't want to say that it was an emotional letdown, because it was the opposite of that, in a sense, but it took a number of hours to set in.

That Monday I got the results was weird. I didn't really loosen up until later in the day. I didn't feel immediate relief at all. I really didn't. I walked back out to the car and I got in and didn't feel anything about it. Then, later in the day, it started to set in and I chilled out and thought, "Oh, this is good. This is good news."

Though I have to go back. Because I got tested within two months of the incident that I am saying is my major incident, they recommended that I go back in six months and get tested again. It could take up to six months for the antibodies to show up in my system, so they're recommending I go back. But I think I'll have a much more confident feeling going back. This first time, I had a lot of doubts, I guess. Or at least I convinced myself that I had some doubts. As the weeks go on, though, I feel better and better about it.

That week turned really strange. I came out negative on the tests on Monday, which was great, but I hardly slept at all that night. I don't know why. But, anyway, I went into the firehouse that next day on maybe an hour and a half of sleep. Then after the call with Skip, I wasn't even tired. I mean, I didn't even feel tired. I should have been asleep on my feet, but that call had me wound up the whole day. I was really wired. And when I went home on Wednesday after the shift, I should have crapped out, but I was wired all that day, too.

It must have been Skip. I kept track of him all that week, and I hardly ever do that. You know how I am. How many MI's have we had this year where you've been with us and seen what goes on? 20, 25? When they're down like that and we can't get them back? Donny figured him for an organ donor. He had been talking to one of the doctors, and apparently when Skip went to CHP, they didn't even give him a physical exam. They said, "We can't see you now.

Come back at 12:30," and they wrote him scripts. That's how that all transpired.

Well, I went to see Skip that Wednesday, the day after his MI. I just went up there and his whole family was there, and they were just all over me. There were like ten people in the room, and they had brought in all kinds of food and stuff. The wife, Kathy, was 100%. She was really cool. She was up and talking the whole time, and she couldn't say enough good about us. High praise for us.

So while I was there, she told me that Skip kept a notebook of his training regimen. The guy was obsessed with working out. He used to run every day on his lunch hour. He had a rower and a treadmill at home. Last year, he did 50,000 sit-ups. That was his obsession, to keep track of stuff like that. I mean, the guy was the picture of health and he was a big guy — 180, 190 pounds probably, almost six feet. Obviously, the picture of health, and CHP fucked him.

I told her I'd get Donny to stop the next workday, which would have been a Saturday, and she said, "When Skip wakes up, he's going to want to see you guys." And I told her, "Well, we want to see him, too," but there was still a nasal gastric tube in him and there was blood coming up through that periodically, and they weren't completely sure what the source of that blood was. Once in a while, he would become agitated for some reason and he'd try to breathe on his own, and then he'd posture a little bit. So I wasn't holding out a lot of hope for him to even wake up, but I didn't say that to Kathy.

Major anterior wall damage. Serious, big-time damage. That's what the doctor had told me. They didn't know what to do. What could you do? That part of his heart was dead. He might have been having the heart attack for a couple of days before he went down, because he had the back pain for that long, at least. I didn't know, one way or the other, looking at him. Maybe that wasn't his day, you know? The doctor was saying that, even with that kind of damage to his heart muscle, stranger things had happened. He could conceivably make it. You can never tell, but they weren't getting any good response to stimulation from him then. He was alive, though, and he wasn't a vegetable. It doesn't often get any better than that, with a big MI, so I felt hopeful about it. That call was all I thought about all week. Really.

Then on Saturday morning, Donny and I stopped in to see Skip again, and that time he was sitting up in bed, and I talked to him. I said, "How you feeling, Skip?" And he just answered me, like it was no big deal that he was sitting up and responding to somebody's question, "Not bad, but I'm really thirsty. I need some water." We couldn't believe it.

So he was off all life support that second time I saw him at Samaritan. He was all on his own for that, but he still had an IV hanging for cardiac meds. There was no neurological deficit, but his thought process was really scrambled. They did a CAT scan on him. He didn't have a stroke. There was no hemorrhage in his head. He didn't blow any gaskets. The ET tube was out of him, but there was still a nasal gastric tube in, because he had some blood in his belly. They weren't sure where that was coming from, and they didn't know where the blood in the lungs was coming from either. Only thing I can think is we could have created a pneumothorax when we were ventilating him: We may have blown a little part of his lung and he got some blood in there that way.

He didn't completely recognize Kathy, and he was definitely spacy that day. He was looking at me but he wasn't looking at me, that kind of thing. Although, obviously, he was showing marked improvement. He had sustained a lot of muscle damage to his heart, but he was holding his own. That was in four days. Who knew what four more days could bring? But yeah, he had made a huge recovery at that point.

Then I got busy and couldn't get up there for a while, so it was maybe two workdays later, which would make it the end of July, that I saw Skip again. There's something called an ejection fraction, which measures the amount of blood that's pumped out of your heart on each pump. Depending on who you are and on your genetics and your personal history, it's anywhere between around 70 and 100%. Skip's was 20%. He was fucked, okay? He was so weak that they walked him about twenty feet, and it took two nurses to hold him up and walk him back and forth. He couldn't even hold himself up. He had enough blood perfusing his brain, but he literally couldn't pump enough blood to sustain himself walking. He had recognized his wife finally, and he realized that he had kids, and that they were his kids, and he knew that he had been some type of mechanic. He had no recall of going to CHP the day of the event, or anything like that. He was way behind on a lot of that stuff. That was a couple of weeks after the MI but it wasn't clear whether, even with rehab, he was going to get a lot more function back.

I stopped going to see him for a while, because I felt really lousy about him, but then it must have been about the middle of August that Kathy called me at home. I had given her all our names, and she must have looked in the phone book. I'm the only Jeff Gordon who's listed in Troy, so I assume I was the first call she made. She told me Skip was supposed to be discharged from Samaritan that weekend. He was going up to Highgate, up past Leonard Hospital. Highgate's a head trauma and therapy place.

So while we were talking, Kathy told me she was a romance novelist. She hasn't been published yet, but she's been submitting a lot, I guess. And she said the day before Skip had his heart attack, she had just been turned down for a book she had written. Apparently, they thought it was going to go through and that was going to be her big break, and she thought that might have been one of the added stressors, which is certainly possible.

Then she started talking about Skip again. She said he could walk with assistance for short distances, but he didn't have a lot of energy. She was going to keep praying and she knew he would be fine, because he used to be such a big runner. He used to run 6, 8 miles a day, and she was saying, "Well, he may never be able to do that again. Maybe he'll only be able to run a mile, but he'll run." I thought she was still in denial about his physical condition, in terms of . . . well, someday he may be able to walk a mile. I don't know if he'll ever be able to run again.

So now here it's what, September 11, and Kathy calls me last night and tells me Skip's home and he's got the okay from his doctor to start jogging again, if he wants to do that. Jesus, can you believe that? Apparently, what happened, the reason he even had the heart attack was . . . I guess everybody has so much plaque in their arteries. As you reach a certain age — 35, or 40, or whatever it is — it starts to build up. What happened to him is the plaque separated somehow from the arterial wall and it caused some sort of aneurysm behind it, like a genetic defect. In most people, it doesn't happen. So that burst, and that's what caused him to have the heart attack. Now they're saying he only had moderate damage, and that it isn't as significant as they previously thought.

Another amazing thing happened. A couple of weeks after he was discharged, they thought he was having seizures. Well, he wasn't having seizures. Apparently, he was just having terrible dreams. When he got into his REM sleep, he was twitching all over the room and all over the bed, and Kathy thought he was having seizures. He was having terrible, terrible dreams that he wasn't remembering when he woke up. They didn't find any indication that he was having seizures.

It was an unbelievable call. It was really the save of the year. He was dead on the ground when we got there, and now the guy is going back to his job. He can't lift heavy weights at work. The most he can lift is 35 pounds. But he's going back to work, and the family wants to come down here. They had a plaque made for us. They want to come down and give us the plaque, the whole family, and not just him and her, but brothers and sisters and kids and relatives. They all want to come down. We're trying to arrange a day. Maybe next Saturday would be best for them, and she wants all the people who were on the call to be here.

You know what Kathy Diamond said to me? "Were you given an award for saving Skip's life?" That's what she said. I told her, "Well, that's a long story, but we're not given awards for saving lives in Troy unless it's a rescue or at a fire. We don't get awards for medical calls."

I understand that we put our lives at risk in rescue situations and at fires, but the person is no less saved and no less alive because it's a medical call. Anyway, it doesn't matter. I'm really happier that this is going the way it's going. It's more satisfying for me to be thanked this way, by the family I've helped, than by being given some award.

11

"*Thus, in what I like to call the Great Asymmetry, every spectacular incident of evil will be balanced by 10,000 acts of kindness, too often unnoted and invisible as the 'ordinary' efforts of a vast majority. We have a duty, almost a holy responsibility, to record and honor the victorious weight of these innumerable little kindnesses . . .*"

— Stephen Jay Gould

This woman's gnarled knees are wider than her thighs, and they swell out like burls on stunted saplings. Under her knees, a thin, aluminum threshold separates the darkened wood strips of her bedroom floor from the stained, threadbare rug in her hallway, where I'm standing, trying to capture the full length of her emaciated body in my camera's viewfinder. The bottom halves of her legs cross that threshold and rest on the rug, right below me, because the wall behind me is too close. I can't move back far enough, even using this wide-angle lens, to fit her ankles and feet into the frame, and that's what I seem to be worried about — fitting all of her into the frame.

When I started this work, almost exactly a year ago, I was shocked by every dead body I saw and unnerved by family members who huddled in corners, crying and comforting each other. Often, on calls during my first couple of months, I couldn't stop myself from crying in empathy. And I was just as often quick to grab an IV bag or lift up the corner of a stretcher, or happy to do whatever I was asked to do, so I could help or fit in, probably.

So what has happened to me in one year? I'm not feeling any thick knot of emotion in my throat, nor am I reaching down to cover this old woman's legs with a blanket before I take the photo. I'm just doing my job, which is to record emergency calls and interviews on cassette tapes, to write notes whenever I can, to shoot dramatic or emotional photographs, and to remember everything I observe. It took the first couple of months to learn how to juggle those tasks on a call, and I'm still trying to understand how to detach my emotions — what any professional journalist does on any given workday — but even that seems a little easier now, on my final day with these firefighters, perhaps because I've accepted the emotional calluses that have formed in the last few months.

Crying during a call meant I couldn't see everything clearly, either optically or emotionally. I learned that early on. And holding a frozen man's arm in the air, so the warmer IV solution could gravitate through the crystallizing limb meant, after all, that I couldn't use both hands and, for me, using only one hand in the back of a moving ambulance usually produced a blurry photo. But I did hold that frozen arm, choosing to help in that instance, even as I kept reminding myself that I was there to document what happened, not to affect or alter the circumstances of it.

Why did I hold that frozen arm? Who did I think I was, anyway? I guess, at many times during this last year, I haven't been so sure. Maybe, in my mid-forties, pretending to be a firefighter suddenly appeared more worthwhile than being a writer or a university professor. Certainly it felt more real, in the way that the newspaper seems real. But also on this job, I didn't have to be alone in a room, imagining dramatic scenes for a novel or a screenplay: I could work with other people who were handling a genuine human crisis, and perhaps I could share in helping them save someone.

Saving people. Wartime reporters and photographers are faced with the extremes of this dilemma all the time. Do you try to save a life, or do you capture that life so others might understand what is happening? Isn't that what saving lives means, in a sense, as well? Although, putting aside for a moment the natural inclination to help in a crisis, is it right to reproduce one person's tragedy so others can experience it vicariously? Is transforming difficult human experience into some form of art truly a moral act: In other words, can seeing it and understanding it improve our lives in any important way?

Take this old woman lying on the floor now. What is most important here? What do we need to know? How to fit her into the frame, or how to help her? For Dave Stevens and Ric Moreno, right now, art isn't even a consideration. Their first questions must be, *Is she alive?* and *Where is she hurt?* Then, *How can we help?* Followed by, *Who is she?*, and *Why is she lying on the floor?* Eventually, *Why are we the ones helping?* or *Where is her family?* and *How can we keep this from happening again?* might be asked as well.

Her name is Elizabeth. She lives on the 2nd floor of 2365 Burdett Avenue, a few houses in from Hoosick Street — two blocks below the house on Hoosick where I grew up, and five blocks above the liquor store where Mike Kelleher was stabbed last September. Elizabeth fell yesterday, "during daylight," she tells us. Nothing hurts except her elbows and her head, in that order. She is being treated for emphysema. She has been losing weight, but she doesn't know why. She doesn't think her doctor knows why, either.

Elizabeth is 76, and she's very weak. She doesn't want to go to the hospital but, at this point, that may not be up to her. From the ambulance driver, we learn that one of her relatives tried to reach her by phone all day yesterday. Finally, at about 9 this morning, Saturday, that relative called for an ambulance. Then Mohawk Ambulance alerted the Troy Fire Department, and now six well-fed men are explaining to this elderly, almost naked, skeletal woman that she really needs to go to Samaritan Hospital.

"I did all this to you, didn't I?" Elizabeth says to Ric Moreno.

"No, you didn't," Ric answers. "That's what we're here for. You didn't do anything to us."

How true is that? It's not her fault that she fell, of course, but everyone in the room is certainly affected by what they see here. Elizabeth has at least done that to us, even if no one is showing it. You can't tell me that none of us took a second to imagine our own mothers, if they're still alive, lying alone and confused on a hard, cold floor when Elizabeth reached over her head to grab Ric's hand. How impenetrable can professional detachment be, after all?

And how quickly did we all leap to the obvious connection — that Elizabeth reminds us of a holocaust survivor or a famine victim? From there, the mental process could easily turn into a headlong rush of memory and association through all we have ever heard or seen or thought was scary about human history and mortality, if we allow that to happen.

Okay, so if it's true that all of these considerations are present, and all are fighting consciously and sub-consciously to be admitted, to be weighed, how can we deal with all of them and still get the necessary work done? That's what people who sign on for public safety jobs, especially in urban areas where the call volume is high, have to contend with on a daily basis: the dead, the dying, the wounded, the scared, the crazy, the sick, the violent, the unwanted, the lonely, the forgotten. How do you face all of that, tour after 24-hour tour of duty, learn to protect your-self physically, psychically, and emotionally, and keep working efficiently? I guess you learn to laugh about it. Or you quit.

Maybe Joe Reilly was actually warning me a year ago, on my first call, when he said that most of the streets in Troy hold some terrible memory for him. As I drive around the city now, on my days off, I remember all the houses where I've seen people die, too, but I don't think I've been at it long enough to laugh about them yet.

Back in the Rescue Squad after Elizabeth has been taken to Samaritan Hospital, Dave Stevens says, "Honestly, 15 hours down isn't really that bad for someone living alone. We've seen them down a day and a half, two days. I don't mean to sound cruel, but it was only 15 hours. That's like if you didn't talk to your mother from dinnertime last night until this morning. That's not so long."

"And someone from her family was calling all along, too," Ric adds.

Suddenly, Frank Ryan turns from his driver's seat and shouts over the sound of the engine, "Did you see the uncashed checks all over the place?"

Ignoring him, I remind Dave, "She needs to eat, and she needs somebody to come by every day and check on her, and she . . ."

"No," Dave breaks in, "she needs somebody to come by and cash all those checks."

Even Ric can't believe what Dave just said, and he stares at him in silence for a few seconds.

"I'm just kidding," Dave says. "That was a joke."

"Whenever it comes to money, leave it to Dave," Ric explains, but he starts to smile now, and Dave laughs and begins to sing: *Money, it changes everything.*

But then he notices I'm not laughing. "Relax," he tells me, "You were having too much trouble in there. That was nothing."

"I didn't want to take a picture of her like that, but I knew I had to."

Dave looks out the window before answering. "It's not that we don't sympathize with her. You just see it so often. You see it all the time."

"Yeah," Ric agrees. "You build up a tolerance over the years."

* * *

It's the last Saturday in September, and Central Station is chuck full of school kids. Most of them are waiting in line for the high ride, staring and waving at the lucky ones who soar up 40 or 50 feet in Truck 2's aerial bucket. The riders yelp with joy a couple of times as they rise, and then they peek over the rim of the bucket and wave back. But a few of the kids are inside the station, checking out the winning posters that line the walls of the common room.

These posters are really why they're all here on a Saturday morning. Since school started up again the day after Labor Day, firefighters have been visiting local elementary and middle schools to teach about fire safety. Then their regular teachers at those schools asked the students to create posters about what they remembered from the fire presentations, and the students whose posters were chosen as winners are here now to receive plaques and certificates and to have a pizza party.

Occupying the right side of this poster next to the well-pockmarked dartboard is half of a light orange house, and this half-house contains eight round windows, each of them quartered by crosses. Two of them, though, are missing lines, so they look like clocks set forever at 3:00 and 9:00. The 3:00 window sits in the middle of a triangle that forms the second floor front of the house, and a long, curved ladder stretches up to that round window from the brown dirt in the foreground. Maybe a firefighter dove through that window and is searching inside for a child hiding from the flames, and that's why the window is missing two of its lines.

A tree in the left half of the poster is bare, though one purple flower has sprouted on each side of it. Behind the house and the tree, pale green hills stretch across the middle of the poster, and a blue-white sky occupies the top of it. Beside the three curvy lines that probably signify birds flying, a circle with a stick-child inside it floats in the air. A diagonal slash passes through the circle and the stick-child. The words *Don't Play With Matches* appear next to it.

In the poster to the left of the Pepsi machine, a girl in a pink dress lies on the ground with flames on each side of her, although the flames resemble triple shark fins or a dragon's back, so the girl looks as if she's riding a dragon through thick clouds. YES ROOL is written above the girl, with no spelling correction, but most of the poster is filled with large blue, green, red, orange, and yellow letters that read

STOP

DROP

And

ROLL If you catch on fire

The kids find their own posters first and point them out to the other kids, but then they all congregate in front of one that is divided into four scenes — 1. Kitchen; 2. Bathroom; 3. Living Room; 4. Workshop — and asks a provocative question at the top: *Can you find all the fire hazards in the pictures?* Then, at the bottom of the poster, instructions appear: *If you can not find out, look under this cardboard.* The kids shout out their answers and then lift the poster to reveal a second poster underneath, where the kitchen and bathroom drawings are now crisscrossed with orange flame-scrawls. A cautionary statement, with a wobbly arrow indicating the flames, is written boldly across the bottom: *This is what could happen — Think before you do something.*

I want to interview the kids, but Jeff Gordon appears and asks me to take a photo. Kathy and Skip Diamond have brought their daughter, Justine, who is nine, and Patrick, their 7-year old son, and their parents and Kathy's sister-in-law and a few other unnamed relatives, and they all came today to thank Jeff and Don Kimmey for saving Skip's life.

"Well, that first night in the hospital, they didn't think he was going to live," Kathy is telling Don when I join them in the watch area. "Or if he did, they thought he'd be a vegetable. They thought there was massive damage. But now they say there was mild to moderate damage."

"That was our big concern, the mental aspect, you know what I mean," Don says. "You can bring the body back."

"I was prepared for the worst, and we would have taken whatever we got. For a while there, his short-term memory was so short that I didn't know what was going to happen. 'Give me a shower, Kath. I need a shower. Kids, give me a shower.' That's what he would ask. Then twenty seconds later, he'd sit up and ask me the same question. He just forgot. And every day, we'd have to tell him that he had a heart attack, and every day it was like he had just heard the news, fresh, and he'd start crying. He's so strong — I mean, just living, that first day. And then the next day, the second day, his heart was beating on its own without medicine. Then the third day, they got him off the respirator."

At this point, Skip jumps in. "That's why my voice, it's not right yet. It's much better, but when I talk a lot, it gets raspy."

And they all keep talking, but I am distracted by Skip's aliveness. He is saying he hardly remembers anything about that day, like it was a normal, forgettable day, while Kathy is telling Jeff that their angels and God were with them because of how she knew she had to be there to help him and how everything fell into place after she dragged him out of the car at Jefferson and First. I watch Patrick holding onto his father's leg, and I see Don notice that and look away for a minute, as if he is remembering what happened to his own dad who never came out of the hospital and I think of my own father, who had a stroke last week.

Now Don reminds Skip that his son isn't going to let go of him for a while and Skip looks down and tells Patrick to just hang onto him, and Don finally says, "I don't blame him." They all continue to talk, but I am just staring at Skip and trying to understand the nature of chance.

He was dead. I saw him. About two months ago, he was lying on the ground, dead, and now here he is, smiling and joking, standing on his own, hugging his kids, kissing his wife, thanking two of the people who brought him back from the dead. Why did Skip Diamond come back, when so many others didn't?

That he did is amazing, of course. That Don Kimmey could send electricity through Skip Diamond's body to reset his heart, give him a shot of Niagara Mohawk juice, as Don likes to call it, and bring this man back to life — yes, that's amazing. Jeff Gordon has been calling it the save of the year, and given how many cardiac arrests they couldn't convert, I have to admit he's right. Not too many come back after their hearts stop.

But don't we see this kind of thing on TV and in the movies all the time: A dead guy's on the ground; paramedics shock him; he comes back to life; the family's together and happy at the close of the show? I have always been cynical about sentimentality, and it's easy to make fun of happy endings. They're clichés we have come to expect from the entertainment industry. Do these happy endings make all the other tragedies bearable? Do we demand that bad news be accompanied by good news to maintain our necessary illusions?

As Kathy describes Skip's time in rehab, I remember Robert Coates, the RPI sophomore who died after a night of heroin use, and Sam Rizzo, the kid in the wheelchair who died in the Lansingburgh fire with his brother and sister, and Olivia Fuller, the obese woman stuck in her bathroom for 27 hours, and how that seemed funny until she died of respiratory arrest in the ambulance, and all the others who have died while I have been riding with these firefighters. I can't stop myself from remembering them, and I'm afraid they will always be with me, but I realize now that Skip Diamond will be, too.

If I need this happy ending to offset the others that turned out badly, then so be it. What's wrong with a happy ending once in a while, anyway? Let this Skip Diamond ending stay with me, and let seeing this moment when his red-haired, freckle-faced son holds onto his leg and his pretty, long-haired daughter laughs like nothing bad ever happened to her father stay with me, too. And let his wife, who kept him alive until professional help arrived, keep describing how everything seemed so beautiful to Skip when he first got out of the hospital to everyone else she meets:

"He said, 'The grass is so green.' And when he saw our house, he said, "Oh, our house is so beautiful.' I mean, it's not beautiful, but everything was beautiful to him."

"I'll tell you, when the Grim Reaper has got you by the pant leg and you shake him off, everything looks nice," Don throws in.

"I don't know," Skip says, "I don't remember," and he smiles at Don, and everyone there laughs, and I take the picture.

* * *

The Diamonds have gone home now, and there's some palpable tension after the visit, though no one will explain what it is. Jeff Gordon, Ric Moreno, Don Kimmey, and I are in the locker room, which sits between the kitchen and the bunkroom, and I've made the mistake of defending emergency medical services in the fire department.

"The truth is, there is a bias against EMS on this job," I say to Jeff. "It's clear, and since there are no awards given to anybody for anything except for rescues and fires, what does that tell you about EMS?"

"Nothing," Ric says, butting in. He is a paramedic himself, of course, but he is also so aggressive at fires that Mike Harrison borrowed the nickname they had for Kurt Russell's character in *Backdraft* and called him "the Bull."

"It tells me that it's a job where you perform, where you need good cognitive ability and intelligence, a cool head, but your body is not at personal risk," Ric goes on.

But I'm not letting him off so easily. "That's not true," I answer. "What about tuberculosis, or hepatitis B, or AIDS? What about all the communicable diseases and blood-borne illnesses that firefighters come in contact with on medical calls?"

What I want to add is, *What about James Hack in end-stage lung cancer, with his lungs exploding out through his mouth and hitting all the firefighters in the face that day? You don't think they felt their bodies were at personal risk in that moment? Or what about Jeff Gordon and the needle stick from some unidentified patient at Samaritan Hospital,* but I don't, because I know that will provoke some caustic comments about Jeff, and then Jeff's defensive responses, and I won't learn how any of them really feel about this EMS vs. fire issue.

"You can protect yourself against all of them," Ric says. "You can't protect yourself against everything that goes on in a fire call or a rescue call."

"Wait, wait, wait a minute. If you've got an EMS call with a patient who has antibiotic-resistant tuberculosis, and he wakes up from a seizure and coughs in your face, you're not physically at risk?"

"Sure you are," Ric agrees, "but I don't look at it the same way at all. Not at all. It's not the same."

"I know what you're saying," I concede. "It takes a lot of guts to run into a burning building and save somebody, or to rappel down into the Poestenkill Gorge for a rescue. I'm not demeaning those things at all, but it seems to me that people can risk their lives on EMS calls, especially ones that turn violent. If firehouse culture sees it as heroic to run into a burning building, but not so heroic to save a life on a medical call, I don't get that."

Don is getting impatient with my questions about something that seems so obvious to him. "Look, we run into a burning building when others are running out," he instructs me. "It takes balls to do that. That's what separates us from most people in society. That's what saves the city of Troy. Most of the guys here can do that.

"I remember, when I first come on the job, I ran into an old jakey bum, and he said, 'Jeez, I couldn't believe you guys the other day.'" Don actually hunches over a little here, assuming the bum's posture, and turns his voice gravelly to imitate his speech. "'I was fucking running out of my building with all the rats, and you assholes were going in. What are you, nuts?'

"And here's a jakey bum, thinking we're nuts for trying to put out whatever shithole he was living in. And he was thinking, *Well, I'm a jakey bum and I'm stupid, but I'm getting the hell out of here and you wackos are going in.*

"You go into a burning building, you're going into the unknown. That is danger. That's an entirely different animal, an entirely different scenario. You don't know what's going on. With medical calls, you can protect yourself. There will be signs that a patient is waking up, or getting up, or doing whatever he's going to do. There's no comparison, really."

"No matter what the circumstances, it doesn't make the family any less grateful for what the firefighters did," Jeff says now.

Maybe Don is uncomfortable because the Diamonds came down to thank him, or maybe it made him miss his own father more. Who knows? But Jeff has seen this stubborn pattern with Ric and Don before, so why prolong the agony.

"They saved the guy's life and they saved the entire family, not just the guy," Jeff continues. "Their gratitude is just as intense on this call as if we had pulled him out of a burning building. That's the bottom line."

"Correct," Don agrees, "because it's all the job. It's all the same job. The thing is, your job, when you swear and put your hand up in the air and take the oath, is public safety. To protect the public. To save the public, and that's what we do with EMS, but in a different manner. It's just another aspect of the job.

"But the other, with the fires, takes balls," Don insists. "As I said before, that's what saves this city. And the thing that makes this city superior to Albany, Schenectady, Glens Falls, Plattsburgh, Syracuse, or wherever, is the interior attack by the people on this job here. It's much more aggressive. You never see three or four buildings burn down in Troy. We got the same construction here as in other cities. The difference is, we go in and put them out. That's the bottom line. We go in and put them out. There are no headlines like FOUR BUILDINGS BURN! here."

"We saved not only his life, but his family's life," Jeff says again, "his kids, his wife's . . ." but Don turns to Ric and begins talking about dinner, so that's it. No true concessions. No closure on the Diamond save. Discussion concluded.

But it doesn't provide much of an answer for me. Don and Ric are two of the best paramedics in the department, and here they are sounding just like Dick Thompson about EMS. They've been bitching about the assistant chief all year long, if not openly feuding with him, and now they're echoing his small-minded, archaic interpretation of the contemporary fire service.

It isn't just about big fires anymore. Like it or not, professional and volunteer fire departments are entrusted with public safety, and the job has evolved into a multidimensional one. Few days, thankfully, hold major disasters for us or for fire departments. Nationally, there has been an average of four times as many emergency medical calls as fires in each of the last five years for professional departments like Troy that handle fire, rescue and EMS services. We better realize that, for many of us, saving our lives one day may depend not on our family doctors or on the medical staff in a hospital emergency room, but on professional or volunteer firefighters, and on how quickly their emergency vehicles can get them to us. Maybe we should be most concerned about what happens to us on the ordinary days, and about who will help us when we run into trouble.

However, there is another part of this debate that interests me. The "balls" part. The macho element. Have Don and Ric been that upset because the 4th Platoon has caught the dramatic fires this year? The 1st Platoon has complained off and on about not having working fires, but I wonder now if their masculine identities have actually been affected by this lack of opportunity to demonstrate their courage? Are those identities really dependent on a received, popular model of masculinity that might make fun of men who provide nurturing emergency medical care for people?

After the last 91 tours of duty with these guys, I can't believe that. How men act and what they say they believe are often at odds, and I have seen Don and Ric care for and comfort too many hurt people in the past year to believe they don't think that emergency medical care is a crucial part of who they are as men. But maybe they can't admit to that, at least not in front of other men. It's easier to bust their balls.

* * *

SIGNAL 30. HOUSE AT 1114 9TH STREET. FULLY INVOLVED. CAR 2, DO YOU COPY?

9th Street is empty at 4 a.m., so Jack Stinson, the new battalion chief, doesn't need to worry as much about people suddenly crossing or cars pulling out as he usually would.

Mike Harrison, the 1st Platoon's battalion chief for most of the last ten years, retired three weeks ago. His last call was for a black cat caught in a sewer drain, and when all the guys said good-bye to him during the nightly, 8 p.m. radio check, not one of them stooped to any easy jokes that mixed water, female anatomies, and superstitions. For that, I guess they received the bonus of a quiet night, because Mike didn't have to go out again.

I wish the same were true for us tonight. I should have gone home after the Diamonds left, and carried the image of Skip smiling with his family and with Jeff and Don in that picture as my final image from this year. But a couple of hours after dinner, we got called to a house near Griswold Heights where a 39-year old mother of two beautiful teenage daughters was having a grand mal seizure. She has cancer of the brain, and her hospice nurse wasn't there when the seizure happened. It was too hard for her to talk about her condition, so one of her daughters had to describe how the cancer started in her breast, spread first to the left lung, then to the right one, and from there to her neck, and how finally it metastasized to her brain.

"I want to say it, but I can't," she said. "I'm sorry. This is terrible."

Her daughter told her it was all right, that she didn't have to be sorry, and Jeff told her, "Take your time, Angela. I'm in no rush. I came here to see you. It's the only reason I came up here tonight."

"God bless you," Angela answered. "I tell you, it's very scary. There's nothing they can do about it, and that makes it scarier."

Then, around midnight, we had another elderly person down at the other end of Burdett Avenue — two old people lying helpless and alone on the same street, on the same day. This one was a 96-year old, retired, RPI chemistry professor who fell in his bathroom and lay there for three days before a neighbor noticed she hadn't seen him and thought to check. He only had some bruises, and he kept flirting with the nurses in the emergency room until one asked him about his wife and he started to cry. As we were leaving, he asked us to put a note on his door for his son, who lived in San Francisco. He was sure his son was flying home to find him, and the note would direct the boy to Samaritan Hospital.

So it was a typical tour until the Signal 30 came in just before 4 a.m. A house fully involved by fire: The 1st Platoon had not heard that for a long time, and several guys actually swung out of bed, corkscrewed into their bunker pants, and sprinted toward the trucks, just like in the movies.

Even going up Hoosick Street, we could see the smoke billowing above the trees, and now, as Jack pulls up in front of the call address, sure enough, the whole place is blazing. Engine 5 pulls up alongside us and blocks our view of the house. Jeff Reilly, Joe's brother and a probie on Engine 5, is pulling a Halligan bar out of a side compartment as Jack and I hurry around the engine to see the fire again.

As Jack starts to transmit the exposures, I can hear the dispatcher calling for Car 2 again, but there's no answer. Car 2 is Dick Thompson, the assistant chief, and he's usually one of the first at a fire, but it is 4 in the morning, after all.

Denny Broughel, who is subbing for Dave Stevens on the Rescue Squad for the second half of the tour, walks straight to one of the two front windows and smashes it with his flashlight. Jeff Reilly ventilates the other window with the Halligan and scrapes the sharp edges out of the frame. Thick smoke rolls out and covers the front of the house, as Denny kneels down to adjust his Nomex hood.

"Over your head," Ric Moreno yells, knowing that when the fresh air collides with the fire inside that room, it will explode out of those two windows. "Over your head," Ric shouts again, just a second before a twisting fist of orange flames jabs through the window on the right and narrowly misses Denny's head.

Ric kicks the front door in now and then steps back to let

the smoke pour out. Terry Fox, behind a picket fence that connects to the corner of the house a few feet from the door, hands
him a charged line. Ric yanks on the heavy line to free up some
slack and then he effortlessly disappears into the smoke, like a
diver entering dark water. If Mike Harrison were here, he'd
probably smile and shake his head and thank God that some
guys are crazy. There's simply no telling what they'll do.

First Platoon at Central Station — September

Terry Fox .... Captain, EMT, Engine 5

Ray Davis .... Lieutenant, Paramedic, Rescue Squad

Jeff Gordon .... Lieutenant, Paramedic, Medic 2

Gary Hanna .... Firefighter, EMT, Engine 5

Jack Stinson .... Battalion Chief, EMT

Don Kimmey .... Firefighter, Paramedic, Medic 2

Matt Magill .... Captain, EMT, Rescue Squad

Ric Moreno .... Firefighter, Paramedic, Rescue Squad

Dave Paul .... Firefighter, EMT, Engine 5

Jeff Reilly ...... Probationary Firefighter, EMT, Engine 5

Frank Ryan .... Firefighter, EMT, Rescue Squad

Dave Stevens ...... Firefighter, Paramedic, Rescue Squad

Bill Patrick

I can't remember all the exact reasons I wanted to ride along with a group of professional firefighters and paramedics and tell their stories. The primary reason, of course, was to immerse myself in a world governed by emergencies so I could see and learn enough to write this book. That was the motivation that I understood. I had been teaching at a university in Virginia before I moved back to Troy, and I needed to experience a job that offered a more compelling brand of danger and service than what I had witnessed working in a college English Department. But there were also darker and more emotional motivations that I didn't fully understand.

When I began riding along, I was in my mid-40s and my second marriage was sailing straight for the rocks. That made living two to three days a week in an all-male firehouse almost a relief, though being on the job felt more like a temporary safe haven than the fulfillment of some clichéd, boyhood fantasy. Although I had always respected what firefighters did, or what I thought they did, I had never wanted to be a fireman when I was growing up. I certainly saw a few house fires in Troy when I was a kid, and I remember one amazing and terrifying blaze that gutted a three-story hotel that had been built in the 1850s on a peninsula called Rockhurst on the eastern shore of Lake

George, near where my grandparents had a summer camp, but I don't remember having any overwhelming desire to run inside that consumed hotel or to stand shoulder to shoulder with those volunteer firefighters and help them try to douse the flames.

Because regular emergency medical services were not offered by fire departments in upstate New York until the early 1980s, I had never associated firefighters with emergency medicine when I was young. And apart from what the television shows Emergency *and* Rescue 911 *had shown me about first response emergency medical care, I learned quickly, once I was actually observing professionals up close, that I didn't know much at all about how firefighters, EMTs and paramedics actually worked to save people. But that aspect — the emergency medical and rescue side of firefighting — was why I had initially wanted to do the project. In my university office, I had stared out the window and wished more than once that I was riding with a rescue squad. Why, specifically, had I wanted to do that?*

My only prior contact with EMTs or paramedics had been in 1979, when I was involved in a serious farm accident. That accident happened on a rainy Sunday in November, so long ago now that it feels like it happened not to me but to some unfortunate stranger in a tragic story I read once and then just couldn't forget. In some vague way, I knew the real reason I was riding along (and signing a sobering consent form that swore I or my family wouldn't sue the Troy Fire Department if I was maimed or killed during my time with them), was to exorcise the guilt and rage and horror that had lodged inside me on that accident day.

November 11, 1979: I was working one day a week at my father's horse farm in Easton, New York, about 10 miles south of Greenwich. My father ran a small, thoroughbred breeding farm, only about 50 acres in all, with a 2-story, log cabin-style house that he had wanted for himself and his new wife and her two young daughters after he left my mother. There was a long equipment shed that was open on one side, where he housed his tractor and his front loader and a low-boy trailer and all the other farm equipment he used. That sat off to your right when you turned down into his long driveway. Straight ahead of you was his only horse barn, but it was a large, state-of-the-art, post-and-beam barn with a spacious hayloft and a manager's apartment on the top. On the ground level sat the office, a tack room, and maybe 10 or 12 stalls and a walking ring. I can't remember right now how many stalls there were in all, but enough to hold a pampered selection of pricey mares and foals that were owned by several wealthy Kentucky and Florida thoroughbred owners who wanted to have well-bred stock that could run in exclusive New York State-bred races. The log house was at the end of the drive.

My father had hired a local guy in his mid-50s named Warren Rodman to be his farm manager. Warren had grown up around Greenwich, but he moved to the West when he was a young man and became a cowboy. He stayed out there for thirty years, riding in rodeos, breaking stock, mending fences, and working for ranchers in Arizona, Colorado and New Mexico. He had only been back in New York State a few years, working on a local road crew, when my father heard about him and offered him the job. Within a year of Warren going to work for him, they had become best friends.

Most of the farm's 50 acres that wasn't too marshy from the creek that wound through the lower third of the property was fenced off for paddocks, and each paddock was supposed to have its own run-in shed for the horses. That November, there was only one paddock that didn't have a finished shed, in the field to the immediate left of the entrance, and Warren and I were digging holes for its corner posts that Sunday morning. My father and his wife weren't there. They had driven down to Troy to be with his wife's daughters at Emma Willard School, so Warren and I were working alone at the farm. It had rained all through the night before, and it was still drizzling in the morning as we worked. The ground was slippery. It was pretty cold, about 40 degrees, and the rainy air wormed its way inside your skin and just made everything that much nastier to grab onto.

Warren had driven the old Ford tractor up near the top edge of the field, fairly close to the town road — Fly Summit Road — and we were using the tractor's power takeoff to run a 12-inch auger. The vertical auger stood maybe 5 feet high with its tip on the ground, and the horizontal shaft from the power takeoff hooked into it and made it spin. There was a bolt sticking out at the connection point, spinning right along with the takeoff shaft, and you couldn't reach in there near it or it would grab your glove and maybe even rip the skin off your knuckles. Warren was sitting on the tractor, feeding it gas and working the controls, and I was steadying the auger inside the holes as it churned down through the slick dirt and rocks.

It was slow digging. Land in the foothills of the Adirondacks isn't much different than the rock-filled soil in Vermont or New Hampshire, and we hit our share of rocks that morning. We'd get down through good dirt a foot or so and then the auger would start to bounce on a stone, and I'd have to bear down harder until it split or shift the tip from side to side and maneuver the auger's spinning blade under an edge of the rock and churn it up and out of the hole. It was pretty tedious work, and the rain didn't make it any easier. By 11 a.m., we'd only finished half the holes. The rain had gotten steadier, and it was tough to get much purchase on anything.

Finally, I hit a stone that wouldn't budge, no matter what trick I tried on it. Warren climbed down off the tractor and planted himself next to me, on my left. There was a curved, yellow steel bar above the spinning takeoff shaft, and Warren grabbed hold of that with both hands and pulled down hard. I kept shifting the auger from side to side, bearing down on it right above the hole. Suddenly, Warren made a weird sound, halfway between a surprised grunt and a nervous laugh. I looked over at him, and saw that the connecting bolt had latched onto his denim jacket. He was leaning back, slamming his boot heels into the mud to get some traction, and pushing away from that bar, all at once. I reached over and tried to pull his jacket off, but he hollered, "Get the tractor."

I ran over to the tractor then, looking frantically for the key to shut the engine off, but I couldn't find it. My father was always worried about accidents and liability on the farm, and he didn't want me *running his equipment, so he had never shown me how to work that tractor. So I jammed all its levers back and forth to kill the power take-off, but nothing worked.*

By then, relentlessly efficient, the bolt had chewed its way through Warren's jacket. His boots kept slipping in the mud. I ran back and grabbed onto him, reaching around him from behind to help him pull free, but the bolt lodged in his skin and yanked him up off his feet. The space in between that overhead steel bar and the spinning takeoff shaft was only sixteen or eighteen inches, about as long as a newborn baby, and Warren was forced through that space twice, bent double and twisted and choking out an involuntary, strangled howl as he hurtled around, as if he were caught in some terrifying breach birth in reverse and had to pass through some unforgiving industrial womb to shift out of our world and move on into whatever world was next for him. As he was dragged up and through, his legs kicked me over backwards and I landed on my left ankle and twisted it sideways.

Warren landed on his back under the takeoff shaft. His coat and shirt had been ripped off and the wadded-up, bloody shreds of them were still snared on the connecting bolt and spinning around on the shaft, though they had wrapped firmly there and only part of the shirttail was slapping against metal as it spun. Warren wasn't moving, but I could see his eyes were open, and I called out his name, twice. He didn't answer. I saw his mouth twitching a little, and I knew, even if I was plunging quickly into shock, that he needed some serious help, and fast.

I couldn't tell what was wrong with my ankle. I didn't think it was broken, but I couldn't put any weight on it. I think in that instant I was hoping it might be broken, maybe because Warren was so hurt he couldn't voluntarily move anything but his eyes, and I felt somehow responsible. I wasn't able to shut the tractor down, or drag him off when he was caught on the spinning bolt, and maybe the pain of knowing that could be lessened if I was badly hurt. Maybe I wanted to be a victim, too, to ease my guilt. I don't know. Even now I don't know all of what's true about that day, but I do know that I was lying there in the mud, scared and shaking, listening to the tractor churn along, and I knew something tragic and irrevocable was happening. I was sure I couldn't walk up to the barn office, where the closest telephone was, so I crawled.

Most rural communities like Greenwich and Easton have volunteer firefighting companies, made up of dedicated men and women who often have day jobs. They don't get to stay at their stations during their shifts, and they have to drive usually long distances twice — first to the station for their emergency vehicles and then to the site of the emergency itself. Those country distances make for long response times, and that morning the volunteer ambulance didn't reach us for about 45 minutes.

After I made the call, I crawled back out, took off my coat, and covered Warren up. He couldn't move his body at all. It was still drizzling, and after the tractor ran out of gas, the rain made a terrible, soft sound as it hit the mud. Warren's eyes were open but glassy, staring vaguely at me, and I held my hand up to cover his face so the rain wouldn't fall into his eyes. A thin line of blood started at the corner of his mouth and wouldn't stop. He tried to talk, but he couldn't get any words out, and the blood gurgled in his throat when he tried. I kept talking to him, telling him how sorry I was and saying it wouldn't be too much longer before the rescue squad got there.

When the volunteers did arrive, they were shocked. It was two older men, in their early 60s maybe, and they stood over us and just stared for a minute. They never even asked me what happened. Then they pulled a collapsible stretcher out of the ambulance, but they couldn't figure out how to assemble it. I was 30 then, impatient and hysterical with grief and my own pain, and I started screaming. What the hell was wrong with them? They couldn't put their own fucking stretcher together? So I grabbed it and threw it together myself. I shouted for them to help me pick Warren up, but they were afraid to move him. They wanted to wait for the head of the rescue squad, who was a paramedic. He was on his way, they said. They were only First

Responders. Maybe this guy's back is broken. Who knows what's wrong with him?

I wasn't about to let Warren lay there in the cold mud any longer. I reached under his legs and his back to lift him, but his back was too soft, too wet, and what bones there were seemed to shift and move away from my hand as I eased him up off the ground. His eyes rolled up and then back and I could see only whites there as I laid him on the stretcher.

A crowd of neighbors had gathered by then, and they formed a loose semi-circle around us. I hadn't even noticed them. But the paramedic had finally arrived. He was much younger than the others, maybe in his mid-30s, a strong, fit-looking guy with a dark beard and wearing a red flannel coat with a hunter's tag on the back. He had a worried look on his face. He immediately grabbed one end of the stretcher and I picked up the other. I was limping on my ankle, trying to hop and not caring about how much it hurt as I carried Warren over to the back of the ambulance, and I was too angry to let either of the older men help me. I climbed into the passenger seat in front, and we drove out onto Fly Summit Road and started toward the closest hospital, Mary McClellan in Cambridge.

The rest of what happened was a montage of surreal images: The paramedic in back started CPR on Warren; when the driver slowed for a black, barking dog in the road, I hollered through my tears at him to run the son of a bitch down and hurry up; a little later, the paramedic slammed his fist into Warren's chest, twice, and cursed; the doctor who was waiting at the emergency bay of the hospital turned away and winced before he reached up to help the paramedic pull out the stretcher; Warren's wife, dazed, put an arm around my shoulders and assured me over and over that it couldn't have been my fault; my father, visibly grief-stricken and looking for answers, said he found a note tacked to his door and wanted me to tell him exactly how it had happened; my first wife, finally jolted into a posture of basic concern, knelt in front of my wheelchair and held both my hands and swore quietly how glad she was it wasn't me who was dead; and, at the end, the two older paramedics sat on a bench outside the operating room, with Warren stretched out inside on a table under a sheet, telling each other there was nothing more they could have done, nothing anyone could have done, that the internal injuries were too massive, that's what the doctor told them, that they had done their best, everybody who was there could see how hopeless it was.

I spent more than ten years unable to speak about that day, though my father did drive me over to Warren's house the night of the accident and insisted that I go in alone and explain everything to his wife and children. And for a few months, I had to be careful when I was driving, because Warren's glassy eyes would suddenly appear and block my vision and I'd have to pull over and stop for a while until the memory faded. But, most of all, I stayed angry about those older volunteers, as if their rationalizations for incompetence were somehow the cause of Warren's death. He had been alive when they arrived, right? If they had just been faster, well then, we might have saved him. That's what I kept believing for a long time.

So what does that have to do with this book? Why would riding with professional firefighters and paramedics, and witnessing more sickness and death in one year than I ever thought I would see in a lifetime, make me think I could resolve Warren's death? I don't really know. Maybe it can't. But it did help me to accept, at the very least, what I did try to do, and it showed me a way to understand those older volunteers on that hospital bench. We can't save everyone, but we can do our best, as foolish and empty as that sounds when we're talking about human lives. I was too young back then to realize that those older men thought they really were doing their best, and that they also needed to find a way to live with themselves when it was all over. There can be considerable art in functioning as a survivor.

People are going to die. Most of us know that, and too much reminds us of it, daily, and the cliché is that we can't save them all. But we can save some, and we can praise those who go to work and try to do that scary, messy job every day, and we can rejoice for those they do save. So much of what firefighters and other rescuers do turns out to be in vain, but seldom because they don't try. And afterwards, everyone who is left has to find a way to live with whatever has happened. Professional firefighters and paramedics, volunteer firefighters, doctors, nurses, EMTs, ambulance drivers, caring police officers, social workers, family and friends who act as caretakers — the list is too long to include everyone who toils on the side of life — all of them are vital to us. Those people, and those occupations, help to affirm that our society chooses creation over destruction. Part of me wants to make it that simple, of course — dividing the world into rescuers and destroyers — so I can choose the more compassionate side and place myself on it. Maybe that helps me exorcise some of my demons, but it may also be true.

Acknowledgments

I could not have written *Saving Troy* without the generosity of many people at the Troy Fire Department. Most of them appear as characters in this book. But I want to thank specifically the members of the 1st Platoon, who put up with my presence, my ignorance, and my questions for eighteen months.

Many men on the 3rd Platoon, including Bill Miller, Dave Gavitt, Ed Cummings, and Eric McMahon were especially helpful when I was riding with them as a videographer.

Gary Favro, president of the Troy Uniformed Firefighters Association, Local 2304, offered constant support during and after my time with the department, as did Tom Garrett, the current chief.

Steve Dworsky, who was City Manager and Public Safety Commissioner, asked Chief Schultz to give me permission to ride along and allowed this project to begin. My hat is off to both of them for taking that risk.

Ed Nare, who was Assistant City Manager, opened some important doors for me, and also provided invaluable information about the Hudson River.

Thanks to Nick Kaiser of the Troy Police Department for helping to keep me safe, and to Kevin O'Connor of Joseph's House for showing me how hard it is to live on the streets.

The New York Foundation for the Arts and the Metropolitan Life Insurance Company awarded me grants that helped to support me as I wrote *Saving Troy*.

Literary agent Don Congdon told me my writing wasn't any good at exactly the right moment: I thank him for his candor then and his genuine support later on.

The Troy Public Library hosted a public reading of the work-in-progress, and *The Record* generously granted me permission to excerpt some of their news stories.

Kathy and Skip Diamond shared intimate details of a harrowing event in their lives with me, and I applaud their honesty and courage.

I owe a great debt of gratitude to friends who read the manuscript in its various states and gave me the encouragement I needed to keep writing: De and Kathy Snodgrass, Marion Roach, Joe Gagen, Chase Twichell, Bob Miner, Serena Fox, Dave Fenza, Paul Grondahl, Tim Cahill, Richard Selzer, Clorinda Valenti, Richard Hoffman, Gene Mirabelli, and Carmel Patrick. All of their suggestions made this a better book.

Finally, I want to thank everyone in my family who cheered me on in what turned out to be a marathon: I wouldn't have finished without you.

A NOTE ON THE TEXT

This book was set in Janson, a typeface long thought to have been made by the Dutchman Anton Janson, who was a practicing typefounder in Leipzig during the years 1668–1687. However, it has been conclusively demonstrated that these types are actually the work of Nicholas Kis (1650–1702), a Hungarian, who most probably learned his trade from the master Dutch typefounder Dirk Voskens. The type is an excellent example of the influential and sturdy Dutch types that prevailed in England up to the time William Caslon (1692–1766) developed his own incomparable designs from them.

Composed by DeMasi Design and Publishing Service
518-877-0404
Printed in China

TERRY FOX

Ric Moreno

CHARLEY WILLSON

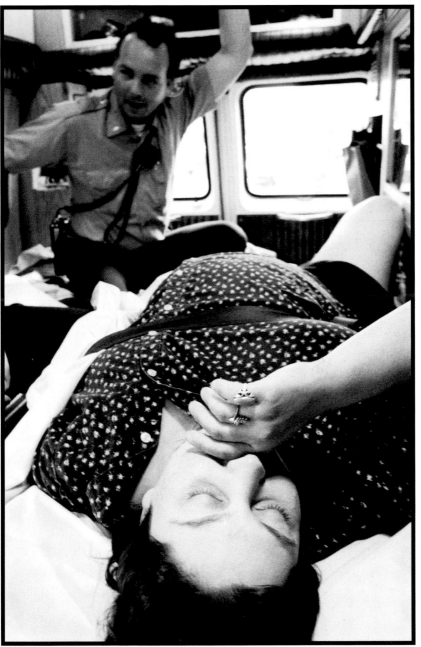

MIKE HARRISON

DAVE STEVENS

DAVE PAUL

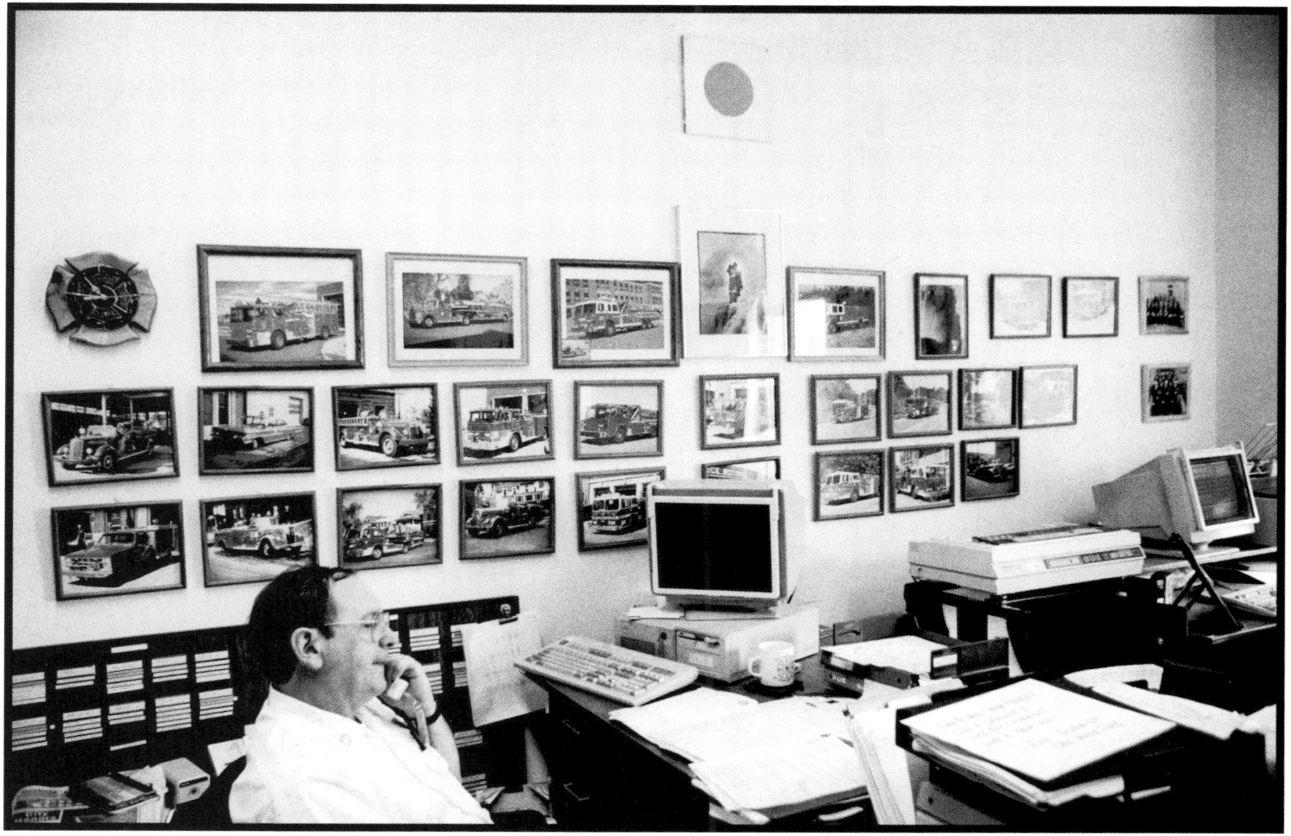

Ed Schultz

MIKE KELLEHER

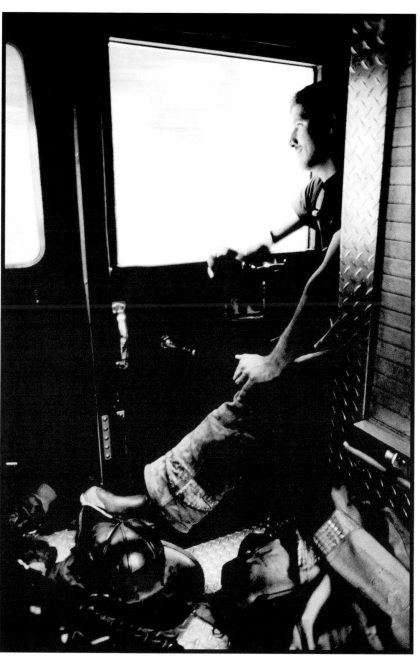

ERIC MCMAHON

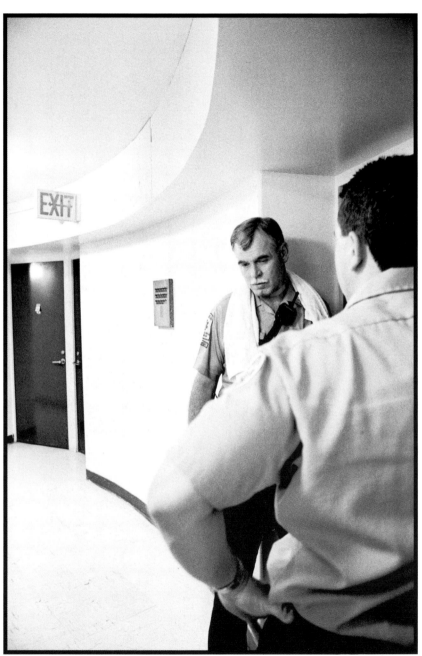

TERRY FOX

RIC MORENO

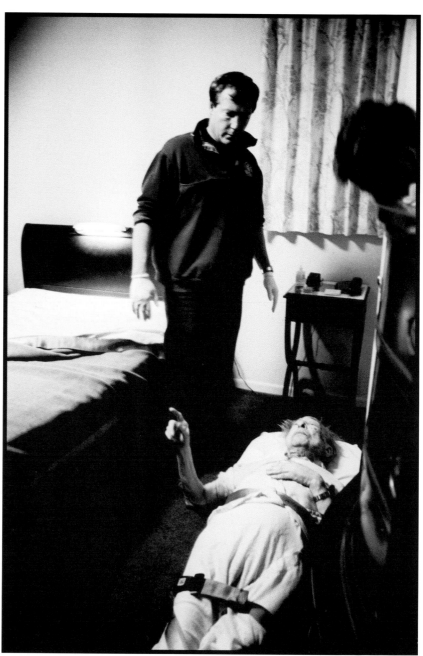

DON KIMMEY

DAVE STEVENS

JEFF GORDON, THE DIAMOND FAMILY, DON KIMMEY

MIKE HARRISON

DON KIMMEY, DAVE STEVENS, TOM MITER

FRANK RYAN, DAVE PAUL

TOM MITER, GARY HANNA, DAVE PAUL